LOVE AND SAINT AUGUSTINE

LOVE AND SAINT AUGUSTINE

HANNAH ARENDT

Edited and with an Interpretive Essay by

Joanna Vecchiarelli Scott

and

Judith Chelius Stark

THE UNIVERSITY OF CHICAGO PRESS

CHICAGO & LONDON

The University of Chicago Press, Chicago 60637
The University of Chicago Press, Ltd., London
Copyright © 1929 by Julius Springer
English translation copyright © 1996 by The Literary Trust of
    Hannah Arendt Blücher
Copyright © 1996 by Joanna Vecchiarelli Scott and
    Judith Chelius Stark
All rights reserved. Published 1996
Printed in the United States of America
16 15 14 13 12 11 10   5 4 3

ISBN-13: 978-0-226-02596-4 (cloth)
ISBN-13: 978-0-226-02597-1 (paper)
ISBN-10: 0-226-02596-9 (cloth)
ISBN-10: 0-226-02597-7 (paper)

Library of Congress Cataloging-in-Publication Data
Arendt, Hannah.
    [Liebesbegriff bei Augustin. English]
    Love and Saint Augustine / Hannah Arendt ; edited and
with an interpretive essay by Joanna Vecchiarelli Scott and
Judith Chelius Stark.
        p.   cm.
    Includes bibliographical references and index.
    ISBN 0-226-02596-9 — ISBN 0-226-02597-7 (pbk.)
    1. Love (Theology)—History of doctrines—Early
church, ca. 30–600.   2. Augustine, Saint, Bishop of
Hippo.   I. Scott, Joanna Vecchiarelli.   II. Stark, Judith
Chelius.   III. Title.
BV4639.A6513   1996
177'.7'092—dc20   95-12866
                                                CIP

Contents

Preface
Rediscovering *Love and Saint Augustine*

Preparing our edited and revised English version of Hannah Arendt's *Love and Saint Augustine* has been a major collaborative effort spanning a decade. Although the number of books, articles, and conferences on Arendt's works increases yearly, particularly in political science, *Love and Saint Augustine* remains an almost unknown text—the last of Arendt's book-length manuscripts to be published in English. Our joint work on the manuscript began in 1985 after a chance encounter at the Patristic, Medieval and Renaissance Studies Association held at Villanova University, where I, as a political scientist, was exploring the dissertation as the missing link between Arendt's "political" and "moral" epistemology and Judith, as a philosopher, was examining Augustine's idea of evil and its relation to political authority. Our paths to Arendt's dissertation follow.

Scott's Path to *Love and Saint Augustine*

At Barnard College and Columbia University, where I studied political theory as an undergraduate and as a graduate Presidential Fellow, the physical presence and intellectual aura of Hannah Arendt were unavoidable. Like Margaret Mead, another eminent woman on the Morningside Heights campus, Arendt was a "presence" at 116th Street and Broadway. Sightings were reported, anecdotes shared. The political science community at Barnard and Columbia, in the grip of the Cold War, elevated Arendt's *Origins of Totalitarianism* and *On Revolution* to canonic status.

Eventually I would go to the United Kingdom (1967–70), where I received my doctoral degree from the University of Strathclyde. Before I left Columbia with a master's degree, however, I continued the work on the history of political thought that I had begun at Barnard, this time with a focus on the radical use of traditional sources in the medieval period, completing a thesis on Marsiglio of Padua's reconstruction of Augustinianism. My professors, Herbert Deane, Julian Franklin, Arthur Hyman, Paul Oskar

Kristeller and Norman Cantor, illuminated the sources of Western political thinking with a passion and precision not unlike Arendt's. Kristeller, in fact, had been her classmate at Heidelberg. As a result, medieval political discourse has never been for me the alien language it often is for political scientists trained primarily in the writings of the moderns.

I began the process of rediscovering Arendt through the medium of her revised dissertation in 1983 after I retrieved not only a copy of the English translation from the Library of Congress but also her annotated retyped manuscript. I had previously read a review of her posthumously published Gifford Lectures and was intrigued by a brief, tantalizing reference to the existence of a translated copy of the dissertation among her papers in the Library of Congress. Given what I thought I knew of Arendt's "politics only" approach to the public world, the undeniable fact that her career had begun with an exploration of Augustine's idea of social life provoked my curiosity. When the text—an oversized pile of manuscript pages —arrived from the Library of Congress, it was double surprise. E. B. Ashton's translation, apparently completed in 1963, had been revised by Arendt in handwritten interlinear and marginal revisions, then partially retyped to include and expand the revisions.

In 1984 Jean Elshtain was coordinating political theory panels for the national meeting of the American Political Science Association in Washington and invited me to present my evaluation of the revised dissertation. Arendt is one of the most widely respected yet controversial figures in twentieth-century political science. Yet surprisingly, my argument for the significance of the dissertation was the first time Arendt's encounter with Augustine had been directly addressed in her chosen American academic discipline. It was also the first time that Arendt's dissertation per se had been taken seriously in political science as more than a standard academic debut. Although heavily indebted to her mentors Martin Heidegger and Karl Jaspers, Arendt's dissertation is her own respectful declaration of independence, which points the way to her later, explicitly political works. Thus, from the beginning, rediscovering the dissertation by means of its 1960s revisions has been controversial and will continue to be so until the whole corpus of her work, in Germany and America, is evaluated and incorporated into the "orthodox" rendering of Arendt's political thought.

Stark's Path to *Love and Saint Augustine*

My interest in both Augustine and Arendt began during my graduate studies in philosophy at Marquette University. There I wrote my master's thesis on "Augustine's Notion of Peace" under the direction of the Augustine scholar Paul Bryne. During the tumultuous days of the late 1960s I plunged into Arendt's works, especially *Between Past and Future, On Revolution,* and her most controversial work, *Eichmann in Jerusalem.* While reading these works, I was delighted to discover a contemporary thinker who was grappling with the most difficult and perplexing issues of our time.

In 1969 I decided to return to New York City, study with Arendt, and thus complete my doctoral studies at the New School for Social Research. During my time at the New School I also worked with Hans Jonas, William Barrett, Aron Gurwitsch, and Arthur Hyman. These were the years in which Arendt was engaged in working through her last major project, the Gifford Lectures, which became *The Life of the Mind: Thinking and Willing.* Augustine figures prominently in this work, especially in the *Willing* volume. The research for my own dissertation on Augustine's early views of the will was carried out under Arendt's direction, including explorations of her dissertation, *Der Liebesbegriff bei Augustin,* which was on reserve at the New School Library. Unfortunately, I did not then glean much from that dense German text, preferring instead to devote my time with Arendt to discussions and disputes about Augustine and his perplexing thoughts on the will. Little did I know at that point that my work with Arendt on Augustine would eventually lead me back to hers. After the publication of *The Life of the Mind* in 1978, I began to appreciate much more fully the depth and duration of Arendt's fascination with Augustine. In 1986 I was invited to present my research in Rome at an international congress sponsored by the Augustinian Patristic Institute celebrating the sixteenth centenary of Augustine's conversion, clearly signaling the importance of *Love and Saint Augustine* among Augustinian specialists.

I have learned, however, that Arendt's ambivalence toward academic philosophy, which (by way of a detour through theology) had been her first love, is mirrored in contemporary philosophy's response to her thought. Her stance derives, among other things, from what she saw as the inherent tensions between philosophy and politics, as illustrated in the temptation to support tyranny, to which philosophers such as Plato and Heidegger succumbed. Even so, she never rejected the German philosophical tradition from which she sprang. Today, research on Arendt in mainstream philosophy conferences and publications remains at the margins of discourse, where political ideas or the writings of women are discussed. Still, Arendt as I knew her would not have bothered about her status among philosophers of "the tradition"; instead she would have praised and encouraged the perilous task of thinking no matter where it occurred.

The Revised Dissertation

As Judith and I worked on the manuscript, it was clear that Arendt had so overwritten the translation with her own annotations and alterations that deciphering it for publication would be a long, complex undertaking. Following the bread-crumb trail of letters, contracts, oblique references, and the recollections of her friends at the New School, we learned that Arendt in 1962 had signed a contract with Crowell-Collier for publication, for which she expected to receive an advance against royalties. Logically, the contract must have spurred revisions to the text, though no direct documentary evidence linking the two has yet come to light. The Ashton manuscript pages, Arendt's revisions, and her retyped pages are all undated.

The most important evidence for dating the "new" revised text is the mirroring of the dissertation in her works of the late 1950s and early 1960s, and the equivalent transfer of terminology from the latter to the revisions of the dissertation. In fact, the new text comes from her most productive period of political theorizing in the United States. The return to Augustine directly infused her revisions of *Origins of Totalitarianism*, her new study *On Revolution*, the essays collected in *Between Past and Future*, and *Eichmann in Jerusalem* with explicit and implicit Augustinian references. At the same time, the revisions demonstrate her continuing commitment to the subject matter, mode of discourse, and conclusions she had produced in 1929. Her research question about "the relevance of the neighbor," her conclusion that Augustinian philosophy is simultaneously both out of and engaged in the world, and her philosophical approach—combining German phenomenology with Christian existentialism—were essentially unchanged, even in the completely different context of New York in the early 1960s. Significantly, neither the pivotal introduction nor Part III was expanded or modified in any way.

Even though the revisions did not alter the character of the dissertation, they unfortunately also did not enhance its accessibility. The new text was a morass of dense, awkward prose literally translated from the German and revised in similar fashion by Arendt. Major chunks of Greek and Latin references survived Ashton's translation and Arendt's subsequent revisions intact. These were then rendered even more impenetrable by additions in Arendt's notoriously unreadable handwriting. Her footnotes, too, were idiosyncratic, containing citation errors and omissions together with her own unusual translations, all of which Ashton had left intact.

Bringing together our familiarity with political science, philosophy,

medieval sources, and Arendt's works, we constituted a team of experts
uniquely prepared to cope with the formidable obstacles entailed in rediscovering the Augustinian foundations of Arendt's political thought. Other
than our own published articles and conference papers in our respective disciplines, Arendt's encounter with Augustine has not been accorded the attention it merits by the Arendt studies community. One possible reason for
the omission in political science is that a critical appraisal of the text requires
familiarity with both medieval and contemporary philosophy, which is not
common among Arendt specialists. Another reason is that the seriousness
with which Arendt engaged Augustine in the dissertation and the obvious
resonances of the text with her American works disturb the status quo in the
field. The following text and commentary are intended to restore the scholarly balance. Using Arendt's own model of natality, we are inserting her dissertation into the public realm of academic debate for the first time.

Together we have been able to decode the text with its many annotations and retypings and "English it" (as Arendt would say) sufficiently for a
broad audience. Arendt's revisions, taken together with the Ashton text,
constitute three phases of textual rediscovery. The first phase is the original
Ashton text; the second is Arendt's initial round of revisions, which we call
Copy A; and the third is her retyped revisions, which we call Copy B. We
have found no evidence in the Library of Congress that points to the dates
of successive revisions, though it is clear that handwritten interlinear additions and subtractions (Copy A) came first. Sometime later, Arendt incorporated her revisions into a second text, which she typed herself and then
further revised by hand (Copy B). Therefore, our text of *Love and Saint Augustine* consists of: Copy B for the first chapter of Part I through the middle
of the first chapter of Part II; Copy A for the introduction, and the rest of
Parts II and III, including the handwritten interlinear revisions that Arendt
did not retype.

We edited both texts to eliminate grammatical and syntactical awk-
wardness, translation difficulties, and footnote errors. Arendt herself heavily revised footnotes in Copy B, moving some into the main body of the text
while adding a substantial number of new notes. Accumulated inaccuracies
were corrected. For example, as she revised Part II, chapter 1 of Copy A and
retyped it as Copy B, she added new footnotes but did not renumber, so that
the text shows footnotes 47a through 47p (B:033 198–200). For reasons unknown, Arendt's typed revisions to the dissertation end at note 47p. Thereafter, the text resumes with Copy A (A:033299) and continues to the end of
the manuscript. For the sake of clarity, we have renumbered the footnotes

VERSION + SEQUENCE IN TEXT		MANUSCRIPT PAGES	ORIGINAL + CURRENT TITLE
A	1	033238	"Table of Contents" (omit)
A	2	033239–40	"Abbreviations" (omit)
A	3	033241–49	"Introduction" (same)
B	4	033131–42	"Part One—Love as Craving/Chapter 1: The Structure of Craving (change to) "Part One—Love as Craving: The Anticipated Future/Chapter 1: The Structure of Craving (*Appetitus*)
B	5	033143–65	"Part One—Love as Craving: Chapter 2: Charity and Cupidity (change to) "Part One—Love as Craving: The Anticipated Future/Chapter 2: *Caritas* and *Cupiditas*
B	6	033166–79	"Part One—Love as Craving: Chapter 3: The Order of Love" (change to) "Part One—Love as Craving: The Anticipated Future/Chapter 3: The Order of Love
B→A	7	Bo33181–2DD Ao33299–313	"Part Two—Creator-Creature: Chapter 1: The Creator as the Source of the Creature" (change to) "Part Two—Creator and Creature: The Remembered Past/Chapter 1: The Origin
A	8	033314–39	"Part Two—Creator-Creature: Chapter 2: Charity and Cupidity (change to) "Part Two—Creator and Creature: The Remembered Past/Chapter 2: *Caritas* and *Cupiditas*
A	9	033340–47	"Part Two—Creator-Creature: Chapter 3: Neighborly Love (change to) "Part Two—Creator and Creature: The Remembered Past/Chapter 3: Love of Neighbor
A	10	033348–73	"Part Three: Social Life (title unchanged)

Handwritten pages:

A		033257–60 033268 (two pages/same number/one out of sequence)	
		033280	
B		033179–80 (partial pages) 033212–27: (partial pages, including brief correspondence)	

German addenda translated by Arendt and added to Copy B:

| B | | 033197–200: Beginning last paragraph, ending where Copy B ends and text returns to Copy A (033299) | |

Footnotes appeared at the end of each chapter in the typed manuscript and so are included in the numbering of the manuscript pages in this table, e.g. the footnotes for Part One, chap. 1 are on pages 033140–42, and so on. The one exception to this is Part Two, chap. 1. Those footnotes are on pages 033201–6 in the Library of Congress collection. *Therefore, the manuscript numbers embedded in the text of this edition do not pertain to footnotes.* Our additions to Arendt's footnotes are set off in brackets.

consecutively; as we return to Copy A, our text simply continues to incorporate Arendt's handwritten marginal and interlinear revisions. Finally, Arendt herself translated German addenda to the dissertation, included in the original 1929 printing, sometime during the process of preparing the dissertation for publication in English. These were included as handwritten pages of notes affixed to Copy A. Some material from these addenda was included in Copy B; the rest was left unincorporated.

Even without Arendt's revisions, the Ashton translation was problematic. Faithful to the text and painfully literal as a result, the translation left thickets of impenetrable phenomenological discourse in place. Awkward phrasing, repetition, and general incomprehensibility were constant difficulties. To the extent possible, without damaging Arendt's apparent meaning, we attempt to clarify the dissertation text for contemporary readers. We have edited translations of Latin terms in the text to achieve consistency. Thus, *civitas terrena* is always rendered as earthly city, *civitas Dei* as city of God, *gemeinschaft* as community, and *societas* as society. The word "creature," which appeared repeatedly in the translation, to the great detriment of readability, is rendered as man or person, except when "natality" and linkage to the "Creator" are at issue. Similarly, neologisms such as "creatural" or "aboriginal" are edited out and rendered in appropriate English usage.

All of the above additions and revisions expand upon rather than fundamentally reorient the original dissertation. The physical appearance of Copy B suggests that Arendt used more than one typewriter in her retyping efforts. This could reflect either the passage of time between episodes of work or the efforts of several typists. Despite the unevenness of typefaces and incompleteness of Copy B, however, Arendt maintained a remarkable continuity between the original translation and her revisions. There is no break in lines of argument, mode of discourse, or subject matter. Unfortunately, there is also no direct or indirect evidence that would help us reconstruct her complete plan for the revisions of Copy B. Hence the question of why the retyped text ends in the midst of Part II, chapter 1 will never be answered. Arendt made some other very minor corrections to Copy A, which she added by hand and typed interlinearly, but whether these preceded or followed her preparation of Copy B is also unknown.

The most likely reason the manuscript was never published is a simple one. Abundant evidence shows that from 1961 onward Arendt was consumed by the Eichmann trial, her reportage in *The New Yorker*, and the subsequent firestorm of criticism. Indeed, the entire period from the late 1950s through 1968 was an extremely busy period in Arendt's life. Her numerous published works, the range and location of her lecture appearances (before academic and general audiences), together with her absorbing concerns with American national affairs (desegregation in Little Rock, the Kennedy election, the Bay of Pigs, the Cuban missile crisis, and the Kennedy assassination) and international events (Khrushchev's speech, the Hungarian revolution, the Suez crisis and its impact on Israel) suggest that she must have had little time or energy left to complete the project. Instead she could, and did, incorporate her dissertation research into her other more overtly political writings and transfer new terms, such as "natality," from them to her dissertation revisions.

In April 1961 Arendt traveled to Jerusalem to cover the Eichmann trial for *The New Yorker*. She prepared her notes and wrote her analysis of the trial during the summer and fall of 1962, right after she had signed the contract with Crowell-Collier to publish the dissertation. Her five-part series on the Eichmann trial appeared in February and March 1963; the book version, *Eichmann in Jerusalem: A Report on the Banality of Evil*, quickly followed in May. Almost immediately a vituperative controversy erupted in the New York community, and eventually around the world, focused on her notorious paradigm of "the banality of evil" and her assertion that Jewish elders had cooperated with Nazi officials in the deportation of their communities.

The controversy raged for years with unrelenting ferocity, assuming a phenomenological existence of its own. Arendt called it simply "The Controversy." Between 1963 and 1969 she tried to respond to the misrepresentations and personal attacks in letters, in talks to the New York Jewish community and student organizations from Hofstra University to the University of Chicago, and in interviews, but this only fanned the flames. By 1969 she returned to her original intention of not responding. Then, too, by the end of the 1960s Arendt was engaged in many other projects at various stages of completion, including editorial work on Walter Benjamin's *Illuminations* (published with her lengthy introduction) and the essays collected in *Crises of the Republic*. With the latter, Arendt ventured into the American political minefields of student violence on campuses and U.S. military involvement in Vietnam. It is no wonder, in retrospect, that the Augustine typescript lay among her papers—unpublished but not forgotten.

The Origin and Reviews of the Dissertation

In analyzing the dissertation, one crucial problem for Arendt scholars has been to explain how a young Jewish student working with the two leading proponents of *Existenz* philosophy wrote her dissertation on Augustine, the Christian bishop and saint. When Arendt's friend and colleague Hans Jonas was asked why this was so, he replied that "such a topic would not have been all that unusual in the German universities of the time." Jonas's sense of Arendt's work on Augustine was that it was "in itself quite an understandable thing," since both Heidegger and Jaspers turned to such thinkers and would have responded to "the existentialist message of Augustine."

In fact, Jonas himself chose Augustine and the problem of freedom for his own first work (*Augustin und das paulinische Freiheitsproblem* [Göttingen, 1930]), but emphasized the Pelagian controversy that dominated Augustine's later works. Jonas speculated that Arendt's topic "grew out of her own reading in combination with Jaspers's work at the time." As he recalled, Christian thinkers such as Augustine, Pascal, and Kierkegaard were a "hot topic" in the German universities; the greatest interest centered on Augustine's *Confessions*. The *Confessions* was a "crucial and pivotal text," Jonas remembers, which prompted students to "self-exploration and the descent into the abyss of conscience." Philosophy students found Augustine's confessional mode to be strikingly "original" compared to that of the Hellenic tradition (Jonas, 1990).

Jonas's sense that Arendt's topic was apt for the time is confirmed by a review of German journals of the late 1920s in which doctoral dissertations were regularly presented and discussed. However, interest in Augustine was not confined to the universities. Protestant circles produced an abundance of theological and pastoral articles on Augustine in which prominent authors addressed the problem of Christianity and modernity. Although Catholic authors also wrote on Augustine, they were more likely to focus their scholarly efforts on Thomas Aquinas as a conservative weapon against the onslaughts of modernism. No doubt Luther's appropriation of Augustine and the great reformer's critiques of scholasticism drove interest in Augustine more firmly into the Protestant camp. Ecumenical interests prevailed at the end of the decade when a flurry of articles, including one by Arendt, marked the fifteen hundredth anniversary of Augustine's death (see "Augustine and Protestantism" in Arendt 1994).

What is striking about the reviews of Arendt's dissertation is their resonance with critical comments made many years later about Arendt's methodology and mode of discourse. Arendt opened her writing career as she would continue it—to rather mixed reviews. Commentators complained about a distorting selectivity in her focus on *caritas*, a misreading of Augustine's role in the historical tradition of political thought, and a failure to address the explicitly theological context and content of his work. Though deemed oblivious to history, tradition, and the established canon of Augustinian scholarship, Arendt was nonetheless given full marks for originality and insight. All agreed she was an important new author, trained in an increasingly visible new methodology (existential phenomenology), whose work warranted serious critical review.

In a short, one-paragraph review in *Kantstudien*, J. Hessen acknowledges Arendt's "meticulousness and sharp mind," yet also asks why she ignored the work of earlier scholars and argues "she could have learned quite a lot from it" (Hessen 1931, 175). The implicit subtext was that as a "phenomenologically educated author" she was an outsider. She had not written her dissertation on Augustine under the direction of a specialist on Augustine nor had she cited the full panoply of research on the saint. A much longer review by Max Zepf in *Gnomon* calls into question Arendt's attempt to take one aspect of Augustine's thought as the object of study and argues further that "the aspect in question is not even an essential and fundamental component of that person's [Augustine's] intellectual world" (Zepf 1932, 101). Missing Arendt's point completely, Zepf thinks Arendt has taken the wrong approach and suggests that the study would have been better had she examined the reasons for Augustine's inconsistencies. The source of the conflicts in his philosophy, says Zepf, can be traced to the two different traditions to which he was heir, "antique philosophy and Christian-Oriental ideas" (ibid., 102).

Arendt, in fact, had made precisely the same point in the dissertation, but in an existential mode of discourse lost on her audience. As in later criticisms of her work in America, Arendt is accused of a narrowly selective use of historical texts in the interest of her own modern agenda. Zepf calls Arendt's dissertation an "instructive and penetrating work," yet—while acknowledging that she may have discovered something new about Augustine's concept of love—he concludes that her "overall beliefs were determined too much by the contrary experience of her intellectual education in order to come to any truly new ideas, especially in this field" (ibid., 104). Finally, H. Eger, a reveiwer in a journal of church history, objects to Arendt's entire approach to Augustine, especially to her claim that she will analyze Augustine philosophically without dealing with the doctrinal elements in his thinking. Arendt's insistence that she could so without losing what is essential in Augustine's thought strikes the reviewer as unconvincing (Eger 1930, 257–59).

Of course, most of these criticisms are valid only if the dissertation is read as a theological analysis within the parameters of academic scholarship on Augustine at the time. But Arendt's effort to import the methodology of the *Existenz* into a traditional field of study was by definition intended to break new ground as her mentors had done. Her argument is that whether or not *caritas* as neighborly love was Augustine's intended point of intersection for the Neoplatonic, Pauline, and Roman traditions he inherited, it in fact fulfilled that very "original" role. Augustine's *quaestio*, "What is the relevance of the neighbor?" has many, possibly irreconcilable, responses for Augustine, all of which Arendt wishes to submit to phenomenological review. As such, the dissertation is far more revelatory about Arendt herself and the early directions in her thinking than it is as a piece of scholarship on Augustine of Hippo.

By 1929 Arendt was well launched on her lifelong path of passionate thinking, positioning herself both inside and outside the tradition of Western thought in order to engage it in radical critique. Because of her chosen Janus-like vantage point, which was characteristic of both Heidegger's and Jaspers's methodology, her early ideas instantly provoked admiration and dismay. Quiet disagreements over Arendt's work that had surfaced in the scholarly journals of theology in late Weimar Germany would evolve into a crescendo of controversy by the 1960s among readers in her newly chosen public world—American political science.

Acknowledgments

As Hannah Arendt would say, to begin at the beginning is an act of memory and gratitude. Having learned from her the importance of telling one's story, Judith and I would like to thank those who have made this particular tale possible. The origin of this project lies in a chance remark made to me more than a decade ago by Doug Scott, who had read a review of Arendt's Gifford lectures and noted a passing reference to the existence of Arendt's dissertation on Augustine, translated into English, in the Library of Congress. We had both been students of Herbert Deanne at Columbia University, and Doug sensed the possibilities. He was right, as usual.

We also owe thanks, which unfortunately come too late, to Mary McCarthy. Like her friend Hannah, she died too soon, but not before offering her characteristically outspoken advice—and an *imprimatur* as the executor of the Arendt Trust. We have been equally fortunate in the support of her sucessor, Lotte Kohler. Last but not least in the publishing history of this text, Liz Murphy, formerly of Harcourt Brace, deserves our very sincere appreciation for her perseverance and professionalism in working together with us and with Senior Editor T. David Brent of the University of Chicago Press, who has brought the project to completion at long last. The complicated contractural hurdles involved have been cleared with good humor and considerable dexterity by David and his staff at the Press, and for that we are very grateful.

Along the way, as we presented and published papers exploring various aspects of Arendt's dissertation, many friends and colleagues have cheered us on and offered much-appreciated advice. Rev. Lawrence Frizzell, director of the Judaeo-Christian Institute at Seton Hall University, translated the German Addenda to Arendt's dissertation and was always available to check translations of Greek and Latin texts. Ralph Walz and John Sweeney at Seton Hall read sections of the dissertation text and offered valuable suggestions. Many librarians provided crucial strategic assistance, including particularly Alice Birney of the Manuscript Division, Library of Congress, who greatly facilitated our access to the Arendt papers and always answered our questions about chronology and legal restrictions with candor and dispatch. In addition, the library of California State University, Long Beach, and the Angus L. MacDonald Library at St. Francis University in Antigonish, Nova Scotia, over the years have patiently accommodated our numerous and sometimes odd requests for materials. Thanks are due to colleagues in our respective disciplines and departments for their interest and support in the form of campus research fellowships and sabbaticals. Judith received a New Jersey Governor's Fellowship in the Humanities in 1990 for the project, and I have put an NEH Summer Institute in 1993 and an NEH Summer Seminar in 1995 to similar use. We also thank my students Karen Schaumann and Claudia Dahlerus, whose computer skills and intelligent insights have enriched this project.

Borrowing Arendt's idea of "natality" once more, we are particuarly grateful to Jean Elshtain, who was there from the start as an unofficial godmother for this "new beginning" in Arendt scholarship at the American Political Science Association meeting in 1984, and who has continued her invaluable support ever since. We would also like to thank Thomas Losoncy and Fr. Joseph Schnaubelt of Villanova University, whose Patristics, Medieval and Renaissance Association meetings have given both of us a venue for our work on Augustine and Arendt over a number of years, and the opportunity to begin our happy collaboration. Finally, we would like to acknowledge Donald N. Levine, who was there at the finish, whose timing was perfect and support invaluable.

Most of all, we thank Donez Xiques and Doug Scott, whose love, assistance, and unflagging confidence in us are beyond telling. And, beginning at our own beginnings, we dedicate this work to our parents, Mabel Campominosi Vecchiarelli and Francis Vecchiarelli, and Hannah Chelius Stark and Charles F. Stark, with love and gratitude.

Joanna Vecchiarelli Scott
August 1, 1995

LOVE AND SAINT AUGUSTINE

HANNAH ARENDT

Introduction

[A:033241] In accordance with the character of Saint Augustine's work, the difficulties of a perceptive interpretation can be shown on three points of principle that govern and delimit any presentation. First, diverse trains of thought appear side by side; second, dogmatic rigidity steadily increased as Augustine grew older; and third, there is a biographically demonstrable development that involves a marked change in the horizon of Augustine's thinking.

This essay will be divided into three parts in order to do justice to the thoughts and theories that run parallel and are usually cited as contradictory. In the area defined by its theme, the three parts will serve to show three conceptual contexts in which the problem of love plays a decisive role. Continuously guided by the question of the meaning and importance of neighborly love in particular, we shall pursue each of the three contexts to this end. Since love of neighbor as a Christian commandment depends on the love of God, which the believer embraces, and on the resulting new attitude toward his own self, each of the first two parts will have to start with the question of what it means to love God and oneself. Each time only a brief conclusion will show the application and will be derived from the question about the neighbor's relevance for the believer who is estranged from the world and its desires. [A:033242] Augustine's every perception and every remark about love refer at least in part to this love of neighbor. Thus the question about the neighbor's relevance always turns into a simultaneous critique of the prevailing concept of love and of man's attitude toward himself and toward God. For it is written, "Thou shalt love thy neighbor as thyself," and only one seized by God and his commandment is able to do so. This critique will never be an absolute critique from some fixed philosophical or theological standpoint. It is a critique only because the respective concept of love claims to be a Christian one. Furthermore, "Christian" will never mean more than "Pauline," because, as Augustine himself notes in his *Confessions*, it is primarily from Saint Paul that his life and thought took their bearings, insofar as both were truly religious rather than determined by Neoplatonic Greek influences.

The parallel trains of thought to be shown here defy systematic conjunction. They cannot even be joined in antithetical form, unless we wish to impose on Augustine a systematic and logical exactitude he never had. The several parts of this essay are linked only by the question concerning the other human being's relevance. For Augustine this relevance was simply a matter of course. Nothing but a belief in the importance of each of the trains of thought shown (an importance verifiable only in the showing itself) can justify the seeming disjointedness of this inquiry. This disjointedness is merely apparent because a single question posed by the author serves as a connecting link, and this disjointedness rests fundamentally on the disjointedness of Augustine's own work, [A:033243] which at the same time makes for its particular abundance and fascination.

Yet, the fact that three independent basic intentions are being treated in three separate parts does not mean that Augustine's writings might be divided into three groups, each containing detailed statements of the respective position. In this view it means that each of his utterances should be interpreted in the direction of one of the three intentions. By interpreting we mean making explicit what Augustine himself has merely implied, and showing by this explication how different intentions go together and mutually influence each other in one and the same context. The inquiry will be analytical throughout, that is, it will be an analysis that attempts to pierce the very recesses not clarified by Augustine himself. The result is a systematic approach that, far from seeking to yoke Augustine to a consistency unknown to him, merely attempts to interpret even seemingly heterogeneous statements and trains of thought in the direction of a substantially common base. In this attempt, the substantial base itself may come to manifest heterogeneous intentions (as, for instance, his twofold conception of the world presented in Part II). These basic intentions determine, and perhaps deflect, each individual statement in a connection that is no longer explicitly transparent. The purpose of this analysis is to demonstrate this connection. Thus, for all its systematic approach in detail, this analysis shows the very disjointedness of the whole.

Augustine's dogmatic subservience to scriptural and ecclesiastical authority will be largely alien to our analyses, which are, [A:033244] on principle, in keeping with their essence and significance, not dogmatically bound. Such intentional detachment from all dogmatic elements may doom the interpretation of a religious author but is relatively easy to justify in Augustine's case. Augustine writes, "They have not understood that 'Do not do to another what you do not wish to have done to you', cannot be varied in any way by any national diversity of customs. When this rule is applied to the love of God, all vices die; when it is applied to the love of our neighbor, all crimes vanish."[1] Preceding the express commandment of neighborly love is another that is independent of any such explicit divine revelation that has become real in Christ. This is the "law written in our hearts."[2] The Christian commandment sharpens this "natural" law, and thus enhances the human community to its highest reality in which all crimes are extinguished. Therefore, we shall be able to limit the scope of interpretation in two ways without being dogmatic. First, we shall ask about this pretheological sphere. Second, we shall seek to grasp what Augustine's exegesis would regard as the specific novelty in the Christian elaboration. Here the postulated and claimed reality of a human life is no longer subjected merely to the law written in human hearts but to the law of God, which commands from the outside. Furthermore, we shall ask why, for a human existence reflecting on itself ("I have become a question to myself"),[3] this divine law should be the only way to its own truth, to the truth prescribed to it in conscience. The right to inquire and interpret is given to us by Augustine himself when he grants to authority merely preparatory and educational functions: [A:033245] "Thus, since we were too weak to discover the truth by clear reasoning, and because, as a result, we had need of the authority of holy Scripture. . . ."[4] Similarly, "Likewise, with regard to the acquiring of knowledge, we are of necessity led in a twofold manner: by authority and by reason. In point of time, authority is first; in the order of reality, reason is prior."[5] In this interpretation no radical breach between authority and reason forces us to become involved in the eternally paradoxical problems of faith, as understood by Saint Paul and by Luther. For Augustine, authority commands from without what we would also be told by conscience, the inner law, if habit had not ensnared us in sin.

Corresponding to this bilateral tendency are the first two chapters in each of the first two parts, while the last chapter in each part will put the case to the test. The first chapter in each part will try to bring to mind the pretheological sphere, from which alone such definitions as "love is a kind of craving *(appetitus)*" or the relation of the creature to the Creator as its source

---

1. *Christian Doctrine* III, 14, 22; see also *Commentaries on the Psalms* 57, 1.
2. Passim. For our question in particular, see *Confessions* II, 4, 9, where Augustine explicitly distinguished this law from the "law of God."
3. *Confessions* X, 33, 50: "Quaestio mihi factus sum."
4. *Confessions* VI, 5, 8.
5. *On Order* II, 9, 26.

can come to be understood. In the second chapter in each part we shall attempt to grasp the specific turn to Christianity, which, in spite of all decisive differences (especially in Part II), comprises the basic intention preceding all specifically theological interpretation. The establishment of fundamental concepts provides the criterion for the individual's fact of being or not being in God's presence as understood by Augustine. Of course, these presentations will not prove whether, in fact, such a pretheological sphere is to be [A:033246] justified at all, or whether the possible being or not being of human existence is truly settled in God's presence.

The disjointedness of Augustine's writings is usually, and to some extent justly, explained by the facts of Augustine's life. He came from the cultural world of late antiquity, and at some time or other was decisively affected by almost all of its trends. After his conversion, in the course of a long process we can trace by biographical dates, he came increasingly under the influence of Christian concepts and religious articles of faith. The ancient rhetor and talented writer turned more and more into the "Father of the Church," the role in which he kept living and working in history. He changed so thoroughly that at the end of his life, in the *Retractations*, he would submit the entirety of his writings to an express revision from this point of view. At first glance it may seem completely irresponsible to ignore this development, as we do in our analyses. Yet it can be said in defense of the attempt at an inquiry of purely philosophical interest, as distinct from an account of Augustine's evolution,[6] that none of the philosophical ideas of antiquity and late antiquity that Augustine absorbed in various periods of his life, from Cicero's *Hortensius* to Victorinus' translation of Plotinus, were ever radically excised from his thinking. The radical choice between philosophical [A:033247] self-reflection and the obedience of religious faith, as actually performed, for instance, by the young Luther, remained alien to Augustine. However faithful and convinced a Christian he became, and however deeply he penetrated Christianity's intrinsic problems by studying Saint Paul's epistles, the Psalms, the Gospels, and the epistles of Saint John, he never wholly lost the impulse of philosophical questioning. Augustine never extirpated this impulse from this thinking. What this means to interpretation is the possibility of tracing the various fundamental intentions independently of the evolutions that bring them to various points. This can only be verified in our concrete analysis. It means the possibility of seeing how the

6. The best treatment of this topic, to my knowledge, is Prosper Alfaric, *L'Évolution intellectuelle de S. Augustin; du Manichéisme au Néoplatonisme* (Paris, 1918). Unfortunately, thus far, this work has not carried Augustine's development beyond Neoplatonism.

Neoplatonic rudiments, though hidden, remain active in each set of Christian problems, peculiarly transforming them (even concealing them) from a purely Christian point of view. From the outset the question never is which is more original, antiquity or Christianity. Our analyses will show not so much what conquered as what guided Augustine's concern. Augustine's starting point, manifested in such utterances as "I have become a question to myself," will be viewed simply as a given phenomenon not subject to interpretation in the framework of this essay. In the framework of our theme, the concept of love, we shall try to clarify the directions in which Augustine's own exegesis and orientation move.

This essay offers three analyses. The first begins with love understood as craving *(appetitus)*, which is the only definition Augustine gives [A:033248] of love. In the presentation of "well-ordered love" at the end of this analysis, we see the incongruities to which this definition of love leads Augustine. Thus we are led to a very different conceptual context, which is incomprehensible from the first analysis and yet in an oddly peripheral sense suggests the attempt of deducing neighborly love from love as craving *(appetitus)*. The second analysis permits us merely to understand in what sense our neighbor is loved in adhering to the commandment of neighborly love. Not until the third analysis is any light thrown on the incongruity of the second. This incongruity is pointed up in the question of how the person in God's presence, isolated from all things mundane, can be at all interested in his neighbor. This is illuminated by proving the neighbor's relevance in a wholly different context. The illumination of incongruities is not tantamount to the solution of problems arising from a relatively closed conceptual and empirical context. It only answers the question of how these incongruities come to appear, that is, what completely different intentions lead to such contradictions, incomprehensible as they are to systematic thought. We must let the contradictions stand as what they are, make them understood as contradictions, and grasp what lies beneath them.

PART I
LOVE AS CRAVING:
THE ANTICIPATED FUTURE

1 / The Structure of Craving *(Appetitus)*

[B:033131] Augustine writes that "to love is indeed nothing else than to crave something for its own sake," and further on he comments that "love is a kind of craving."[1] Every craving *(appetitus)* is tied to a definite object, and it takes this object to spark the craving itself, thus providing an aim for it. Craving is determined by the definitely given thing it seeks, just as a movement is set by the goal toward which it moves. For, as Augustine writes, love is "a kind of motion, and all motion is toward something."[2] What determines the motion of desire is always previously given. Our craving aims at a world we know; it does not discover anything new. The thing we know and desire is a "good" *(bonum)*, otherwise we would not seek it for its own sake. All the goods we desire in our questing love are independent objects, unrelated to other objects. Each of them represents nothing but its isolated goodness. The distinctive trait of this good that we desire is that we do not have it. Once we have the object our desire ends, unless we are threatened with its loss. In that case the desire to have *(appetitus habendi)* turns into a fear of losing *(metus amittendi)*. As a quest for the particular good rather than for things at random, desire is a combination of "aiming at" and "referring back to." It refers back to the individual who knows the world's good and evil and seeks to live happily *(beate vivere)*. It is because we know happiness that we want to be happy, and since nothing is more certain than our wanting to be happy *(beatum esse velle)*, our notion of happiness guides us in determining the respective goods that then became objects of our desires.[3] Craving, or love, is a human being's possibility of gaining possession of the good that will make him happy, that is, of gaining possession of what is most his own.

This love can turn into fear: "None will doubt that the only causes of fear are either loss of what we love and have gained, or failure to gain what

1. *Eighty-three Different Questions* 35, 1 and 2.
2. Ibid., 1.
3. *Enchiridion* 28, 104 and 105; *The Free Choice of the Will* II, 16, 41; *Sermon* 306, 3 and 4; [*The Happy Life* 2, 10].

we love and [B:033132] have hoped for." Craving, as the will to have and to hold, gives rise in the moment of possession to a fear of losing. As craving seeks some good, fear dreads some evil *(malum)*, and "he who fears something must necessarily shun it."[4] The evil that fear makes us shun is whatever threatens our happiness, which consists in possession of the good. So long as we desire temporal things, we are constantly under this threat, and our fear of losing always corresponds to our desire to have. Temporal goods originate and perish independently of man, who is tied to them by his desire. Constantly bound by craving and fear to a future full of uncertainties, we strip each present moment of its calm, its intrinsic import, which we are unable to enjoy. And so, the future destroys the present. Whatever can be taken away from a lasting enjoyment for its own sake cannot possibly be the proper object of desire.[5] The present is not determined by the future as such (although this, too, is possible with Augustine, as we shall see below), but by certain events which we hope for or fear from the future, and which we accordingly crave and pursue, or shun and avoid. Happiness *(beatitudo)* consists in possession, in having and holding *(habere et tenere)* our good, and even more in being sure of not losing it. Sorrow *(tristitia)* consists in having lost our good and in enduring this loss. However, for Augustine the happiness of having is not contrasted by sorrow but by fear of losing. The trouble with human happiness is that it is constantly beset by fear. It is not the lack of possessing but the safety of possession that is at stake.

This enormous importance of security—that nothing subject to loss can ever become an object of possession—is due to the condition of man and not to the objects he desires. Good and evil are good and bad for one who wants to live happily. Although all men want to live happily, each one means and seeks something else by happiness, and by the goods which constitute it. Hence the questions arise: what is good? what is evil? Each one understands something different by them. However, all are agreed on one point, namely, wanting to live. Thus the happy life *(beata vita)* is actually life itself. And it also follows that a life in constant peril of death is no true life, because it is continually threatened by the loss of what it is, and is even certain to lose it some day. "The true life is [B:033133] one that is both everlasting and happy,"[6] and "since all men want to be happy, they want also to be

---

4. *Eighty-three Different Questions* 33.
5. Ibid., 35, 1.
6. *Sermon* 306, 7. [In the original German text of the dissertation, the footnote following this citation contains a reference to *The City of God* XI, 28, in which Augustine writes about the process of returning to God: "There our existence will have no death, our knowledge no error, our love no obstacle." Another text from *The City of God* XIV, 25 corresponds more exactly to

immortal if they know what they want; for otherwise they could not be happy."[7] Thus the good love craves is life, and the evil fear shuns is death. The happy life is the life we cannot lose. Life on earth is a living death, *mors vitalis*, or *vita mortalis*. It is altogether determined by death; indeed it is more properly called death.[8] For the constant fear that rules it prevents living, unless one equates being alive with being afraid.[9]

This basic fear guides all our fears of specific evils. By putting an end to life, death is at the same time the cause of the constant worry of life about itself—the endless concern about its transient happiness—and about life after death. But, as Augustine writes, "what if death itself cuts off and puts an end to all worries along with all feeling?"[10] Is there no consolation in death? Augustine has no answer other than to summon up the "authority of the Christian faith" with its claim that life is immortal.[11] Do not all men agree that they want to live? Only where there is no death, and hence no future, can men live "without the anguish of worry."[12] In their fear of death, those living fear life itself, a life that is doomed to die. Hence, their fear teaches them the true nature of life. "All things shun death, since death is the contrast of life; it follows necessarily that life, shunning its opposite, also perceives itself."[13] The mode in which life knows and perceives itself is worry. Thus the object of fear comes to be fear itself. Even if we should assume that there is nothing to fear, that death is no evil, the fact of fear (that all living things shun death) remains. Hence, "either the evil we fear exists, or evil is the very fact of fear."[14] The fearless security of possession reigns only where there is nothing to be lost. This fearlessness is what love seeks. Love as crav-

---

Arendt's reference in the German original: "Therefore, life will only be truly happy when it is eternal."]

7. *The Trinity* XIII, 8, 11.

8. *Confessions* I, 6, 7: "vita mortalis"; ibid. X, 17, 26: "in homine vivente mortaliter" [in man living as mortal]; *The City of God* XII, 21: "If indeed it is to be called life, when it is really a death."

9. *Sermon* 306, 7.

10. *Confessions* VI, 11, 19: "It is not for nothing and meaningless that the dignity and authority of the Christian faith are spread throughout the whole world. Such great and wonderful things would never have been done for us by God if the life of the soul were to end with the death of the body."

11. Ibid.

12. *Letter* 55, 17.

13. *The Free Choice of the Will* II, 4, 10.

14. *Confessions* VII, 5, 7. ["Thus did I conjecture that your finite creation was filled by you (God), the infinite, and I said, 'Behold God and behold what God has created. . . . Being good, he has created good things. Behold how he encircles and fills all things! Where then is evil and whence and by what means has it crept in here? . . . Therefore, either there is an evil that we fear, or the fact that we fear is itself an evil.'"]

ing (appetitus) is determined by its goal, and this goal is freedom from fear (metu carere).[15] Since life in its approach to death is constantly "diminished" and thus keeps losing itself, it is the experience of loss that must guide the determination of love's adequate [B:033134] object (the amandum).

Thus the good of love is established: it is "what you cannot lose against your will."[16] Thus we see that the good that gives man happiness is essentially defined by Augustine in two heterogeneous contexts. First, the good is the object of craving, that is, something useful that man can find in the world and hope to obtain. In the second context, the good is defined by fear of death, that is, by life's fear of its own destruction. All other accidents of life, which man does not have in his hand, are traced back to his lack of power over life itself. "Which man could live as he would since the mere fact of living is not in his power?"[17] Analogously, death is interpreted in two ways: first, as the index of life's lack of control over itself, and second, as the worst evil encountered by life—its adversary pure and simple. As this utmost evil, death comes to the living from the outside and they shun it, while with such terms as vita mortalis men are viewed as mortals to begin with. Life and death belong together. The consciousness of this impotence, in which life is regarded as inherently mortal, contradicts the definition of love as craving because craving, in line with its meaning as a quest, makes us strive for something that can be achieved, though we may fail to achieve it. Only when death is regarded as the utmost evil, meeting life from the outside, is the unity of the argument (love as craving) preserved.

The reason for this incongruity lies in Augustine's terminology, which he took over from the tradition of Greek philosophy even when he wished to express experiences that were quite alien to it. This is especially true of the appetitus reflections, which can be traced back to Aristotle via Plotinus. Aristotle defined death as the "evil most to be feared" without, however, insisting on this fear for his understanding of man.[18] Yet it is precisely in the twofold interpretation of death that the twin rudiments of this whole set of problems become manifest. For the present we can make this point: life

---

15. Eighty-three Different Questions 34.
16. The Free Choice of the Will I, 16, 34; Sermon 72, 6.
17. The City of God XIV, 25. ["In our present state, what human being can live the life he wishes, when the actual living is not in his control?"]
18. Aristotle, Nicomachean Ethics III, 1114b26. For the origin of appetitus (in the Greek, desire or appetite), see Nicomachean Ethics I, 1094a1, 1095a16; and Plotinus, Enneads III 5, 4 and VI, 8, 2–8. For Aristotle's influence on Plotinus's Neoplatonism, see Gerhard Nebel, Plotinus Kategorien der Intelligiblen Welt (Tübingen, 1929). For Augustine's dependence on Greek tradition and the way it was handed down, see Harald Fuchs, Augustin und der antike Friedensgedanke (Berlin, 1926), reprinted in Neue Philologische Untersuchungen (Berlin, 1965).

characterized by death craves something that, in principle, it cannot obtain, and pursues it as though it were at its disposal.

Every good and every evil lie ahead. [B:033135] What lies at the end of the road we keep walking all our lives is death. Every present moment is governed by this imminence. Human life is always "not yet." All "having" is governed by fear, all "not having" by desire. Thus the future in which man lives is always the expected future, fully determined by his present longings or fears. The future is by no means unknown since it is nothing but the threatening or fulfilling "not yet" of the present. However, every fulfillment is only apparent because at the end looms death, the radical loss. This means that the future, the "not yet" of the present, is what we must always fear. To the present, the future can only be menacing. Only a present without a future is immutable and utterly unthreatened. In such a present lies the calm of possession. This possession is life itself. For all goods exist for life alone, to protect it from its loss, from death.

This present without a future—which no longer knows particular goods but is itself the absolute good *(summum bonum)*—is eternity. Eternity is what "you cannot lose against your will." A love that seeks anything safe and disposable on earth is constantly frustrated, because everything is doomed to die. In this frustration love turns about and its object becomes a negation, so that nothing is to be desired except freedom from fear. Such fearlessness exists only in the complete calm that can no longer be shaken by events expected of the future. The good, which can be understood only as a correlative to love defined as craving and which is unobtainable for mortal life, is projected into an absolute present commencing after death. Even though this present becomes an absolute future for mortal life, it is still being craved and thus it lies ahead just like any other good expected in the future. The sole exception to this is the life whose expectations aim at the absolute future and can no longer be disappointed. However, as the object of craving becomes pure calm and the pure absence of fear, the good retains its negativity and lack of content. These qualities have arisen from the senselessness of craving for a life seen essentially from the viewpoint of death. For this kind of life, the will to possess and the will to dispose of something have become simply absurd.

There can be no doubt that death, and not just fear of death, was the most crucial experience in Augustine's life. [B:033136] With exquisite eloquence he describes in the *Confessions* what it meant to him to lose his friend, and how "he became a question to himself" as a consequence of this loss. After "the loss of life of the dying" followed "the death of the living." This was the experience that initially turned the young Augustine toward himself when he had first fallen in love with philosophy at age nineteen after reading Cicero's *Hortensius* (one of his lost works, an exhortation to practice philosophy).[19] Still, according to Augustine, the decisive motive for his conversion to Christianity was the "fear of death," for nothing else had so strongly recalled him from "carnal pleasures."[20] Under these circumstances, it was almost a matter of course that the apostle Paul finally convinced Augustine, for nowhere else in the New Testament is the fact of death, life's imminent and final "no more," invested with such decisive importance.[21] The more Christian Augustine grew in the course of a long life, the more Pauline he became.

Fearless possession can be achieved only under the conditions of timelessness, equated by both Augustine and Plotinus with eternity. Thus, Augustine proceeds to strip the world and all temporal things of their value and to make them relative. All worldly goods are changeable *(mutabilia)*. Since they will not last, they do not really exist. They cannot be relied upon. Plotinus writes:

> For what is does not differ from what always is, just as a philosopher does not differ from a true philosopher. . . . We add to "what is" the word "always" and to "always" the word "being", and thus we speak of "everlasting being". This means: What always is, that is truly.[22]

But even if things should last, human life does not. We lose it daily. As we live the years pass through us and they wear us out into nothingness.[23] It seems that only the present is real, for "things past and things to come are not"; but how can the present (which I cannot measure) be real since it has no "space"?[24] Life is always either no more or not yet. Like time, life "comes from what is not yet, passes through what is without space, and disappears into what is no longer."[25] Can life be said to exist at all? Still the fact is that

19. *Confessions* IV, 4, 7–9.
20. Ibid., VI, 16, 26.
21. Ibid., VII, 21, 27.
22. See especially Plotinus's treatise on "Time and Eternity," *Enneads* III, 7, 6. ["There is, of course, no difference between Being and Everlasting Being; just as there is none between a philosopher and a true philosopher. The attribute 'true' came into use because there arose, what masqueraded as philosophy. For similar reasons 'everlasting' was adjoined to 'Being,' and 'Being' to 'Everlasting,' and we have 'Everlasting Being.' We must take this 'Everlasting' as expressing no more than Authentic Being."]
23. *Sermon* 109, 4; see also *Sermon* 38, 5.
24. *Confessions* XI, 21, 27.
25. Ibid. Time without space is immeasurable nor can it be held on to; see also *Confessions* XI, 27, 36.

man does measure time. Perhaps man possesses a "space" where time can be conserved [B:033137] long enough to be measured, and would not this "space," which man carries with himself, transcend both life and time?

Time exists only insofar as it can be measured, and the yardstick by which we measure it is space.[26] Where is the space located that permits us to measure time? For Augustine the answer is: in our memory where things are being stored up. Memory, the storehouse of time, is the presence of the "no more" *(iam non)* as expectation is the presence of the "not yet" *(nondum)*.[27] Therefore, I do not measure what is no more, but something in my memory that remains fixed in it.[28] It is only by calling past and future into the present of remembrance and expectation that time exists at all. Hence the only valid tense is the present, the Now. Plotinus writes, "Generally speaking, the past is time ending now, and the future is time beginning now."[29] The Now is what measures time backwards and forwards, because the Now, strictly speaking, is not time but outside time. In the Now, past and future meet. For a fleeting moment they are simultaneous so that they can be stored up by memory, which remembers things past and holds the expectation of things to come. For a fleeting moment (the temporal Now) it is as though time stands still, and it is this Now that becomes Augustine's model of eternity for which he uses Neoplatonic metaphors—the *nunc stans* or *stans aeternitatis*—although divesting them of their specific mystical meaning.[30] Augustine writes:

> Who will hold [the heart], and fix it so that it may stand still for a little while and catch for a moment the splendor of eternity which stands still forever, and compare this with temporal moments that never stand still, and see that it is incomparable . . . but that all this while in the eternal, nothing passes but the whole is present.[31]

Clearly, this harks back to Plotinus:

> That which "neither has been nor will be, but simply exists," that which standing still possesses existence because it is neither in the

26. Ibid., XI, 21, 27.   28. Ibid., XI, 27, 35.
27. Ibid., XI, 28, 37.   29. Plotinus, *Enneads* III, 7, 9.
    30. For Augustine's use of mystical terms while discarding their original meaning, see Karl Holl, "Augustins innere Entwicklung," *Preussische Akademie der Wissenschaften* (1928): 24, and Max Zepf, "Augustins Konfessionen," *Heidelberger Abhandlungen Zur Philosophie* 9 (1926): 28.
    31. *Confessions* XI, 11, 13.

process of change toward the future nor has it been changed [in the past]—that is Eternity.[32]

What prevents man from "living" in the timeless present is life itself, which never "stands still." The good for which love craves lies beyond all mere desires. If it were merely a question of desiring, all desires would end in fear. And since whatever confronts life from the outside as the object of its craving is sought for life's sake (a life we are going to lose), the ultimate object of all desires is life itself. Life is the good we ought to seek, namely true life, which is [B:033138] the same as Being and therefore endures forever. This good, which is not to be obtained on earth, is projected into eternity and thus becomes again that which lies ahead from outside. For man, eternity is the future, and this fact, seen from the viewpoint of eternity, is of course a contradiction in terms.

The reason the contradiction arises is that eternity as everlasting life is desired like any other object, a "good" among goods, even though the highest. The object of craving can only be a thing I can possess and enjoy, and it is therefore quite characteristic that in this context Augustine can even speak of God as an "object of enjoyment." Augustine writes, "For whatever is not a thing is altogether nothing," and "the proper things to enjoy are Father, Son and Holy Spirit."[33] This slip of the pen, if such it were, is all the more revealing as Augustine clearly distinguishes between love for another person and love for things.[34] This should be noted quite apart from the fact that the Confessions offer overwhelming evidence for the preponderance of personal love in the range of Augustine's experience. Thus life, too, becomes a "thing," an object that disappears from the word and, like all other objects of our desires, does not endure. From this perspective of desire, life is looked upon from the outside (from outside the living person) as something that occurs in the world and mutably clings to the immutable in order to gain permanence from it. Such permanence is granted by eternity, the object of desire.

32. Plotinus, *Enneads* III, 7, 3; see also Plato, *Timaeus* 37c–38a.

33. *Christian Doctrine* I, 2, 2. ["For whatever is not a thing is absolutely nothing, but not everything is also a sign." Ibid., I, 5, 5: "The proper object of our enjoyment, therefore, is the Father, Son and Holy Spirit, the same who are the Trinity, one supreme Being, accessible to all who enjoy Him, if, indeed, He is a thing and not rather the cause of all things, or perhaps both thing and cause."] See also ibid., I, 7, 7.

34. Etienne Gilson draws attention to this distinction in *The Christian Philosophy of St. Augustine* (New York: Random House, 1960), 311 n. 40: "On this point, as on many others, Augustine's terminology is rather flexible. As far as can be judged from the different texts, the most general meaning of the word *charity* would be a 'person's complete love for another person' (as opposed to his love for things)." However, Augustine's terminology is more than "flexible," and he usually uses the word *diligere* for personal love.

As it takes an object to determine and arouse desire, Augustine defines life itself by what it craves. Life craves the goods occurring in the world, and thus turns itself into one of them only to find out that things *(res)*, if compared to life, are of almost sempiternal permanence. Things endure. They will be tomorrow what they are today and what they were yesterday. Only life vanishes from day to day in its rush toward death. Life does not last and it does not remain identical. It is not ever-present and, indeed, is never present, since it is always not yet or no more. No earthly goods can lend support to life's instability. The future will strip it of all of them and in death it will lose itself along with its acquisitions. True, all worldly goods are good as such, being created by God. It is only a life that clings to them, and will always be deprived of them in the future, that also turns them into changeable *mutabilia*. Augustine writes, "For we [B:033139] call 'world' not only this fabric which God made, heaven and earth . . . but the inhabitants of the world are also called 'the world.' . . . Especially all lovers of the world are called the world."[35]

The world is constituted as an earthly world not just by the works of God but by the "lovers of the world," that is, by men, and by what they love. It is the love of the world that turns heaven and earth into the world as a changeable thing. In its flight from death, the craving for permanence clings to the very things sure to be lost in death. This love has the wrong object, one that continually disappoints its craving. The right love consists in the right object. Mortal man, who has been placed into the world (here understood as heaven and earth) and must leave it, instead clings to it and in the process turns the world itself into a vanishing one, that is, one due to vanish with his death. The specific identification of earthly and mortal is possible only if the world is seen from the point of view of mortal man. Augustine's term for this wrong, mundane love that clings to, and thus at the same time constitutes, the world is *cupiditas*. In contrast, the right love seeks eternity and the absolute future. Augustine calls this right love *caritas:* the "root of all evils is *cupiditas*, the root of all goods is *caritas*."[36] However, both right and wrong love *(caritas* and *cupiditas)* have this in common—craving desire, that is, *appetitus*. Hence, Augustine warns, "Love, but be careful what you love."[37]

---

35. *Homilies on the First Epistle of John* II, 12.

36. *Commentaries on the Psalms* 90, 1, 8. [Augustine cites Eph. 3:17, "that you may be rooted and grounded in love *(in caritate),*" and 1 Tim. 6:10, "For the love of money is the root of all evils."

37. Ibid., 31, 5. [The next sentence reads, "*Caritas* says: love of God and love of neighbor; *cupiditas* says: love of the world and love of this age *(saeculum)*."

PART I
LOVE AS CRAVING:
THE ANTICIPATED FUTURE

2 / Caritas and Cupiditas

[B:033143] Love understood as craving desire *(appetitus)*, and desire understood in terms of the Greek tradition from Aristotle to Plotinus, constitutes the root of both *caritas* and *cupiditas*. They are distinguished by their objects, but they are not different kinds of emotion: "just as temporal life is cherished by its lovers, thus we should cherish eternal life, which the Christian professes to love."[1] Desire mediates between subject and object, and it annihilates the distance between them by transforming the subject into a lover and the object into the beloved. For the lover is never isolated from what he loves; he belongs to it. "What else is love except a kind of life that binds, or seeks to bind, together some two things, namely the lover and the beloved? And this is so even in external and carnal love."[2] Hence, in *cupiditas* or in *caritas*, we decide about our abode, whether we wish to belong to this world or to the world to come, but the faculty that decides is always the same. Since man is not self-sufficient and therefore always desires something outside himself, the question of who he is can only be resolved by the object of his desire and not, as the Stoics thought, by the suppression of the impulse of desire itself: "Such is each as is his love."[3] Strictly speaking, he who does not love and desire at all is a nobody.

The quest for worldliness changes man's nature. This quest transforms him into a worldly being. In *cupiditas*, man has cast the die that makes him perishable. In *caritas*, whose object is eternity, man transforms himself into an eternal, nonperishable being. Man as such, his essence, cannot be defined because he always desires to belong to something outside himself and changes accordingly. Hence, he is seen by Augustine in his isolation as separated from things as well as from persons. However, it is precisely this isola-

1. *Sermon* 302, 2; see also *Letter* 127, 4.
2. *The Trinity* VIII, 10, 14.
3. *Homilies on the First Epistle of John* II, 14. ["Rather hold fast to the love of God, that as God is forever and ever, so you may also remain forever and ever; because such is each one as is his love."]

tion he cannot bear. If he could be said to have an essential nature at all, it would be lack of self-sufficiency. Hence, he is driven to break out of his isolation by means of love—whether *cupiditas* turns him into a denizen of this world or *caritas* makes him live in the absolute future where he will be denizen of the world-to-come. Since only love can constitute either world as man's home, "this world is for the faithful [who do not love the world] what the desert was for the people of Israel"—they live not in houses but in tents.⁴ Would it not then be better to love the world in *cupiditas* and be at home? Why should we make a desert out of this world? The justification for this extraordinary enterprise can only lie in a deep dissatisfaction with what the world can give its lovers. Love that desires a worldly object, be it a thing or a person, is constantly frustrated in its very quest for happiness.

[B:033144] Desire, the craving for something, can only be stilled by the presence of the desired object, which the craving constantly anticipates. To be with the beloved stills love and brings about a calm quietude. The motion of love as desire comes to an end with the possession of the beloved and the holding *(tenere)* of its object. Only in possession does isolation really end, and this end is the same as happiness. For "no one is happy who does not enjoy what he loves. Even those who love things they should not love, think themselves happy not because they love but because they enjoy" whatever they desire.⁵ Hence, for happiness, which is the reversal of isolation, more is required than mere belonging. Happiness is achieved only when the beloved becomes a permanently inherent element of one's own being. Augustine indicates this closeness of lover and beloved by using the word *inhaerere*, which is usually translated as "clinging to" and occurs chiefly as *inhaerere Deo*, "clinging to God," expressing a state of being on earth that is not Godforsaken.

Happiness occurs when the gap between lover and beloved has been closed, and the question is whether *cupiditas*, the love of this world, can ever attain it. Since the ultimate goal of the lover is his own happiness, he actually is guided in all his desires by a desire for his own good, that is, for something that is inside himself. In *cupiditas* I seek what is outside, outside myself *(extra me* or *foris a me)*, and this search is vain even if it is the search for God.⁶ Self-love is the root of all desire, of *caritas* as well as of *cupiditas*. And the reason that self-love, which starts with forsaking God, is wrong and never attains its

---

4. Ibid., VII, 1; see also *Tractates on John's Gospel* XXVIII, 9: "At the present time, then, before we come to the land of promise, namely the eternal kingdom, we are in the desert and live in tents."

5. *The City of God* VIII, 8.

6. *Confessions* VI, 1, 1, and *True Religion* 39, 72.

goal is that such love aims at "things which are outside [the lover] who is thus driven outside himself."[7] Thus in *cupiditas* man wants not himself but the world, and in having the world he desires to become part and parcel of it. Originally he is not part of the world, for if he were of the world, he would not desire it. To be sure, man is also isolated from God. Both *caritas* and *cupiditas* testify to a fundamental isolation of man from whatever might bring him happiness, that is, to a separation of man from his very self. It is precisely by the pursuit of what is outside my self that *cupiditas* makes me miss my aim—myself.

Goods outside myself are not within my power, and among them is the highest good, life itself. *Cupiditas* desires and makes me dependent upon things that, in principle, are beyond my control, [B:033145] that is, which I "can lose against my will" *(invitus amittere possum)*. Indeed, the fact that life, which is cut off from what it needs, craves at all means that man is not independent and self-sufficient. His original isolation from his own good testifies to his dependence. On the road to what he needs to be able to be at all, man encounters the outside world, and since he can never close the gap between this outside and himself, he is enslaved by it. In his discussion of free will, or rather of freedom of choice (especially in *The Free Choice of the Will*), Augustine opposes not *caritas* but freedom to *cupiditas*, which here is called *libido* or desire, and like *cupiditas* is defined as the love of things one can lose against one's will. For this reason Augustine considers *cupiditas* more hostile to a "good will" capable of freedom than anything else.[8] In this process of belonging to what is "outside myself," I am enslaved, and this enslavement becomes manifest in fear. Freedom in this context means nothing but self-sufficiency, and Augustine's train of thought often seems to follow almost verbatim the thinking of the Stoic philosophers. Sentences such as the following could just as well have been written by Epictetus: "All that is not in our power cannot be loved and valued highly. . . . Who does not love them, will not suffer from their loss and will despise them altogether."[9] As with the Stoics, fear expresses in its most radical form our lack of power over life itself and is the existential reason for this ideal of self-sufficiency. Hence, we see that contempt for the world and its goods is not Christian in origin. In this context God is neither the Creator nor the supreme judge nor the ultimate goal of human life and love. Rather, as Supreme Being, God is the quintessence of Being, namely self-sufficiency, which needs no help from the outside and actually has nothing outside itself. So strong is Augustine's

7. *Sermon* 96, 2.
8. *The Free Choice of the Will* I, 16, 34.
9. Ibid., I, 13, 27.

dependence upon these non-Christian currents of thought that he even uses them occasionally for a description of God: "God needs no assistance from anything else in the act of creation as though he were one who did not suffice himself."[10]

Undoubtedly, insofar as Augustine defines love as a kind of desire, he hardly speaks as a Christian. His starting point is not God who revealed himself to mankind, but the experience of the deplorable state of the human condition, and whatever he has to say in this context is far from original in late antiquity. All the late philosophical schools had this analysis of man's existence in common, and it speaks for Augustine's sense [B:033146] of philosophical relevance that he turned to Plotinus rather than to the Stoics in his early philosophical endeavors. According to Plotinus, "desire pulls outward and implies need; to desire is still to be drawn, even [if drawn] toward the good." Obviously, "need, inexorably desiring satisfaction, is not free in face of that to which it is forced."[11] From this it follows that craving for God is just as unfree as love of the world. Augustine tries to avoid this conclusion by stating that God is identical with man's own good, but this results in the further difficulty that God is then no longer understood as being outside man, and Augustine indeed sometimes speaks of God "circulating within us."[12] However, this difficulty is minor compared to the simple fact that the very act of desiring presupposes the distinction of an "inner" act and its "external" object, so that desiring by definition can never attain its object, unless the object, too, is within man and so within his power. Plotinus, unlike Augustine, is quite consistent in his speculations: freedom exists only where desire ceases to be. For Plotinus this freedom can be actualized in this life by virtue of the *nous*, the human spirit, whose main characteristic it is that it relates only to itself. From the viewpoint of life, this state in which man's spirit relates to itself is a kind of death. For to the extent that we are alive and active (and desire is a form of action), we necessarily are involved in things outside ourselves and cannot be free. Only the spirit has its origin not in something outside itself and hence is it own good. Freedom, according to Plotinus, "must be referred not to the doing, not to external

10. Ibid., I, 2, 5.
11. Plotinus, *Enneads* VI, 8, 4; VI, 8, 2.
12. Etienne Gilson comments on *Sermon* 163, 1, 1 (in *The Christian Philosophy of St. Augustine* [New York: Random House, 1960], 141–42) in the following: "To live by charity we must do two things: move towards God, i.e., towards charity, and possess charity even now as a pledge of future happiness, i.e., possess God. Indeed, charity is not only the means whereby we shall obtain God; it is God already possessed, obtained and circulating, so to speak, within us through the gift He has made us of Himself." [Gilson then refers to *Sermon* 163, 1, 1 in which Augustine writes of *caritas* as God "circulating within us" ("deambulat in nobis Deus").]

things done, but to the inner activity, to the Intellection, to virtue's own vision."[13]

No matter how much Augustine's theory of freedom, as expressed in *The Free Choice of the Will*, owes to Plotinus, he was a Christian when he wrote the treatise, and this is why the Neoplatonic terminological framework never quite works. For Augustine, man's highest good cannot be his own spirit and happiness cannot come from reliance on any human power even though it be the highest. The highest good of a created being must be his Creator, and there is no doubt that the Creator is not inside his creature in the same way as the spirit, the *nous*, is certainly inside man. Thus, Augustine's uncritical use not only of Stoic but also of Neoplatonic categories could not help but lead him into inconsistencies, if not into outright contradictions. We shall see later that Augustine, [B:033147] although he never became fully aware of the inadequacy of part of his terminology, knows of an entirely different kind of *caritas*, namely, of a love that stands in no relation whatsoever to either *appetitus* or *cupiditas*, and therefore is truly of divine and not of human origin. This entirely different kind of love is the *caritas* that is diffused *in cordibus nostris*, "the love that is shed in our hearts" (Rom. 5:5). In this sense *caritas* indicates not God's "circulating" presence within us, but the grace bestowed by the Creator upon his creature.

The reason Augustine found it so difficult to rid himself of Plotinus's terms long after he had formally disowned him was that no one had more convincingly conceived of man's utter strangeness in the world he is born into and had more plausibly shown the depth of the gulf between man and world, which manifests itself in human appetites and desires, than had Plotinus. This must have been Augustine's deepest pre-Christian experience, and he found in Plotinus its very philosopher. However, the distinction between these two thinkers is as great as their affinity. There had never been anything in Augustine that could compare with Plotinus's noble serenity, his "self-sufficiency," or, to speak in the language of the time, his complete contentment in being alone with himself. As Gilson rightly pointed out, for Plotinus, but never for Augustine, the soul itself was divine.[14] Plotinus carried, in a sense, all the things within himself that Augustine desired. And it is for this very reason that Plotinus did not know fear, that is, the very experience that prompted Augustine's conversion.

Therefore, if Augustine, like Plotinus and not unlike the Stoics, actually holds that the thing to be loved is fearlessness, and then equates this fear-

13. Plotinus, *Enneads* VI, 8, 6.
14. Gilson, *The Christian Philosophy of St. Augustine*, 110.

lessness with self-sufficiency, he does not really say the same thing, because Augustine never believed that such fearlessness or self-sufficiency can be obtained by man in this world, no matter how much he might strain all his capacities of mind and spirit. To be sure, true being means "not being in want" and the corresponding attitude would be fearlessness. However, the specific quality of being human is precisely a fear that nothing can remove. This fear is no idle emotion, but rather the manifestation of dependence. Desire is not bad because the "outside" is bad. Rather, desire is bad and slavish because it entails dependence on what is, in principle, unattainable. This does not contradict the previous statement that all craving is determined by its object and turns into *caritas* or *cupiditas* by what it seeks. For it is only by its pursuing [B:033148] what is outside that craving turns the neutral "outside" into a "world" strictly speaking, that is, into a home for man. Only the world constituted by the "lovers of the world" *(dilectores mundi)* is an evil, and only desire *(appetitus)* for this "evil" turns into *cupiditas*. Still, the main characteristic of this evil is that it is "outside," and the outside as such enslaves and deprives of freedom. For freedom is essentially freedom from fear. No one who depends upon what is outside himself can be fearless. As we shall see later, *caritas* is free precisely because it casts out fear *(timorem foras mittit)*.

The tie to the world, which is actualized in *cupiditas*, must be cut because it is governed by fear. Living in *cupiditas*, man belongs to the world and is estranged from himself. Augustine calls this worldliness in which the self gets lost "dispersion." By desiring and depending on things "outside myself," that is, on the very things I am not, I lose the unity that holds me together by virtue of which I can say "I am." I thereby become dispersed in the manifoldness of the world and lost in the unending multiplicity of mundane data. Out of this dispersion, Augustine calls upon the One God "to gather [him] in from the dispersion wherein [he] was torn asunder."[15] Since dispersion brings about loss of self, it has the great advantage of distracting from fear, except that this loss of fear is identical with loss of self. I flee from my own self, which must die and lose all its possessions, in order to cling to things that are more permanent than myself. Augustine writes that "men who desire what is outside are exiled from themselves."[16] This self-loss comes about by curiosity, an oddly selfless "lust of the eyes" (1 John 2:16), which is attracted by the things of the world. Lust of the eyes desires to know the things of the world for their own sake, without any reflection upon

15. *Confessions* II, 1, 1.
16. *Commentaries on the Psalms* 57, 1.

the self and without in the least seeking pleasure of any kind. For pleasure, sensual pleasure *(voluptas)*, seeks whatever is pleasing to the senses as the beautiful is pleasing to the eyes, the melodious pleasing to the ears, the soft to the touch, and the fragrant to the sense of smell. However, vision is distinguished from the other senses in that it knows of a temptation "by far more dangerous" than the mere attraction by the beautiful. The eyes are the only sense that also wishes to see what may be contrary to pleasure, "not for the sake of suffering pain, but out of a desire to experience and to know."[17] While sensual pleasure is reflected back upon the pleasure seeker, so that, for better or worse, he never can lose himself altogether, the desire to know, even if it attains its goal, brings no profit whatever to the self. In knowing [B:033149] or in the quest for knowledge, I am not interested in myself at all. I forget myself in much the same way the spectator in the theater forgets himself and all his worries over the "marvellous spectacle" before his eyes. It is this non-sensual love for the world that makes men go "to search out the hidden works of nature, which are outside *[praeter]* ourselves, which to know is altogether useless, and wherein men lust for nothing but knowledge itself."[18]

Whoever wishes to say "I am," and to summon up his own unity and identity and pit it against the variety and multiplicity of the world, must withdraw into himself, into some inner region, turning his back on whatever the "outside" can offer. It is in this context that Augustine definitely departs from contemporary philosophical teachings, Stoic and Neoplatonic, and strikes out on his own. For unlike Epictetus or Plotinus, he did not find either self-sufficiency or serenity in this inner region of the self. Augustine does not belong to those "who can act well within themselves so that actual deeds will result from this *(qui aliquid boni vobiscum intus agistis unde facta procedunt)*. On the contrary, may God see 'where I am . . . and have mercy and heal me' (Psalm 6:2)." For the more he withdrew into himself and gathered his self from the dispersion and distraction of the world, the more he "became a question to himself" *[quaestio mihi factus sum]*.[19] Hence, it is by no means a simple withdrawal into himself that Augustine opposes to the loss of self in dispersion and distraction, but rather a turning about of the ques-

17. *Confessions* X, 35, 55.
18. Ibid. [Arendt's emphasis in this translation is on the human propensity to be attracted to the "outside" world and then to become lost and, as Augustine would say, to forget oneself in that world. A more literal translation of the text would read: "From the same motive (curiosity) human beings proceed to search out the secrets of nature which are beyond our ken—things which offer us no benefit in knowing and which people only desire to know for the sake of knowing."]
19. Ibid., X, 33, 50.

tion itself and the discovery that this self is even more impenetrable than the "hidden works of nature." What Augustine expects of God is an answer to the question "Who am I?"—the certainty of which all previous philosophy had taken for granted. Or, to put it another way, it was because of this new quest for the self that he finally turned to God, whom he did not ask to reveal to him the mysteries of the universe or even the perplexities of Being. He asks to "hear about myself" from God and thus "to know myself." "Seeking God outside myself," in the splendid manifestations of his creation, he had not found "the God of my heart." His mind (the "light of my eyes") "was not with me; for it was inside, while I was outside."[20] When he recalled himself and "entered the inner regions," it was under God's guidance. Augustine was able to find himself only because God was his helper.[21] Self-discovery and discovery of God coincide, because by withdrawing into myself I have ceased to belong to the world. This is the reason that God then comes to my help. In a way I already belong to God. Why should I belong to God when I am in quest of myself? What is the relationship, [B:033150] or perhaps, the affinity between self and God?

Augustine gives an answer to this question in Book X of the *Confessions*. The question he raises is: "What do I love when I love *my* God?"[22] The emphasis I added contains the answer to our question. His quest here is for the God of the human heart, and if this is also a quest for the Supreme Being, then it is only so in the sense that this Being (God) is the essence of this heart. For "when I love *my* God," I love not "the beauty of bodies, nor the splendor of time, nor the brightness of light, the friend to these eyes, nor the sweet melodies of all kinds of songs," yet I still "love some kind of light, and some voice, and some odor," and these belong to "my inner man" as surely as beauty belongs to bodies and brightness to light and sweetness to melodies, except that these properties, now located inside, beyond the reach of the outside world, no longer need adhere to perishable matter and become sheer essences—the pure light that "shines within my soul can be contained by no space, what sounds there, no time snatches away, what smells there no wind can disperse . . . and no surfeit will separate me there from whatever is close to me."[23] In other words, this God who is *my* God, the right object of my desire and my love, is the quintessence of my inner self and therefore by no means identical with it. Indeed, this relationship is no more identical than beauty, the quintessence of all beautiful bodies, can be said to be identical to any one body. And just as body may be consumed but not beauty, light

20. Ibid., X, 3, 3; VI, 1, 1; VII, 7, 11.   22. Ibid., X, 7, 11.
21. Ibid., VII, 10, 16.   23. Ibid., X, 6, 8.

may be extinguished but not brightness, the sounds come and go but not the very sweetness of music, the dark "abysses" of the human heart are subject to time and consumed by time, but not its quintessential being that adheres to it. To this quintessential being I can belong by virtue of love, since love confers belonging: "Hold fast the love for God, that as God is eternal, so you too may remain in eternity: since such is each as is his love."[24] Man loves God because God belongs to him as the essence belongs to existence, but precisely for this reason man *is* not. In finding God he finds what he lacks, the very thing he is not: an eternal essence. This eternal manifests itself "inwardly"—it is the *internum aeternum*, the internal insofar as it is eternal.[25] And it can be eternal only because it is the "location" of the human essence. The "inner man" who is invisible to all mortal eyes is the proper place for the working of an invisible God. The invisible inner man, who is a stranger on earth, belongs to the invisible God. Just as my bodily eyes are delighted with light because their proper good is brightness, so the "inner man" loves God because his proper good is the eternal.

It is in this sense that God is being called the "highest good," namely, the good of goods, as it were, or the good we actually crave in the pursuit of all other goods. Hence, God is the only true correlative of desire. And since desire craves for possession, we cannot but wish to have and hold this good of goods as we wish to have and hold all other goods.[26] Insofar as man loves this [B:033151] "highest good," he loves no one but himself, that is, that of himself which is the true object of all self-love: his own essence. However, since this human essence is immutable by definition *(incommutabilis)*, it stands in flagrant contradiction to human existence, which is subject to time and which changes from day to day, from hour to hour, appearing through birth from non-being and disappearing through death into non-being. So long as man exists, he *is* not. He can only anticipate his essence by striving for eternity, and he will *be* only when he finally holds and enjoys *(frui)* it. The right kind of self-love *(amor sui)* does not love the present self that is going to die but that which will make him live forever. When man begins to search for his essential self in this present life, he first discovers that he is doomed to die and that he is changeable *(mutabilis)*.[27] He finds existence instead of essence, and existence is unreliable. An existing, changeable self cannot always remain present and identifiable: "While you have with you something which you must lose, and either in death or life let go, it cannot be with you always."[28] Hence the moment when "you discover that you are

24. *Homilies on the First Epistle of John* II, 14.
25. *Confessions* IX, 4, 10.   27. *True Religion* XXXIX, 72.
26. *The Free Choice of the Will* II, 9, 26.   28. *Sermon* 125, 11.

changeable by nature, you must transcend yourself."[29] This "transcendence" goes beyond time and tries to catch eternity, "eternal life" versus "temporal life."

However, since this eternity cannot be understood by a temporal being except in terms of absolute futurity, it can be actualized only in the form of radical negation of the present. In other words, because self-love loves the present, it must turn into self-hatred. This is the case not because self-love as such stands accused of wrongful pride and glory (as in Paul), but because an absolute futurity can be anticipated only through the annihilation of the mortal, temporal present, that is, through hating the existing self *(odium sui)*. Life's own essence, its inherent "good," must transcend and even negate life insofar as all worldly life is determined by its opposite, by death, which is its natural and inherent end. Hence, life's true end or goal must be separated from life itself and its present existential reality. Life's true goal is being projected into an absolute future. However, this projection somehow does not work. No future, not even absolute futurity, can ever deny its origin in ordinary human temporality. An event expected from this absolute future is structurally no different from other events expected within the limitations of earthly life. This is the reason that eternal life, expected as a future event, finds its correlation in desire and appetite, that is, in human faculties that cannot but expect their "goods" from [B:033152] outside. In this conceptual context, *caritas*, like any love, must be understood as craving and is distinguished from *cupiditas* by its object alone. From this it follows that man's own life, insofar as it is a "happy life," has turned into a good expected from the outside. In other words, man's present life is being neglected for the sake of his future, and loses its meaningfulness and weight in comparison with that true life which is projected into an absolute future and which is constituted as the ultimate goal of present, worldly human existence.

That the "highest good" on earth is "possessed" in the act of striving for it is, of course, a contradiction in terms. Just as true self-love can be actualized paradoxically only in self-hatred, so "possession" can here only be actualized by oblivion. In longing for and desiring the future, we are liable to forget the present, to leap over it. If the present is altogether filled with desire for the future, man can anticipate a timeless present "where the day neither begins with the end of yesterday, nor is ended by the beginning of tomorrow; it is always today."[30] This is properly called divine "time," that is, the time of him whose "today is eternity."[31] This anticipation, namely that

---

29. *True Religion* XXXIX, 72.   31. *Confessions* XI, 13, 16.
30. *Enchiridion* 14, 49.

man can live in the future as though it were the present and can "hold" *(te-nere)* and "enjoy" *(frui)* future eternity, is possible on the ground of Augustine's interpretation of temporality. In contrast to our own understanding, time for Augustine does not begin in the past in order to progress through the present into the future, but comes out of the future and runs, as it were, backward through the present and ends in the past. (Incidentally, this was the Roman understanding of time, which found its conceptual framework solely in Augustine.) Moreover, as far as human existence is concerned, past and future are understood as different modes of the present. Augustine writes, "There are three times; a present time about things past, a present time about things present, a present time about things future," for the future exists only as expectation, and the past as memory, and both expectation and memory occur in the present.[32] Hence, to live in expectation to the point of oblivion is still a way of living in the present. This is the only way of complete self-obliteration: "God must be loved in such a way that, if at all possible, we would forget ourselves."[33]

However, this forgetfulness is by no means only characteristic of the love of God. Since craving is the basic mode of human existence, men always "forget over something," namely, over whatever they happen to desire. Desire itself is a state of forgetfulness. Hence, while "the soul has forgotten itself out of love [B:033153] for the world, let the soul now forget itself out of love for God."[34] Whatever man loves and desires, he always forgets something. Craving the world, he forgets his self and forgets the world; discovering that he cannot find his self except in the craving for God, he forgets his self. Although desire arises out of the will to be happy *(beatum esse velle)* and thus refers back to the self, it forgets this origin, cuts itself loose from this anchor, and becomes entirely absorbed by its object. This change of the point of reference that occurs in the course of desire, such that the lover forgets himself in the pursuit of the beloved, is the "transit" *(transitus)* characteristic of all craving.[35] The "transit" indicates the moment when the lover no longer loves with reference to himself, when his whole existence has become "loving." In a similar way, *caritas*, the craving love of God, achieves the "transit" to the future eternity.

In so doing man not only forgets himself, but in a way he ceases to be himself, that is, this particular person with this particular place in time and space. He loses the human mode of existence, which is mortality, without exchanging it for the divine mode of existence, which is eternity. Insofar as

---

32. Ibid., XI, 20, 26; XI, 28, 37.   34. Ibid.
33. *Sermon* 142, 3.   35. Ibid.

human existence is temporal, its mode of being is from an origin toward an end. The transit achieves oblivion of the "from" over the "toward," whereby the forgetting of the origin obliterates the entire dimension of the past. "Extended" *(extentus)* toward what lies ahead *(ante)* and is "not yet" *(nondum)*, man forgets and disdains his own worldly past along with the world's multiplicity from which he recollected himself. The temporal future (all that is not yet) moves from the future into the present and then into the past. However, the absolute future that is reached in the transit remains forever what it is—sempiternally imminent, immovable by any human conduct and forever separated from human mortality. Since nothing can be done about it, the only proper human attitude toward it is expectation, an expectation in either hope or fear. It is hoped for by those who belong to God by virtue of *caritas* and feared by those who belong to this world from which they must part in death. This is why the Christian creed is constituted by hope. Indeed, *love* of and *hope* for the tenets of *belief* make it Christian and distinguish it from the superstitious belief in demons.[36] In its constant imminence this absolute future cannot distract. In straining forward to it, man lives "not distended but extended" *(non distentus sed extentus)*, even though its result is self-oblivion or self-transcendence.[37] [B:033154] Augustine writes that "no one attains Him unless he transcends himself."[38]

The examination of human existence from the viewpoint of durability has shown that temporality is its dominant character: "wasting time and being wasted by it" *(devorans tempora, devoratus temporibus)*.[39] To Augustine, being and time are opposites. In order to *be*, man has to overcome his human existence, which is temporality: "Hence so that you too may be, transcend time."[40] Therefore, the "transit" consists in transcending temporality, and what needs to be forgotten, and is forgotten, is mortality. Just as the lover forgets himself over the beloved, mortal, temporal man can forget his existence over eternity. The transit is the forgetting. Moreover, despite all disclaimers that the highest good for man should not lie outside, the transit leaps from itself to that which lies outside it. And this is inevitable so long as love is understood and defined as desire. Hence, the first advice: "Do not go outside; return into yourself," since it leads to finding "your nature changeable," is followed by the second advice: "transcend yourself as

36. *Letter* 194, 11 on belief in demons.
37. *Confessions* XI, 29, 39.
38. *Tractates on John's Gospel* XX, 11.
39. *Confessions* IX, 4, 10.
40. *Tractates on John's Gospel* XXXVIII, 10 for the important discussion of the non-being of time.

well."[41] Thus it is not only the world, but human nature as such, that is transcended.

The greatest difficulty this self-forgetfulness and complete denial of human existence raises for Augustine is that it makes the central Christian demand to love one's neighbor as oneself well nigh impossible. The difficulty arises from the definition of love as desire and from the definition of man as one who remains always wanting and forever isolated from what gives him happiness, that is, his proper being. Even *caritas* mediates between man and God in exactly the same way as *cupiditas* mediates between man and the world. All it does is mediate. It is no manifestation of an original interconnectedness of either man and God or man and world. Since every desire is determined by and dependent on its object, man's way to himself (which started under the rubric of Greek autarchy and Stoic self-sufficiency) must end in self-denial and in self-forgetfulness for the sake of the world or for the sake of God. It should be obvious that this kind of self-denial, even if it is called *caritas*, is actually pseudo-Christian. (We shall discuss this point in greater detail in Part II, chapter 2.)

The "good" of which man is deprived and which he therefore desires is life without death and without loss. God as the object of love (as desire) is nothing but the manifestation of this "good."[42] By anticipating eternity (the absolute future) man desires his own future self and denies the I-myself he finds in earthly reality. In self-hatred and self-denial [B:033155] he hates and denies the present, mortal self that is, after all, God's creation. The criterion of right and wrong in loving is not self-denial for the sake of others or of God, but for the sake of the eternity that lies ahead. From this it follows that man should not love in this life, lest he lose in eternal life. If he spends his love ill, he has hated, and if he spends his hatred well, then he has loved.[43] To love God means to love oneself well, and the criterion is not God but the self, namely the self who will be eternal.

> "He who knows how to love himself, loves God; but he who does not love God, even though he loves himself as nature bids him, is better said to hate himself since he acts in a way to be his own adversary."[44]

This love of God is the love of the self that will be (the immortal self) and the hatred of the self that is (the mortal self). This self-hatred is not the same as Christian self-denial, which springs from the awareness of being

41. *True Religion* XXXIX, 72.   43. *Tractates on John's Gospel* 51, 10.
42. *Confessions* I, 13, 21.   44. *The Trinity* XIV, 14, 18.

created and hence is subject to the Creator's call for obedience in faith. Nor is it the denial of the ideal of self-sufficiency, which Paul denounced as "boasting." Rather this self-hatred is the last, desperate consequence of self-love that desires, but never attains, its own "good." The misery of man consists in that, unlike God, he does not "derive happiness from himself as his own good," and that his "good" lies outside himself, which then must be searched for and desired. In this search man must "forget" his self over the good he desires, and he runs the risk of losing himself altogether if he forgets himself over the goods of the world.[45] Desire has the function of procuring the "good" from which happiness will result. The trouble with the wrong desire, the love of the world, is not so much that man does not love God as that "he does not stay in himself but [by virtue of having dismissed God] has gone out of himself as well."[46]

Love as desire looks to eternity for its fulfillment. According to Augustine the consummation occurs in the act of seeing because he understands vision as the most perfect mode of possession. Only the seen object stays and remains present as it is. What I hear or smell comes and goes, and what I touch is changed or even consumed by me. In contrast, the act of beholding is pure "enjoyment" (frui) in which no change occurs as long as it lasts. In the absolute calm and stability of eternal life, the relation of man to God will be an eternally lasting, beholding "enjoyment," and this, as it were, is the only adequate attitude of man to God. This is a far cry from Pauline Christianity. For Paul love is by no means a desire that stands in need of fulfillment. What stands [B:033156] in need of consummation is belief, and the end of belief, not of love, is vision. It is not belief but love that puts an end to human Godforsakenness. Love is "the bond of perfection" even on earth. As such, love is not the manifestation of craving, but the manifest expression of man's attachment to God. The reason that caritas is greater than faith and hope is precisely because caritas contains its own reward and will remain what it is in this life and the next. That is the meaning of the famous verses in Paul's first epistle to the Corinthians (1 Cor. 13). Prophecies shall fail, tongues shall cease, and knowledge, such as men possess it in this life, shall vanish. Only "love never fails." We love God with the same love here

---

45. *The City of God* XII, 1: "However, a being whose happiness springs from his own goodness instead of from another's, cannot be unhappy, since he cannot lose himself." [From the content of this text, it is clear that Augustine is referring to God, who is self-sufficient being and goodness. All other beings (creatures) who are capable of happiness (rational) must seek for and find happiness outside themselves with true happiness to be found only in the attainment and enjoyment of God.]

46. *Sermon* 330, 3.

on earth as in the hereafter. Love and nothing else overcomes human nature on earth and man's being of and belonging to the "world." This love does not seek and depend on its object but really transforms the lover—"such is each as is his love." In Paul's understanding love will not "increase in the future when we shall see face to face."[47] Nor will love cease when man has attained "happiness," that is, when he has and beholds ("enjoys") what he merely "loves" and desires on earth.

The crucial importance that love of neighbor had for Paul as the possibility of "perfection" even in this world is not shared by Augustine, at least not in this conceptual context in which love is understood as desire (*appetitus*). For this is not the kind of love of which Augustine, in an altogether different context, writes that it has the power to "make God present."[48] In this context Augustine can write that "if you love God you are in heaven even though you are still on earth."[49] All desire craves its fulfillment, that is, its own end. An everlasting desire could only be either a contradiction in terms or a description of hell. Hence, when Augustine writes that "only *caritas* stays forever"[50] and that "after this life only *caritas* will remain," since instead of believing we shall know and instead of hoping we shall possess, he refers necessarily to a different kind of love.[51]

The fulfillment and end of desire is "enjoyment" (*frui*). This is the goal toward which love aims and which constitutes "happiness." Happiness is achieved when all striving has come to an end and when man dwells in the immediate neighborhood of the thing he desired. A thing is sought for its own sake (in *caritas* or in *cupiditas*) if its possession puts desire to rest. Thus, nothing can be said to be "loved" which is sought for the sake of something else. And so, enjoyment and desire have this in common: they are concerned with things for their own sake.[52] Their opposite is *use* (*uti*), which uses things as a means for obtaining something else. The goal of love is [B:033157] the "good" whose attainment marks the end of love as such. Love exists only for the sake of this "enjoyment" and then it ceases. The end of love is surrender either to the world or to the future eternity where all action and all desire have come to rest. However, the first possibility—surrender to the world—is never the true end of love since "temporal things cannot extinguish *cupiditas*."[53] Temporal things are loved more before we have them,

---

47. *Retractations* I, 6, 4.   50. *Sermon* 158, 9.
48. *Sermon* 378.   51. *Soliloquies* I, 6, 13.
49. *Commentaries on the Psalms* 85, 6.   52. *Christian Doctrine* I, 4, 4.

53. *Commentaries on the Psalms* 105, 13. [Arendt added these texts: Desire "for things which are sought for the sake of something else should not be called cupidity" (*Soliloquies* I, 11, 19); and "to enjoy means to cling to something with love for its own sake" (*Christian Doctrine* I, 4, 4).]

that is, we cannot enjoy them. Moreover, they can be lost, and death, the loss of the world, will deprive us of all of them.

Human life, with its happiness cast into an absolute future by virtue of "transcending" and "forgetting," is harnessed to this "for the sake of" *(propter)*. All earthly goods are viewed under the aspect of love's final goal, for whose sake alone they possess their relative legitimacy. "For the sake of" expresses the interrelationship of all desirable goods. Only the "highest good" lacks all relations because in causing desire to cease it breaks off all relationships.[54] This complete isolation is expressed by the term "for its own sake" *(propter se ipsum)*, and insofar as the meaning of the *propter* consists in pointing to something else, the phrase *propter se ipsum* (where the thing and the sake for which it exists coincide) contains a paradox and thus negates itself. The paradox indicates that "enjoyment" stands outside all human-temporal categories and hence can only be hinted at *via negativa*. Enjoyment is the existential state that is unrelated to anything except to itself. All desire is harnessed to this "for the sake of," that is, it loves "the highest good for its own sake" and all other "goods" insofar as they may lead to the highest. The road to "happiness" is pointed out by desire and leads to "enjoyment" by way of "usage." The right object of enjoyment determines the objects of right usage: "Things to be enjoyed make us happy. Things to be used help us who tend toward happiness."[55] Since *caritas* is tied to the "highest good," it relates to the world only insofar as the world is of some use for attaining the ultimate goal. "To use a thing is to employ what we have received for us to obtain what we want, provided that it is right for us to want it." Hence, if the object of desire is God, the world is related to God by using it. Since it is used, the world loses its independent meaningfulness and thus ceases to tempt man. The right attitude to the world is to use it: "the world is there for usage, not for enjoyment."[56]

Since *caritas* is harnessed to the "for the sake of," it is manifest in right usage and enjoyment: "And *caritas* itself could not have been more tellingly designated than by the words 'for Your sake.'"[57] This qualification, "for

---

54. *Christian Doctrine* I, 38, 42. ["There is this difference between temporal and eternal goods, that something temporal is loved more before we have it, but becomes worth less when it has come into our possession. It does not content the soul whose true and appointed abode is eternity."]

55. Ibid., I, 3, 3.

56. Ibid., I, 4, 4.

57. *The Way of Life of the Catholic Church* I, 9, 15. ["Tribulation, distress, persecutions, hunger, nakedness, and danger all affect human beings profoundly in this life. Therefore, all of these words are summed up in that one text from the Old Law where it says, 'For your sake we are afflicted' (Ps. 42:23). All that remains is the sword, which does not inflict a life of pain and

Your sake," annihilates all bonds between man and the world. It [B:033158] establishes the proper distance between them, that is, the definitive distance between user and used which tolerates no affinity and no belonging. A life governed by *caritas* aims at a goal that, in principle, lies outside the world, and thus outside *caritas* as well. *Caritas* is but the road that connects man and his ultimate goal. Stretching out in this purposive direction, *caritas* possesses a provisional sort of eternity. By the same token the world, as a mere means toward this end, loses its awesome character and gains some sense by being made relative through this process. Love as desire always faces this alternative of either use or enjoyment. This is as true for divine love as it is for human love: "For if God neither enjoys nor uses, I cannot see how He would love."[58] Far from being enjoyment, *caritas* itself merely desires it. *Caritas* "desires to see and to enjoy."[59] Once it is liberated from the unrest of desire, the true perfection of enjoyment lies in the future. No one, not even a "just and holy man, is perfect" in this life.[60] However, since the longed-for object of *caritas* is itself eternal and cannot be lost or missed, a provisional sort of eternity comes about that manifests itself in this life as absolute fearlessness.

In the transcending expectation of eternity, death becomes relative. Death has died.[61] It has lost its importance for the living. Without death there can be no fear of loss, and fearlessness is primarily freedom from fear of loss. This is why "the freedom of *caritas* may rise above the servitude of fear."[62] Since man's own life (insofar as it is a true life) is projected into the future as an outside good to be pursued, he has become its master. His own self, not as it is but as it will be, has become self-sufficient. This future self-sufficiency manifests itself on earth in the faculty of desire. We have seen that this projection into an absolute future is possible only if one's own life is posited as a correlative of *appetitus*. In this context, the basic perplexity comes to light in the experience of death (that life cannot dispose of itself) and is solved through the concept of *caritas*. *Caritas* knows no fear because it knows no loss. Death is transformed into the worst evil (as contrasted with the "highest good") for a life governed by *cupiditas*.

At this point, as Augustine explains in an argument against the Stoics, it

---

hardship, but takes away life altogether. To this corresponds the words: 'We are regarded as sheep for the slaughter.' And surely, *caritas* could not have been better expressed than by the words, 'for your sake.'"]

58. *Christian Doctrine* I, 31, 34.

59. *Soliloquies* I, 6, 13.

60. *Christian Doctrine* I, 39, 43.

61. This point is one that Augustine usually makes in reference to quotations from the Scriptures; see, for example, *Tractates on John's Gospel* XLI, 13.

62. *Eighty-Three Different Questions* 36, 2.

is no longer so much a question of coming to terms with death but with life: "For there are those who die with equanimity; but perfect are those who live with equanimity."[63] *Caritas* comes to terms with life and the world by "using" them freely, that is, without being bound by them. Indeed, this freedom is provisional: "not yet [B:033159] whole, not yet pure, not yet full freedom, because not yet eternity."[64] However, in its purely negative characterization, this freedom corresponds exactly to the ideal of self-sufficiency. Life on earth is not independent even in *caritas*. Life on earth remains subject to the fear of losing the "highest good." Hence, for the present time, human life remains tied to desire and fear: "Desire and fear lead to every right act; desire and fear lead to every sin."[65] If we succeed in freeing ourselves from the world, we become the "slaves of *caritas*" *(servi caritatis)* and subject to "chaste fear" *(timor castus)*. This chaste fear arises out of *caritas* and has the task of shielding us from *cupiditas*. *Cupiditas* knows the fear of God but as fear of punishment, just as it knows belief in God without hope or love. This fear is inauthentic for the very reason that it does not spring out of love itself. It arises out of secondary considerations. In contrast, true fear *("chaste fear")* dreads to lose the object of love's striving and thus is part and parcel of *caritas* itself. And this fear "*caritas* possesses; in fact, only *caritas* possesses it."[66] For this is not the "fear that deters us from an evil that might happen to us, but it keeps us in a good which cannot be lost."[67] Thus, the freedom of *caritas* is a future freedom. Its freedom on earth consists in anticipating a future belonging for which love as desire is the mediator. The sign of *caritas* on earth is fearlessness, whereas the curse of *cupiditas* is fear—fear of not obtaining what is desired and fear of losing it once it is obtained.

63. *Homilies on the First Epistle of John* IX, 2.
64. *Tractates on John's Gospel* XLI, 10.
65. *Commentaries on the Psalms* 79, 13.
66. *Homilies on the First Epistle of John* IX, 5.
67. *The City of God* XIV, 9.

PART I
LOVE AS CRAVING:
THE ANTICIPATED FUTURE

3 / The Order Of Love

[B:033166] The future freedom, anticipated in *caritas*, serves as the guide and ultimate standard for the right understanding of the world and the right estimation of everything that occurs in it—of things as well as persons. What should and what should not be desired and who should and who should not be loved are decided with reference to the anticipated future, as is the degree of desire and love to be spent on whatever occurs in the present. The anticipated future establishes the order and measure of love *(dilectionis ordo et mensura)*.[1] According to Augustine, such a hierarchical order of love always exists. Insofar as it is a worldly order, there is a natural hierarchy for bestowing love—first come our close relatives, then our friends, and finally people we do not know.[2]

As a Roman, Augustine calls the right conduct of men in this world their "virtue." He writes in his political work, *The City of God*, that "a brief and true definition of virtue is the order of love."[3] The difference between this worldly hierarchy and the order that arises out of the anticipated future is that the worldly hierarchy loves and desires whatever or whomever it loves and desires for its own sake, although the degree of intensity will vary. However, the order constituted by the anticipated future prescribes that nothing and no one be loved or desired for its own sake: "Each man insofar as he is a man should be loved for the sake of God, and God for his own sake."[4]

From the viewpoint of the anticipated future, the world is not only not eternal, it never exists for its own sake. Hence, man's proper attitude to the

---

1. *The Trinity* VIII, 8, 12; IX, 4, 4; see also *Christian Doctrine* I, 27, 28: "well-ordered love"; *The City of God* XV, 22 (for the definition of virtue as the order of love).

2. *Christian Doctrine* I, 28, 29.

3. *The City of God* XV, 22: "Hence it seems to me that a brief and true definition of virtue is the order of love. [That is why in the holy Canticle of Canticles, Christ's bride, the city of God, sings, 'Order in me my love.']"

4. *Christian Doctrine* I, 27, 28.

world is not "enjoyment" *(frui)* but "use" *(uti)*. Men should use the world freely and with the same independence from it that characterizes the master in his use of means and tools. The relevance of means and tools is determined by the ultimate purpose of the user. And so the world, which is harnessed to the "for the sake of," receives its meaning from the purposiveness of the user. Viewed from this perspective, the world is set into a definite order—it is the order of the relative importance of means toward a definite end. And since it is man, the user, who decides about means and ends, this order is not "objective" (determined by the world), but "subjective" or anthropocentric. Just as man is for the sake of God, the world is for the sake of man. The relation of man to a thing *(res)*, that is, to everything that exists, is determined by love as desire. Thus, love of the world, [B:033167] guided by an ultimate transmundane purpose, is essentially secondary and derivative. Striving for the "highest good" which is not of this world, the world in its independent "objectivity" has fallen into oblivion, even though the lover himself still belongs to it. From the absolute future, to which *caritas* prompted him to surrender, man returns necessarily to the world as it now exists, only to find that the world has forfeited its original significance, and that in loving or desiring it he no longer loves or desires it for its own sake. Yet in the absolute future he has at the same time acquired a point of reference that lies, in principle, outside the world itself, and which therefore can now serve as regulator of all things inside the world as well as of the relationships by which they are interconnected. The unifying guiding thread of this regulatory point of reference is the "highest good" while its object is the existing world. We saw above how, in the search for his own self, human existence itself becomes the object of craving and desire; that is, a "thing" that is loved as though it were objectively extant, a "true life" outside the present life. This "reification" of existence is completed precisely by its projection into a future of timeless stability. He who returns from the absolute future to regulate the world will see even his own present existence as a "thing" among things, to be fitted into the rest of what exists.

In order to understand fully the consequences of this operation, we must be aware that Augustine's *amor sui*, love of self, can have two very different meanings: the "love of self" that gives rise to perplexed self-searching ("I have become a question to myself") is totally different from the unperplexed self-love that results from this ordered *caritas*.[5] It is not only the world but also the self that is carried into the oblivion of the present over the future. The attitude of man toward his self is not decided upon in either love

5. *Confessions* X, 33, 50.

or hatred. Rather, love or hatred are almost automatic results of the general estimate of the world to which the self belongs in the present. The source of this estimate is the "highest good" and the ordered regulation that is derived from it. In this order the "I" is like everything else—a mere "thing" to be used for the true life to come. The fact that the world is made relative involves the individual as well, insofar as he "views" himself as part of the world outside of himself, as the object of his striving. In the love that follows from this order, pseudo-Christian self-denial becomes real and effective, [B:033168] ruling a human life that through *caritas* is harnessed to the highest good.

In the order derived from the absolute future, what has been regulated is encountered only as purely extant. The regulator, whose objectivity toward the world and himself is guaranteed by the loving anticipation of the desired good, is no longer concerned with either the world or himself. With this unconcerned objectivity he determines what ought to be loved. Love itself is a consequence of this determination. The same is true for the degree of intensity that love will spend on its object, depending upon the order that assigns each to its proper place. Everyone is loved as much as he ought to be, no more and no less.

> He lives a just and holy life who is an impartial appraiser of things.
> He is a person who has a well-ordered love and neither loves
> what he ought not, nor fails to love what he should. He does not
> love more an object deserving only of lesser love, [nor love
> equally what he should love either more or less, nor love either
> more or less what he should love equally].6

Therefore, the commandment "Love thy neighbor as thyself" is understood in its literal sense by Augustine, "Love of one's neighbor recognizes as its limitation the love of one's self," and he who "loves his neighbor more than himself" is guilty of transgression.7 Obviously, the love of self and neighbor in this context stands in curious contradiction to the original definition of love as desire, which seeks a thing for its own sake, is affected by it, and consequently depends upon it. To a certain extent, this difficulty is less obvious in the Latin text than in my translations, because the Latin translation of the Greek New Testament could accommodate three Greek terms for love—*eros, storge, agape*—with the corresponding Latin: *amor, dilectio,*

---

6. *Christian Doctrine* I, 27, 28.
7. *On Lying* 6, 9.

caritas.[8] It is true, as Gilson remarks, that Augustine's use of these terms is "rather flexible."[9] Moreover, Augustine frequently uses them synonymously and even emphasizes this repeatedly.[10] Still, Augustine had three terms at his disposal where we have only one, at best two, love and charity. Augustine generally, but not consistently, uses *amor* to designate desire and craving (that is, for love in its largest, least specific sense); *dilectio* to designate the love of self and neighbor; and *caritas* to designate the love of God and the "highest good." However, to give but one instance of Augustine's terminological inconsistency, he also distinguishes occasionally between licit and illicit *caritas.*[11] An even greater difficulty arises if we ask why man, existing in and anticipating the absolute future, using the world and everything in it (including his own self and his neighbor) should establish this kind of emphatic relationship that is implicit in all kinds of love and is demanded of the Christian [B:033169] explicitly: "Thou shalt love thy neighbor as thyself." Obviously there is no answer to this question in the present conceptual framework except the divine commandment itself, which appears here like a *deus ex machina.* However, this is not to say that neighborly love has no place in Augustine's thinking. On the contrary, we shall meet it again in an altogether different context developed as the specifically Christian and particularly explicit version of the natural, prereligious, and secular law of not doing to others what we would not have them do to us *(quod tibi fieri non vis, alteri ne feceris).*

However, love that has yielded to the right order can no longer be understood as craving and desire because its direction is not determined by any particular object but by the general order of everything that is. This order includes the lover, although the order of love is designated from the standpoint of man, the lover. For this hierarchy distinguishes between what is above us *(supra nos)*, what is beside us *(iuxta nos)*, and finally what is beneath us *(infra nos)*. Clearly, what is above us is the highest and must be loved most, and what is beneath us, our body, must be loved least.[12] What is above us is the "highest good" and therefore to be loved for its own sake; whereas everything else—our own selves, our neighbors, our bodies—must be loved

---

8. *The City of God* XIV, 7; see Harnack, "Der Eros in der alten christlichen Literatur," *Sitzungsbericht der preussischen Akademie der Wissenschaften* (1918):85.
9. Etienne Gilson calls attention to this "flexibility" in Augustine's terminology in *The Christian Philosophy of St. Augustine* (New York: Random House, 1960), 311 n. 40.
10. *The City of God* XIV, 7.
11. *Sermon* 349, 1–3; see also Gilson, *The Christian Philosophy of St. Augustine,* 311–12 n. 40.
12. *Christian Doctrine* I, 23, 22.

for the sake of the highest: "Whatever else should strike us as lovable, let that be carried along in the direction where the whole impetus rushes."[13] Still, since this "highest good" is seen from the perspective of one's own absolute futurity, the resulting order remains bound to my own self. Not everything, but only what stands in some relation to myself, is included in the order of love. And this relation is established in the community *(societas)* of those who, like myself, can achieve happiness only in regard to God and "the highest good" and therefore are "closest to me" *(proximi)*, my true neighbors. In a similar way, I establish this relation to my body as the appurtenance of my earthly existence. Therefore, there is a difference between the mere use of the world *(uti)* in complete alienation from it and this love that also is directed toward the world, even though it is not permitted to enjoy its objects for their own sake *(frui)*.

> Not everything which should be used should be loved, but only that which through a certain community with us is related to God as for instance a man [B:033170] or an angel; or what . . . is related to ourselves as for instance our body.[14]

Angel, man and body—"what we are and what is beneath us belong to us by an undisturbed law of nature."[15] At this point it becomes manifest that Augustine's categories of opposition, that is, the opposition between use and enjoyment *(uti* and *frui)*, between means and end, are no longer adequate and that we dealing with a kind of love that actually cannot be understood or defined as craving. Obviously, only what is above me or beneath me can be fitted into this scheme. What is beside and next to me, I-myself and my neighbor, is neither to be "used" nor to be "enjoyed." This love can actually be explained only in an altogether different context, which we shall present and discuss later (see below, Part II, chapter 3 and Part III). In the context of love as desire, these relationships concern us only insofar as they, too, are ordered from outside, that is, from the viewpoint of the "highest good." And it is no accident that the consistent explication of a unified conceptual context—with love always defined, explicitly or implicitly, as craving—runs into considerable difficulties at this point and can no longer be isolated from different contexts. The strong influence of Stoic and Neoplatonic terminology on Augustine's early thought takes its revenge here, and the result is all the more confusing as these "formal concepts remain unchanged through-

13. Ibid., I, 22, 21.   15. Ibid., I, 26, 27.
14. Ibid., I, 23, 22.

out all the stages" of his development.[16] To the extent that Augustine, when speaking of the quest for and the love of self, thinks in terms of the ideal of autarchy and self-sufficiency, he cannot but arrive at an ideal of absolute isolation and independence of the individual from everything "outside" this self over which the self has no power. And this "outside" includes not only my "neighbors" but also my own body. This is an alienation from the world, which is much more radical than anything requested or even possible in orthodox Christianity.

Augustine's order of love is an indication of the utterly derivative character of all relations that go beyond the mere use of worldly data. Since Augustine never denied the factual character of these relations, they constitute a true perplexity for him. For his attempts to integrate neighborly love, the specifically Christian relationship with the world, are by no means merely dictated by his adherence to the Christian Scriptural tradition. It is rather the projection of happiness and fulfillment into an absolute future and hence the impossibility of perfection in the present that bring him back to the actual problem of how to live in this world. The notion of sheer self-sufficiency in "enjoyment" to be expected in the future is Stoic and Neoplatonic in origin, but the notion of this future itself, [B:033171] as well as the possibility of an ordering of the present from the standpoint of an absolute future, is quite uncharacteristic of Stoicism as well as Neoplatonism. Indeed, insofar as the future is anticipated in desire, the "highest good" is drawn into the present and can dominate and regulate life in this world. However, the fact of death that will part man absolutely from the world and his present existence is not minimized. Man cannot reach either perfection or happiness as long as he lives in this world. He can only strain forward to it (extentus esse) and then come to terms with the world. And the order of love prescribes the rules, as it were, according to which this provisional reconciliation with the world and the present is to be achieved. However, insofar as this well-ordered love, derived from the absolute future, is still supposed to remain *love* (namely, the desiring and caring for something for its own sake), it is bound to founder. The love of my neighbor is at best a secondary consideration for a desire whose aim transcends mankind and the world, both of which have a justifiable existence only to the extent that they can be "used" for the sake of something that is radically different and separated from them.

16. See the interesting remarks concerning Augustine's terminology in discussing freedom in Hans Jonas, *Augustin und das paulinische Freiheitsproblem: Ein philosophischer Beitrag zur Genesis der christlich—abendländischen Freiheitsidee* (1930; reprint, Göttingen, 1965), 23.

In the order of love the neighbor occupies a place beside my self, that is, on the same level of the tripartite hierarchy. From this it follows that I should "love him as myself." He occupies this place because he *is* like myself; he, too, can "enjoy God" *(Deo frui)*. He is my neighbor only insofar as he has entered into the same relationship with God or the absolute future. Hence, those with whom I live together in this world can be divided into those whom I help and those by whom I am helped in this sustained effort. Augustine writes, "Of all those who are able to enjoy God with us we love either those whom we help or those by whom we are helped."[17] The emphasis in this neighborly love is on mutual help, and this insistence is the clearest sign that love remains harnessed to the "for the sake of" category, which rules out meeting my fellow men (in their concrete worldly reality and relation to me) in their own right. Augustine is aware of the problem this creates for human relationships and of the danger, one could say, of degrading men into mere means for an end. "It is a great question," he observed, "whether men should enjoy or use each other, or whether they should do both." And it is with some reluctance that he comes to the conclusion:

> For if we love somebody for his own sake, we enjoy him; if for the sake of something else, we use him. [B:033172] But it seems to me that he should be loved for the sake of something else. The happy life is grounded in what must be loved for its own sake; and the thing which constitutes this happy life is not yet at our disposal, although the hope for it consoles us in the present time.[18]

This hope is at the same time actualized in love and determines its order. This means that love is derivative—derived from hope. It is not love that disclosed to me my neighbor's being. What I owe him has been decided beforehand according to an order that love follows but has not established. The establishment of the order that assigns to each thing its proper place can originate only from outside. This demands an objectivity and a basic lack of concern with the particular entities being arranged. The "outside" is the absolute future anticipated in hope. The lack of concern or the objectivity of this "ordered love," standing in flagrant contradiction to the very essence of love in all its forms, is conspicuously manifest when Augustine tries to explain the commandment "Love thy enemies" in this context. He writes, "Hence it comes to pass that we even love our enemies: for we do not

17. *Christian Doctrine* I, 29, 30.
18. Ibid., I, 22, 20.

fear them since they cannot snatch from us what we love."[19] This fearless-ness is not inspired by love. On the contrary, we saw that what makes love, defined as desire, unbearable is the constant fear—that must accompany love—of losing its object. Well-ordered love presupposes that the lover is out of danger. His appetite is stilled. He loves men as such, not because they are particular men but because "they have rational souls which I love even in thieves."[20] This objectivity marks one who has become indifferent to the world and to himself. A consequence of the strange dialectics of the equa-tion of love and desire is that self-oblivion grows eminently real. The pseudo-Christian self-denial has reached its peak. To the question "Who is my neighbor?" (*Proximus quis*—literally, "Who is next to me?") Augustine always replies, "Every man" (*Omnis homo*).[21] The answer is equivocal. It can mean literally everyone is next to me; I have no right to choose; I have no right to judge; all men are brothers. However, it can also mean that every member of the human species is equally near, that is, not everyone in his concrete uniqueness, but in the sense that every man shares the most ab-stract quality of being human with all others: "I love men because they are men" and not animals.[22] Furthermore, Augustine writes that "he who lives according to God . . . will not hate a man because of this vice nor love the vice because of a man, but he will hate the vice and love the man."[23] [B:033173] In other words, he loves his neighbor in sublime indifference regardless of what or who he is. In either case, neighborly love cannot be determined as desire or craving. Nevertheless, Augustine had to give an ac-count of neighborly love in this terminological context. The result is that he had to declare love derivative and to claim that there is no other alternative for relating to a desired object except either use (*uti*) or enjoyment (*frui*). This clearly results in a degradation of love, which contradicts the central place love occupies in Augustine's thought.[24] The love of my neighbor, or

19. Ibid., I, 29, 30.

20. *Soliloquies* I, 7; see also *Christian Doctrine* I, 2, 7, 28 and III, 16, 24.

21. [Arendt did not provide specific citations, although she did note Augustine's *Letters, Commentaries on the Psalms*, and *Sermons* in the footnotes, undoubtedly intending to furnish the specific citations at a later time. The citations are as follows: *Commentaries on the Psalms* XV, 5; Psalm 25, 2; *Eighty-Three Different Questions* 53, 4; *The Lord's Sermon on the Mount* I, 19, 59; *The Trinity* VIII, 6, 9.]

22. *Soliloquies* I, 7.

23. *The City of God* XIV, 6.

24. Gunnar Hultgren discusses this fundamental difficulty in his important study *Le Commandement d'Amour chez Augustin: Interprétation philosophique et théologique d'après les écrits de la période 386-400* (Paris, 1939): "La conception de la *beata vita* qui trouve son achèvement en Dieu comme *summum bonum* n'aide pas Augustin à résoudre le problème de l'amour du pro-cain. Et bien que la distinction *frui-uti* prenne comme point de départ l'amour en tant qu'aspi-

generally love between human beings, derives from a source altogether different from appetites and desires. A different concept of love comes into play, which we shall trace in the following chapters.

---

ration au bonheur, il est bien manifest que la définition de tout amour outre l'amour de Dieu comme une 'utilisation,' définition qui résulta logiquement de cette distinction implique en réalité l'introduction d'une nouvelle notion d'amour que l'on ne peut faire dériver uniquement du schéma eudémoniste. Ces difficultés et ce manque de clarté nous obligent à envisager autrement le problème et à voir s'il n'est pas possible d'en trouver une explication et une solution dans une manière différente d'envisager le *summum bonum*." It is on this last point that I would disagree with Hultgren. I think, and hope to show, that it is precisely the notion of God as *summum bonum* that creates the difficulty.

PART II
CREATOR AND CREATURE:
THE REMEMBERED PAST

1 / The Origin

[B:033181] In the conceptual context of Part I, where love was defined as desire, man took the bearings for his conduct in the present world from the future. His present mode of existence was hope and anticipation. However, by virtue of love he could anticipate the possession of the "highest good," and by returning, as it were from eternity, he could objectively establish the order and the extent of desire to be bestowed on the things of this world. In this ordering, the original self-love and with it the love of his neighbor were bypassed. Even though all desires not only aim at something but refer back to the subject that seeks happiness, the anticipated attainment of man's "highest good," which lies in an absolute future, blots out self-love and thus invalidates all present standards and motivations for love and desire. Hence, there arose the following specific incongruity. The commandment "Love thy neighbor as thyself" disclosed itself as meaningless if love is defined as desire, that is, as an emotion whose object by definition lies in the future. From this we may conclude that the definition "love is a kind of craving" is inadequate. In contrast, all desires seem to reckon with a kind of love that is nondesirous. In order to meet this kind of love in its proper context so as to be able to distinguish it from the context of desires, we now return once more to the original proposition: Love is desire.

We saw that craving is a combination of "aiming at" and "referring back to" (see above, Part I, chapter 1). We aim at what we hope will make us happy. And since we are mortal, we cannot hope for any secure possession of whatever we may desire because life itself, the presupposition of all happiness, is not in our possession. Therefore, since craving takes its bearings from the present notion of happiness, it must be forever frustrated. Hence, a life determined by desire, if it understands itself, must project the desired "happy life" into an absolute, timeless future as a "good" it never has but can only expect from the outside. In other words, if the desires of mortal men are not to be entirely futile, they must lose the original reference back to the desiring self in the very process of desire because of its utter unreliability.

Desiring must end in self-oblivion (see above, Part I, chapter 2). Nonetheless, this self-oblivion by no means signifies [B:033182] a liberation from desires or an openness for relating to things or persons that would be free from wanting to have them. On the contrary, it signifies that the whole person has become desire and is "extended" to the future by losing the holding-back power, the reference back to the self and its present notion of happiness. The horizon of human experience is now strictly limited by the future from which alone the relevant "good" or "evil" is to be expected.

However, while this total, uninhibited direction toward the future seems to follow logically from the structure of desire, it leaves out, or rather neglects, the simple fact that in order to desire happiness we must know what happiness is and that this knowledge of the desired object necessarily precedes the urge to possess it. Within the context of desire, this knowledge appears as the "referring back" to the self for whose sake man aims at whatever he desires. Since this context takes its bearings exclusively from the future, it leaves out the temporal character of the knowledge that precedes desire. From the viewpoint of desire, this knowledge points back to the past out of which the very notion of a "happy life" arises so that man can desire it at all and then project it into the future.

I can only seek that thing of whose existence I have some kind of knowledge. For Augustine this knowledge is preserved in man's memory, which he equates with self-consciousness as such. He writes that "just as we call memory the faculty of remembering things past, thus we may without absurdity also call memory what in the present enables the mind to be present to itself that it may understand by virtue of its own thought."[1] Augustine likens the way I recall what escapes my memory to the way I know, and possibly love or desire, what I am seeking. If it were altogether forgotten I would not recognize it. Indeed, I would not even know that I forgot something.[2] This can be easily understood in the case of "corporeal images," where only an effort of the will is required to bring back to me the image of the city of Carthage that I saw before. However, "it is indeed wondrous (*mirabile*) that the mind should see in itself what it saw nowhere else," for example, "what is means to be just."[3] In the same way we who seek the happy life and have no way of knowing what it is like know enough of its possible existence to seek and desire it. The way we know what the happy life is like is to know that it would be impossible if immortality were incompatible with human nature.[4]

1. *The Trinity* XIV, 11, 14.
2. Ibid., XI, 7, 12.
3. Ibid., VIII, 6, 9.
4. Ibid., XIII, 8, 11. ["In order for a man to live happily, he must first be alive."]

The knowledge of the possible existence of the happy life is given in pure consciousness prior to all experience, and it guarantees our recognizing the happy life whenever we should [B:033183] encounter it in the future. For Augustine this knowledge of the happy life is not simply an innate idea, but is specifically stored up in memory as the seat of consciousness. Hence, this knowledge points back to the past. When happiness is projected into the absolute future, it is guaranteed by a kind of absolute past, since the knowledge of it, which is present in us, cannot possibly be explained by any experiences in this world. The possibility of such remembrance is made plausible by an analysis of the way memory works in general. Augustine asks, how do I remember the "happy life"? He answers:

> Is it like the way we remember joy? Perhaps so, for even when I
> am sad, I remember joy, just as when I am miserable, I remember
> the happy life. But I never saw, or heard, or smelled, or tasted joy
> with a bodily sense. I experienced it in my mind when I rejoiced
> and knowledge of it has clung to my memory.[5]

Hence, it is the nature of memory to transcend present experience and guard the past, just as it is the nature of desire to transcend the present and reach toward the future. Since all men wish to be happy and no one can pretend that "he is not experienced in it, it is recognized that it [the happy life] is found in memory, whenever the words 'happy life' are heard."[6]

In this analysis, upon which the argument for a possible transmundane recollection partially rests, Augustine is making a definite statement about this mode of recollection. The happy life is not recalled as past, pure and simple, without further relevance for the present. Insofar as the happy life is remembered, it is part and parcel of the present and inspires our desires and expectations for the future. The point about remembering joy when we are sad is that we hope for its eventual return, just as in remembering it while in a state of joy we actually fear that sadness may come back. Only insofar as it is remembered as this specific potentiality can the "happy life" become the ultimate guide for all human endeavor. Only because this recollection actually must transcend the present life in this world can it become the guarantee for a transmundane future. "Where then and when did I experience my life as happy that I should recall it?" For whenever we remember anything, "we don't judge it to be something new, but recalling it we assert that

---

5. *Confessions* X, 21, 30.
6. Ibid., X, 21, 31. [Arendt worked the following footnote in the original text into the body of the dissertation.]

this is indeed what has been said." Hence, when I look for God or the happy
life, I actually "walk in the space of my memory and I do not find [them]
outside it."[7] It is the function of memory to "present" (make present) the
past and deprive the past of its definitely bygone character. Memory undoes
the past. The triumph of memory is that in presenting the past and thus
depriving it, in a sense, of its bygone quality, memory transforms the past
into a future possibility. What has been can be again—this is what our memory [B:033184] tells us in hope or in fear.

> From that same abundant stock, also, I combine one and another
> of the images of things, whether things actually known by experi-
> ence or those believed in from those I have experienced, with
> things past, and from them I meditate upon future actions, events
> and hopes; and on all this I again meditate as though they were
> present.[8]

This clearly shows that desire is not free-floating, arising, as it were, from
nowhere. Our craving and the relationships we establish through it only
seem to be in our own power. In truth, craving and its relationships depend
upon a preexisting reference whose object was forgotten in desire's exclusive
direction toward the future. Memory thus opens the road to a transmundane past as the original source of the very notion of the happy life. The
quest for this life is not thereby transformed into craving desire for the
"highest good." On the contrary, "if a weak soul demands to be happy, it
must ask *whence* a holy soul is happy."[9]

Thus, the whole question in this context does not turn about goals and
whither I shall go, but about origins and *whence* I come, and not about the
faculty of desire but the faculty of remembrance. Desire is truly directed
toward a transcendent, transmundane future because it rests ultimately on
the desire for an everlasting happy life. In a similar way, since recollection
presents a knowledge that necessarily lies before every specific past, it is also
truly directed toward a transcendent and transmundane past—that is, toward the origin of human existence as such. For remembrance in Augustine
is primarily recollection, "collecting myself from dispersion." This recollection is not simply guided by a desiring love for the highest good, which is
God, but by "the love of Thy love," which neither is nor could be the object
of desire.[10] The search for the origin begins with recollection from dispersion. And the *amor amoris Dei*, under whose auspices the recollection goes

---

7. Ibid., X, 24, 35.   9. *Tractates on John's Gospel* XXIII, 5.
8. Ibid., X, 8, 14.   10. *Confessions* II, 1, 1.

about its business, already presupposes a relation with God that the simple *amor Dei*, the craving for God, seeks to establish. To recall the past and to recollect myself from dispersion is the same as to "confess." And what leads to remembrance, recollection, and confession is not the desire for the "happy life"—although happiness, too, can be discovered and above all guaranteed as legitimate only in the dimension of memory—but the quest for the origin of existence, the quest for the One who "made me." Hence, transcending the faculties [B:033185] of perception, which we have in common with the animals, and rising gradually "to Him who made me," Augustine arrives at "the camps and vast palaces of memory."[11] There he finds the notion of the "happy life," which is his origin and as such the quintessence of his being. The absolute future turns out to be the ultimate past and the way to reach it is through remembrance. By recalling a past that is prior to all possibilities of earthly, mundane experience, man who was created and did not make himself finds the utmost limit of his own past—his own "whence." The dependence of desire *(appetitus)* upon the general wish to be happy thus implies a deeper and more fundamental mode of human dependence than desire can ever detect when it acts in accord with its own phenomenological meaning. To understand this dependence and its consequences is the task of this chapter.

This dependence was already manifest in desire insofar as desire refers back to the self and not only aims at the desired good. This is the dependence of the one who is created upon his Creator. That man in his desire to be happy depends upon a notion of happiness that he could never experience in his earthly life, and that such a notion, moreover, should be the sole determinant of his earthly conduct, can only signify that human existence as such depends on something outside the human condition as we know and experience it. And since the concept of happiness is present in us through a consciousness that is equated with memory (that is, since happiness is not an "innate" but a *remembered* idea), this "outside the human condition" actually means *before* human existence. Therefore, the Creator is both outside and before man. The Creator is *in* man only by virtue of man's memory, which inspires him to desire happiness and with it an existence that would last forever: "Hence I would not be, my God, I would not exist at all, if you were not in me," namely, in my memory.[12]

> You, O Lord, who live forever and in whom nothing dies, since
> before the beginnings of the centuries and before anything that

11. Ibid., X, 7, 11–8, 12.
12. Ibid., I, 2, 2.

can be called 'before,' you *are* . . . and with you stand fixed the
causes of all changeable things and the immutable origins of all
that is mutable and [with you] there live the sempiternal reasons
of everything that is irrational and temporal.[13]

Only in referring back from mortal existence to the immortal source of this
existence does created man find the determinant of his being. For in the
Creator who "made him," the "reason for making man" must necessarily
precede [B:033186] and survive the "act of creation."[14] Every particular act
of love receives its meaning, its raison d'être, in this act of referring back to
the original beginning, because this source, in which reasons are sempiternal *(rationes sempiternae)*, contains the ultimate and the imperishable "reason" for all perishable manifestations of existence. "Thus while not every
creature can be happy . . . the one that has this capability cannot achieve
happiness itself since it was created out of nothing, but only through the one
from whom it is."[15]

It is important to realize that though man was made "out of nothing,"
he does not come from nothingness or nobody-ness. Man's cause of existence is the one who *is*. If man returns to where he came from, he finds his
Creator. To refuse this return *(redire)* is "pride" *(superbia)*:

May the soul be confounded in order to return, who prided itself
on not returning. Pride then hindered the soul's return. . . . The
soul is being recalled to itself which went away from itself. And as
the soul went away from itself, it also abandoned its Master.[16]

Since the "return to oneself" is an act of recollection, it is identical to a return to the Creator. Man loves himself by relating to God as his Maker. Just
as desire, striving for the "happy life," derives its meaning from a memory
that recalls it, however vaguely, from a transcendent region, so the creature
in its createdness derives its sense of meaningfulness from a source that precedes its creation, that is, from the Maker who made it. The source as Creator antedates the created object and has always existed. Since the creature
would be nothing without this source, its relation to its origin is the very
first factor establishing it as conscious entity. The very fact that man has not
made himself but was created implies that the meaningfulness of human existence both lies outside itself and antedates it. Createdness *(creatum esse)*

13. Ibid., I, 6, 9.
14. *Literal Commentary on Genesis* VI, 9, 16.
15. *The City of God* XII, 1.
16. *Sermon* 142, 3.

means that essence and existence are not the same. The Supreme Being (*summe esse*) that bestows being upon man by creating him is also the "Primal Being" (*primitus esse*), meaning that which is first and compared with which everything else is secondary and derivitive.[17] Hence, to "return to God" is actually the only way in which a created thing can "return to itself." "For if you wish more and more to be, you will approach that which is in the highest degree."[18] In other words,

> you will see that you are the more miserable the less you approach that which is in the highest degree. And you may even believe that it would be better not to be at all than to be miserable if you lose sight of what *is* in the highest degree. [B:033187] Nevertheless, you wish to be because you are from Him who is in the highest degree.[19]

The difference between "the species of rational mortals" and other created things, such as "beasts, trees, stones," is that the former possesses consciousness, hence memory, and therefore can relate back to its own origin.[20] Only insofar as this reconnection is established can a created thing be said to *be* truly. Without it, man's existence, like the existence of the world, is utterly perishable. For Augustine it is a matter of course that true Being and perishability are mutually exclusive.[21] Hence, Augustine writes that "man is something so long as he adheres to him by whom he was made a man. For if man withdraws from God, man is nothing."[22] This adhesion is not a matter of will and free decision; it expresses a dependence inherent in the fact of createdness. Desire also makes man dependent (see above, Part I, chapter 2). He depends upon the desired object. However, this dependence arises out of the specific inadequacy of life and is always determined by the future, from which he expects "good" or "evil" in hope or fear. By contrast, man's dependence rests not on anticipation and does not aim at something, but relies exclusively on remembrance and refers back to the past.

To put it differently, the decisive fact determining man as a conscious, remembering being is birth or "natality," that is, the fact that we have entered the world through birth. The decisive fact determining man as a desiring being was death or mortality, the fact that we shall leave the world in

---

17. *The Way of Life of the Manichaeans* II, 1, 1.
18. *The Free Choice of the Will* III, 7, 71.
19. Ibid., III, 7, 70; III, 7, 20.
20. *The City of God* XII, 1.
21. *The Way of Life of the Manichaeans* II, 1, 1; *The Nature of Good* 19.
22. *Commentaries on the Psalms* LXXV, 8.

death. Fear of death and inadequacy of life are the springs of desire. In contrast, gratitude for life having been given at all is the spring of remembrance,
for a life is cherished even in misery: "Now you are miserable and still you
do not want to die for no other reason but that you want to be." What ultimately stills the fear of death is not hope or desire, but remembrance and
gratitude: "Give thanks for wanting to be as you are that you may be delivered from an existence that you do not want. For you are willing to be and
unwilling to be miserable."[23] This will to *be* under all circumstances is the
hallmark of man's attachment to the transmundane source of his existence.
Unlike the desire for the "highest good," this attachment does not depend
upon volition, strictly speaking. Rather, it is characteristic of the human condition as such. Augustine's reflections on human existence in this Creator-
creature [B:033188] context arise directly from Jewish-Christian teaching
and are obviously much more original than the more conventional considerations centering on desire and fear that were discussed in Part I, chapter 1.

Everything that is created exists in the mode of becoming: "the heavens
and the earth proclaim that they have become, for they change and alter."
Since the verb *fieri* (to become) is also the passive form of *facere* (to make), to
become and to be made are virtually identical for Augustine. By contrast,
the Creator "truly is because he remains unchangeably."[24] As such, the Creator is in principle prior to everything else *(ante omnia)*. Nothing is "becoming in him" and all things, insofar as they are in him, "are sempiternal."[25]
Only things that are in the mode of becoming indicate something that precedes their existence and that lies *before* them: for "whatever has not come
into being and yet *is* contains in it nothing which was not there before."[26]
Since created things have come into existence, they change and alter. Their
coming into existence was the first change, from non-being into being, and
the law of change will from then on preside over their destinies. Strictly
speaking, their mode of being is neither Being nor non-Being, but something in between. They are not simply, but only in relation to something
else: "While [God] remains in himself, whatever is out of him must turn
about back to itself." We saw that this is a capacity only human beings possess, "insofar as every creature has the limitation and goal *[terminus]* of its
nature within itself by not being what He is."[27] God is immutable and un-
alterable Being. Thus created man is related to Being, which is essentially

23. *The Free Choice of the Will* III, 6, 64.
24. *Confessions* XI, 4, 6; VII, 11, 17.
25. *The Free Choice of the Will* III, 3, 24.
26. *Confessions* XI, 4, 6.
27. *Literal Commentary on Genesis* VI, 18, 34.

the very antithesis of his own mode of existence. Nevertheless, man finds in this opposition to himself his own being, in the way that all changeable, perishable tables have their "true being" in the notion or the blueprint of the "idea" of table *(sempiterna ratio)*. When life is seen in its mutability as coming into existence and passing away, and hence as neither altogether being nor altogether not-being, it exists in the mode of relation. In this sense human life does not possess the Being from which it comes. For being "made out of nothing it can be deficient," nor does it possess the nothing from which it was made.[28] However, since even mutability can exist only on the ground of an immutable Being ("without an immutable good there would be no mutable goods"),[29] human life exists in relatedness to Being.

Once called into existence, human life cannot turn into nothingness. [B:033189] "A mind that turns from the highest good loses the quality of being a good mind, but not the quality of being a mind."[30] However, no matter how closely it adheres to the "highest good," it will never "become" true Being: that is, eternal, unchangeable, or self-sufficient.[31] Strictly speaking, human existence *is* not at all, which of course does not mean that it "is" nothing. Rather, human existence consists in acting and behaving in some way or other, always in motion, and thus opposed in any way to eternal "enduring within itself" *(permanere in se)*.[32] All that is created is seen in the image of human life, coming out of nothingness and rushing into nothingness. To the extent that even this precarious mode of existence is not nothing, it exists in relating back to its origin. It is the hallmark of human life that it can explicitly adopt this reference and consciously hold on to it in *caritas* (see above, Part I, chapter 2). However, the reference as such does not depend upon what man does or fails to do in *caritas* or *cupiditas*; it is a constitutive element of human existence and indifferent to human conduct.

This relatedness of human existence is actualized in imitation. To imitate, as well as to refer back to one's origin, is a general characteristic of human existence before it becomes a consciously adopted way of life. Even wickedness could not exist without being related to the Supreme Being and imitating it. "All who have withdrawn from You and boast of themselves against You imitate You perversely. But even in thus imitating You they

---

28. *The City of God* XII, 8.
29. *The Trinity* VIII, 3, 5.
30. Ibid.
31. *Confessions* VII, 11, 17. ["I saw other things below you, and I saw that they are not altogether existent nor altogether non-existent. They are because they are from you; they are not since they are not what you are."]
32. *The Way of Life of the Manichaeans* II, 6, 8.

demonstrate that You are the Creator of the whole of nature." Does not even pride *(superbia)*, which is the vice of vices because it wants to imitate God instead of serving Him, "imitate his height"? Is not this imitation of God "perverse" because it actually wants to be where God is, that is to be "one lifted above all"?[33]

Such perversion may arise out of the nothing from which man was made. However, for Augustine it is a perversion of being, and not a falling into nothingness, that is constitutive of vice and sin, although he occasionally calls these evil acts those that approach nothingness *(appropinquare nihilo)*: "Man does not so forsake as to be altogether nothing . . . but to be approaching nothingness."[34] Human conduct, as opposed to the highest Being in which to be and to act coincide in the simplicity of One, is determined throughout by this imitation.

> Being is nothing else but being one. Hence, inasmuch as something [B:033190] achieves unity, to that extent it is . . . for simple things are through themselves. However, those that are not simple imitate unity through the harmony of their parts and these exist inasmuch as they do this successfully.[35]

In brief, imitation belongs first among the basic structures that rule human conduct, so that even seeming desertions must be understood as mere perversions. Second, imitation can be actualized explicitly through love: "They loved by believing; they imitated by loving."[36]

It is not just perishability but also temporality that stands as the stigma of all created things. Only men, who know that they were born and will die, actualize this temporality in their very existence. God "was always and is" and will be; whereas "we were not and are" and will not be.[37] Other things once existed, but are not now; or they will exist, but were not and do not now exist. In all these cases, essence precedes existence: "For the essence *(ratio)* that is established as a created thing antecedes in the word of God the creature that is established."[38] Since the whole creation is but was not, it had a beginning. And everything that began exists in the mode of becoming. Thereby, the whole creation is already subject to mutability. It has not always been what it is, but has become so.

33. *Confessions* II, 6, 14; II, 6, 13.
34. *The City of God* XIV, 13.
35. *The Way of Life of the Manichaeans* II, 6, 8.
36. *Commentary on Paul's Epistle to the Galatians*, chap. 24.
37. *Homilies on the First Epistle of John* I, 5.
38. *Literal Commentary on Genesis* II, 8, 17.

Augustine distinguishes between the beginning of the world and time, both of which existed before man and the beginning of man. He calls the former *principium* and the latter *initium*. *In principio* refers to the creation of the universe—"In the beginning God created the heavens and the earth" (Gen. 1:1). However, *initium* refers to the beginning of "souls," that is, not just of living creatures but of men. Augustine writes that "this beginning did in no way ever exist before. In order that there be such a beginning, man was created before whom nobody was." Furthermore, man was created into time, but time itself was created simultaneously with the world, namely, together with motion and change. Not only is time unthinkable without the existence of "some creature by virtue of whose movement time could pass," but movement is unthinkable without the notion of passing time.[39] Moreover, the beginning that was created with man prevented time and the created universe as a whole from turning eternally in cycles about itself in a purposeless way and without anything new ever happening. Hence, it was for the sake of *novitas*, in a sense, that man was created. Since man can know, be conscious of, and remember his "beginning" or his origin, he is able to act as a beginner and enact the story of mankind.

Everything that has a beginning, in the sense that a new story begins with it (*initium* and not *principium*), must also have an end, and therefore [B:033191] cannot truly *be*. He who "is and truly is . . . is without beginning (*initium*) and without end."[40] In contrast, man "is simultaneously in life as well as in death; that is, in life in which he lives until it is totally taken away, but in death through which even now he dies while life is taken away."[41] His end starts working in him from his beginning. While this life that approaches death is and is not at the same time, it also has as its source eternal Being. Seen from the perspective of human life, this Being has as its outstanding characteristic that it was before life began, will be when life has passed away, and therefore lies ahead of it in the future. Being relates to human life as that from which it comes and to which it goes, and is "before" (*ante*) man in the twofold sense of past and future.

Through remembrance man discovers this twofold "before" of human existence. As we saw (see above, Part I, chapter 1), memory has the function of recalling the past and of making it present again to the mind. In this process of re-presenting, the past not only takes its place among other things present but is transformed into a future possibility. In remembering past joy

39. *The City of God* XII, 21; XI, 6.
40. *Commentaries on the Psalms* 134, 6.
41. *The City of God* XIII, 10. [Arendt eliminated the footnote that followed in the original text.]

we can hope for its return in the future, just as the remembrance of past sorrow instills in us the fear of impending disaster. This is the reason why the return to one's origin *(redire ad creatorem)* can at the same time be understood as an anticipating reference to one's end *(se referre ad finem)*. Not until beginning and end coincide does the twofold "before" acquire its proper meaning. For the person who turns back to the absolute past, the Creator who made him, the Whence-he-came reveals itself as identical to the Whither-he-goes. Thus the postulated eternity of Being makes beginning and end interchangeable in terms of the temporal creature's reference to its own existence. Since Being is "immutable," it is simultaneously the ultimate limit of both the farthest removed past and the most distant future. The Creator remains forever identically the same, independent of his creation and whatever may happen within it. His eternity is not a different temporal mode, but strictly speaking, no-time. Even his "operations" cannot be temporally understood "in intervals of time," except that one may say that they are all happening "at the same time *(simul)*."[42]

The temporal image of the no-time that is eternity is the present, sempiternal "today," and this absolute present coincides, of course, with the absolute past as well as the absolute future. However, man whose existence is determined by the three tenses of time and by the very fact of his having come into existence *(fieri)*, can only reunite [B:033192] this temporal extension through memory and expectation. In so doing he also unites into a whole his own existence, which otherwise would be nothing more than an orderly succession of temporal intervals. Through this mental concentration that saves him from "distraction," that is, from losing himself to one moment after another, man approaches the sempiternal "today," the absolute present of eternity. The fact that the past is not forever lost and that remembrance can bring it back into the present is what gives memory its great power *(vis)*.[43] Since our expectations and desires are prompted by what we remember and guided by a previous knowledge, it is memory and not expectation (for instance, the expectation of death as in Heidegger's approach)[44] that gives unity and wholeness to human existence. In making and holding present both past and future, that is, memory and the expectation derived from it, it is the present in which they coincide that determines human existence. This human possibility gives the man his share in being "immutable"; the remotest past and the most distant future are not only,

42. *Literal Commentary on Genesis* V, 12. [Arendt eliminated the following footnote.]
43. *Confessions* X, 17, 26; X, 8, 14.
44. Martin Heidegger, *Being and Time*, trans. John Macquarrie and Edward Robinson (New York: Harper and Row, 1962), 279–304, sect. 46–52.

objectively speaking, the single twofold "before" of human life, but can be actualized as such while man is still alive. Only man, but no other mortal being, lives toward his ultimate origin while living toward the final boundary of death. Since he can concentrate through remembrance and anticipation his entire life into the present, man can participate in eternity and thus be "happy" even in this life. For "the happiness by which the soul itself becomes happy does not come about except through participation in this life which lives forever, is unchangeable and of eternal substance; that is, in the life which God is."[45] The presentation of past and future in which both coincide annihilates time and man's subjection to it.

To sum up: Man initiates the quest for his own being—by asserting "I have become a question to myself."[46] This quest for his own being arises from his being created and endowed with a memory that tells him that he did not make himself. Hence, the quest for his Being is actually the quest for his origin—for the Creator of the creature. In this quest, which takes place in memory, the past comes back into the present and the yearning for a return to the past origin turns into the anticipating desire of a future that will make the origin available again. In other words, by virtue of man's quest for his own being, the beginning and end of his life become exchangeable.

This phenomenon of the exchangeability of human life's beginning and end gives rise to three questions. [B:033193] First, what is Augustine's concept of Being, according to which he then can determine man's "true being" (vere esse) as an encompassing whole that appears to man as the twofold "before" of absolute past and absolute future? Second, which property of temporal life in this world enables man, by "returning to the self" (redire ad se), to discover something he can by no means experience in it? For the "true being" of created man is never immanent in temporal worldly life. His true being antedates this world in principle, and it is the source of creation that itself does not belong to it. Third, what sort of a world is it into which created man is born and to which he both does and does not belong?

In Augustine's thought, the first question and the last two are answered in two wholly heterogeneous and, to an extent, mutually exclusive contexts. Augustine's understanding of Being is derived from the Greek concept that identifies Being with everlastingness or endurance, "for being refers to what remains."[47] This Being, as we shall see, is nothing but the sempiternal structure of the universe. In contrast, Augustine's understanding of the

45. *Tractates on John's Gospel* XXIII, 5.
46. *Confessions* X, 33, 50.
47. *The Way of Life of the Manichaeans* II, 6, 8; "'By corruption all things cease to be what they were and are brought to non-permanence, to non-being, for being entails permanence.'"

world is guided by the Christian teaching that conceives of all mundane existence as being created, thereby precisely denying its endurance. Augustine
is also guided by the specifically Christian distinction between world and
universe, in which the former is understood as the human world constituted
by men.[48] The following difficulty arises from these two heterogeneous assumptions: on the one hand, man's quest for being is answered by the structure of the universe in its totality, of which man himself is a part. On the
other hand, in the Christian view of creation, by saying "I have become a
question to myself," man has begun to ask himself out of the world in his
quest for "true being." Our task is to show how Augustine's definition of the
Creator and of eternity as the twofold "before" grows out of these two intentions whose diametrical opposition he must reconcile. Not surprisingly,
we shall find that for the Creator-creature relationship the Christian worldview is by far the more important and decisive one. Nevertheless, this is no
reason to neglect Augustine's indebtedness to Greek philosophy, which is
most apparent in his conception of the universe. Moreover, it was only by
deflecting the Christian conceptual context that Augustine could arrive at
his notion of the twofold "before."

According to the Greek philosophical tradition as Augustine knew it,
Being meant the cosmos in its entirety because it remains forever identically
the same, regardless of the variability of its parts. [B:033194] Every part of
the universe *is* only to the extent that it is a part of Being, participating and
fitting into the whole, and "any part that does not conform to its specific
whole is out of place." It is the function of the parts to set and keep in motion
(*agere*) the whole, and they do this "by passing away and succeeding" each
other, by growing and withering away, so that the parts never exist simultaneously.[49] Just as "a great house obviously is not greatness," but receives its greatness by participating in greatness, which must be prior to all
things we then call great, thus the whole cosmos, which is Being, is "prior to
and by far superior" to everything that *is* only by virtue of participating in
it.[50] To be sure, the universe seen as God's creation must be understood as
containing all things simultaneously, for "God created all things at once,"
and they exist in a hidden way "just as all those things which in time grow
into a tree are invisibly in the very seed and [in this sense] simultaneous"
with the whole of creation.[51] However, the parts themselves, which come

48. See Rudolf Bultmann, "Die Eschatologie des Johannes-Evangeliums," *Zwischen den Zeiten* 1 (1928).
49. *Confessions* III, 8, 15; IV, 10, 15.
50. *The Trinity* V, 10, 11.
51. *Literal Commentary on Genesis* V, 23, 45.

into existence and pass away, are unaware of this simultaneousness. Since men themselves are parts of the whole, they cannot for this very reason ever see it: "Wherever you turn to see it, you will see parts."[52] "We ourselves, by virtue of our mortality, are embedded in a part [of the order of the universe] and cannot perceive the universe in which the parts that offend us fit in quite aptly and decently."[53] For Augustine, the temporal tenses of parts arise from this inconceivable simultaneity.

In this context, the mortality of man is no more than a special case of the temporality of the parts in the universe. In this way, temporality is not based on man's mutability and transiency, but is inherent in the relationship between parts and the whole. Time exists because, for the part, simultaneousness unfolds itself in the guise of a sequence. The *simul*, the "all at once" of eternity, is transformed into a sequence for everything that is not eternal. However, eternity is the essential structure of the whole, that is, of the universe. For although the universe has been created and had a beginning and thereby must also perish and come to an end, Augustine is by no means sure that "a total destruction" will ever come to pass. Augustine quotes Paul (I Cor. 7:31–32): only [B:033195] "the figure of this world," that is, as it appears to us, "passes away, not its [intrinsic] nature."[54] In other words, what endures independently of the parts' coming and going is the imperishable harmonious whole in which the parts find their place. If sequence is the mode in which the whole appears to the parts, time is the mode in which man understands it. Augustine writes:

> They attempt to grasp eternal things, but their heart flutters
> among the changing things of past and future and is still futile.
> Who will catch hold of it [the heart] and make it fast so that it
> stands firm for a little while, and for a little while may seize the
> splendor of eternity standing still forever, and compare this with
> the times that never stand still, and see that it is without compar-
> ison? Let [the heart] see that a long time could not possibly be
> long unless it be composed of many transient motions which can-
> not extend themselves all at once *[simul]*, but that in eternity
> nothing can be transient since the whole is present; and surely, no
> time is ever totally present. And let the heart see how every past is
> propelled out of the future, and every future follows from the
> past, and all past and future are created and flow out of what is
> ever present.[55]

52. *Sermon* 117, 5.
53. *The City of God* XII, 4.
54. Ibid., XX, 14.
55. *Confessions* XI, 11, 13.

This is the way eternal Being, understood as the ever-present universe, appears to its parts that come into being and pass away. Only the species, the human race but not individual men, participates in the universe's simultaneity and as such is somehow of the same nature. The human race actually exists only in form of individual men. That is the way eternity "operates" *(agere)*. Hence, existence, but not essence, in the universe is actualized through time. The same is true for man's life: his whole life exists through "the actions of man which are its parts." This life itself, insofar as it is believed to be eternal, must possess the same character of original simultaneity as Being (the universe).[56]

This interpretation has grave consequences for the understanding of human life. The whole is by definition the totally encompassing and as such is indifferent to its parts. In its immutability the whole constitutes the parts that have no meaning outside of their integration into the whole *(totum)*. In this relationship between the whole and its parts, the sequence of the parts, by virtue of which the whole exists, is of no importance. Therefore, human life is divested of the uniqueness and irreversibility in which temporal sequences follow each other from birth to death. These temporal sequences are parts that exist only [B:033196] because earthly life lacks simultaneity and therefore is temporal. In this view Being is equated with the universe and is the encompassing whole where time is not. It is the eternal present that shows all things simultaneously and thus encompasses the parts in their temporal transiency. Since no part in this universe, no human life and no part of this life, can possess its own autonomous significance, there can be no "evil" *(malum)*. There are only "goods" *(bona)* in their proper order, which may merely *seem* evil from the transient perspective of the individual *(singulum)*. This quality of goodness does not arise from the particular things themselves, but is bestowed upon them by the universe:

> Even particular things are good, since the admirable beauty of the universal consists of all of them. . . . In this universe even what is called evil is well ordered and put into its proper place and thus recommends to us even more eminently the good things that they may please us more and be more worthy of praise when they are compared with evil things.[57]

For are not all things created by God? How could God have created evil?

56. Ibid., XI, 28, 38.
57. *Enchiridion* 3, 10 and 11.

[God] made all natures, not only those which persevered in virtue
and justice, but also those that were to sin; and the latter [He
made] not that they should sin, but that they might decorate the
universe whether they wished to sin or not to sin.[58]

As the universe, Being is neither the sum total of its parts nor can it be easily
equated with God as creator, who obviously makes his creation from the
outside. Being is for Augustine, as it was for the Greeks, the everlasting, forever lawful structure and the harmony of all the parts of the universe. The
appropriate interpretation of wickedness, difficult enough to arrive at, is
then as follows:

He who has become wicked out of [his own] will and has lost the
universe he possessed through obedience to God's precepts, still
remains fitted (ordinatus) [as part into the whole] in such a way
that he who did not wish to act lawfully is acted upon by the law.[59]

In other words, that person is wicked who tries in vain to escape the predetermined harmony of the whole. It is the structure of this all-encompassing
harmony that as the "eternal law is impressed upon us," as it is impressed
upon every singular entity, so that the best of men is the "well-ordered man"
(homo ordinatissimus).[60] If Augustine in the same context says that everything that "is just and lawful in temporal law is derived from eternal law," he
does not necessarily think of [B:033197] God as the eternal lawgiver, but
rather that the laws determining the motions and actions of the parts are
necessarily derived from the law of the encompassing whole.

It is difficult to overestimate the enormous influence this concept of Being as the all-encompassing universe exerted on Augustine's thought. This
is most manifest in passages in which the perfection of man or other created
things is derived from the Creator and not from Being as such. Even in such
an obviously Christian context, the other strictly "Greek" thought echoes
through as in the following text: "The perfection of each thing does not lie
so much in the universe whose part it is, but in Him through whom it is and
in whom the universe itself is."[61] Obviously, if man is nothing but part of the

---

58. *The Free Choice of the Will* III, 11, 32.
59. *On Music* VI, 11, 30.
60. *The Free Choice of the Will* I, 6, 15; I, 8, 18.
61. *Literal Commentary on Genesis* IV, 18, 34. [Arendt eliminated the rest of this footnote,
where she had remarked: "How strongly Augustine is dominated by the concept of the universe
as the encompassing, and of man as the part encompassed, may be seen from a quotation in

universe and has no direct relationship to God as his Creator, he cannot very well "return" *(redire)* or "refer back" *(referre se)* to his origin. Augustine hardly ever used these terms in contexts in which the universe and Being are discussed. The part of a whole has no beginning to which it could refer back. The universe, [B:033198] whose universality the part can never comprehend, is not an origin but the higher order into which the part is integrated. As such the universe is the eternal framework that determines, but does not create, its structural and other properties.[62] This universal order is as it is throughout eternity, and so is that which it orders, even though individual entities may come and go, grow and perish in their singularity. The part can be exchanged and replaced at any time precisely because of its perishability. The part exists only for "the beauty of the whole" *(pulchritudo universitatis)*, not for its own sake. An individual self, such as man possesses, is both enclosed and lost in the eternally identical simultaneity of the universe. Here the "before," in the sense of the Creator, has lost its meaning. If man and his life are parts of some encompassing whole, they cannot be said to have an origin and their mortality has become irrelevant.

These speculations about everlasting Being and the universe are Platonic in origin. Augustine's concept of the world partly belongs to a tradition that reached from Plato to Plotinus. The problem of a beginning of the universe, which becomes so perplexing for Augustine, who knows of a definite beginning through the Creator, had been troubling this tradition from its very start. In the *Timaeus* Plato declares categorically that the cosmos "has come to be, starting from some beginning"; and he adds, "It is a hard task to find the maker and father of this universe, and having found him it would be impossible to declare him to all mankind." However, Plato is not interested in this maker who is more like a human craftsman than a divine creator and has fashioned the world according to some eternal model. What does interest Plato is this model which is quite open to human understanding and is "comprehensible by rational discourse . . . and always in the same state."[63] Thus, we find in Plato three factors that account for the universe: the maker, the model, and the product. According to Plato, it is the model that has no beginning, is "everlasting" *(aidion)*, and without any change. However, the product has come into being, has a beginning, and is also everlasting by virtue of "imitating" the model according to which it was fash-

---

which the perfection of man, as of all created things, is sought in the Creator, and yet man appears as an integrated part of the universe." Arendt then inserted the citation from the *Literal Commentary on Genesis* into the text of her chapter.]

62. *Confessions* I, 6, 9.
63. Plato, *Timaeus* 28c, 29a.

ioned, but in constant change. In this sense the product is sempiternal Becoming.[64]

It is only in Augustine that the "imitation" indicates dependence upon the Creator, whereas in Plato it indicates clearly the dependence upon the model that is above both the maker and his product. Augustine was quite conscious of this important distinction—for Augustine Becoming can never be eternal as it is in Plato.[65] And while according to Augustine time itself was created, having a beginning and an end, time for Plato, though also brought into being, is the "moving image of eternity," consisting of the everlasting motion of the heavenly bodies.[66] It is true that the universe (the cosmos) is but the "image" of the eternity of true Being without any Becoming. Thus, the universe is neither autonomous nor independent of eternity. On the contrary, the cosmos and all its parts in their manifoldness receive their Being from the One (they are *kath' hen*).[67] However, the "imitation" guarantees the universe its everlasting Being though in the form of sempiternal change. The universe is not just a "copy"; it is a mirror that mirrors true Being. Insofar as this Becoming is also everlasting *(aei)*, it is independent of its own beginning. By being what it is, "everlasting Becoming": *(aei genesthai)*, the universe constantly reaches that eternity (the *aion*) according to which it was fashioned. This *aion* remains as the eternal "pattern" *(paradeigma)*, whereas the cosmos (called here and throughout the *Timaeus* "the Heaven") "has been and is and shall be perpetually throughout all time."[68]

In Aristotle's analysis this Platonic cosmos has already lost its beginning. Aristotle holds that the whole universe "is single and eternal, having no beginning and no end of its whole existence, containing and embracing in itself infinite time."[69] The cosmos itself is equated with [B:033199] holding together all its possible variations *(systasis* versus the *diatheseis)*. Since these variations occur in bodies *(somata)*, they are limited and therefore changeable. However, the whole is prior to its parts and can survive their coming and going, that is, their changeability. Aristotle writes, "Prior to Becoming there was always this keeping-together which preceded it and of which we cannot say that it changed, since it never came into being."[70]

64. Ibid., 29b–d.
65. *The City of God* XII, 11, 12, 14, and 16 for Augustine's arguments against the eternity of cosmos.
66. Plato, *Timaeus* 37d.
67. Ibid., 30c.
68. Ibid., 38c.
69. Aristotle, *On the Heavens* II, 1, 283b 26–31.
70. Ibid., I, 10, 280a 24.

Since this whole, the system of the heavenly bodies, moves in a circular movement, it has neither beginning nor end. It moves eternally "around the earth."[71] The eternity of the whole is not bestowed upon it through "imitation" of some eternal pattern beyond it, but, on the contrary, is inherent in it. For, as Aristotle points out explicitly in his argument against Plato,

> If, as is written in the *Timaeus*, the elements moved without order before the cosmos came into being, their movement was necessarily either forced upon them or in accordance with their nature. If the latter was the case, the cosmos was necessarily in existence.[72]

In other words, the very order of the cosmos, that is, what makes it a cosmos, must somehow exist before chaos could become cosmos. This is only another way of saying that the beginning of the cosmos is unthinkable.

The last, and for Augustine, most important representative of Greek philosophical thinking about Being and the universe was Plotinus, whose thought Augustine frequently renders almost verbatim.[73] Plotinus, too, is convinced that the cosmos is everlasting, with no beginning and no end: "That the cosmos never began, for this would be absurd, as has been pointed out, gives confidence in its future."[74] Becoming is again an "imitation" and, since Becoming imitates eternal Being, it is itself sempiternal and everlasting. Consequently the world "did not begin and will not end." All particular things and individual organisms are embedded as parts in the order *(taxis)* of the whole, although their own constitution is entirely different from the constitution of the whole. The cosmos as a whole stands under the order to remain as it is forever, whereas the parts have a centrifugal tendency and are bound to the whole by a bond that does not arise out of their own nature. There is simply no place to which they could escape. This disparity seals man's fate in the cosmos.

> If one of these parts moves according to its nature, it makes those suffer to whom this movement is against their own nature, whereas the former as parts of the whole are well. Those who cannot bear the order of the whole perish . . . since they cannot escape the order. . . . [B:033200] If, however, they could fit them-

71. Aristotle, *The Meteorologics* I, 2, 339a 15–30.
72. Aristotle, *On the Heavens* III, 2, 300b 16.
73. See especially Louis Grandgeorge, *S. Augustin et le Neo-platonisme*, (Neudruck der Ausgabe, Paris, 1896; reprint Frankfurt 1966), who has collected a number of passages together with the respective passages from the *Enneads*.
74. Plotinus, *Enneads* II, 1, 4.

selves into the order of the whole they would suffer nothing from it.[75]

The reason that Plotinus was so important for Augustine's own thought is that Plotinus, in contradistinction to his ancient predecessors, is primarily interested in the fate of man in this everlasting cosmos. Hence, Plotinus raises the question of the origin of evil, which is of no great interest to either Plato or Aristotle but is of compelling significance for Augustine. The point on which Augustine parts company with Plotinus is in his understanding of "imitation." For Augustine imitation is not identical with Becoming as such. All creatures are subject to Becoming, but in Augustine's thinking imitation is only characteristic of man. Nonetheless, Plotinus's notion of evil, that one should "not think it to be anything but . . . a lesser good and a continuous diminution,"[76] echoes through most of Augustine's discussions of this question. In a similar way, the general concept of Being as "the order of the whole" (Plotinus' *taxis tou holou*) and of men as parts of this Being is decisive for Augustine's concept of "the well-ordered man" *(homo ordinatissimus)*, whom Augustine distinguishes from the evil man as a "part" that has become wicked because it did "not agree with its whole."[77]

[A:033299] While this view of the cosmos, derived from the Greek tradition, is not really the primary focus of Augustine's later writings, it plainly deflects his concept of the world *(mundus)*, which we shall now consider. As Augustine writes about the world, "Therefore, nothing happens in the world by chance. This having been established, it seems to follow that whatever is done in the world is done partly by divine agency and partly by our will."[78] We share in events in the world by our will. And insofar as things also happen as a result of divine action, God is not the eternal, all-encompassing one who embraces us and our actions—the relationship is half and half. Thus, the world is the place where things happen. Outside of the world, in a sense, stands whoever makes them happen, be it man or God. In any case, events in

75. [Arendt notes here that she is "paraphrasing *Enneads* II, 9, 7, of which this is the general meaning." The standard translations differ somewhat. Compare Stephen McKenna's translation (Plotinus, *The Enneads* [London: Faber and Faber, Ltd., 1956], 139) with Émile Bréhier's bilingual Greek-French edition (Plotin, *Ennéads*, vol. 2 [Paris, 1924], 120).]

76. Plotinus, *Enneads* II, 9, 13.

77. *Confessions* III, 8, 15. [The notion of order and its application to the human being as *homo ordinatissimus* was an important theme that appeared in many of Augustine's writings. For example, see *The Free Choice of the Will* I, 8, 18: "Whatever it is by which man is superior to beasts, whether mind or spirit or whether either of them is the correct term (we find both in the Scripture), if this governs and controls all the other elements of which the human being is composed, then he is well-ordered in the highest degree." See also, I, 7, 16; I, 10, 20.]

78. *Eighty-Three Different Questions* 24.

the world are partly constituted by man who inhabits the world. Yet, what is this world in itself? Augustine answers, "For the 'world' is the name given not only to this [A:033300] fabric which God made, heaven and earth; but the inhabitants of the world are also called the world . . . all lovers of the world are also called the 'world.' "[79] So the world consists of those who love it. The concept is twofold: first, the world is God's creation (heaven and earth), which antedates all love of the world; and second, it is the human world, which constitutes itself by habitation and love *(diligere)*.[80] What "happens by our will" turns heaven and earth into the world in this second sense. By being thus constituted this world is initially brought into being, but not out of nothing, as in the case of the creation. Rather, it is from the divine fabric *(fabrica Dei)*, from the pre-existing creation, that man makes the world and makes himself part of the world. Augustine asks, "Why are sinners called the world? Because they love the world, and by loving it dwell in the world; as in speaking of a house, we mean the fabric as well as the residents."[81] What happens by our will is guided by the love of the world *(dilectio mundi)*, which for the first time turns the world, the divine fabric, into the self-evident home of man. When living man finds his place in the pre-existing creation he is born into, he turns the fabric of creation into the world.[82]

Love for the world, which makes it "worldly," rests on being "of the world" *(de mundo;* see below note 87). Just as God's creation is not worldly as such, neither is man who is of the world already worldly. We shall see later what this concept of "worldliness" really means. Man has the chance of not wanting to be at home in the world and thus keeping himself constantly in a position to refer back to the Creator: "Do not love to dwell in the building, but dwell in the [A:033301] Builder."[83] God's creation is found in existence, and as the creature finds the world, he also finds himself "of the world" and

79. *Homilies on the First Epistle of John* II, 12.

80. See M. Heidegger, "Vom Wesen des Grundes," *E. Husserl-Festschrift* (Halle, 1929), 86–87. In outlining the history of the concepts of the world, the Augustinian one is mentioned among others. Heidegger also distinguishes two Augustinian meanings of *mundus:* on the one hand, it is *ens creatum* (which in our context coincides with the divine fabric, heaven and earth), and on the other, it is the world conceived as the lovers of the world. Heidegger interprets only the latter: "World, therefore, means the *ens in toto,* as the decisive How, according to which human existence relates to, and acts toward, the *ens.*" While his interpretation is thus confined to illuminating the world as "living with the world at heart," and the other world concept, though mentioned, remains uninterpreted, the aim of our interpretation is precisely to make this twofold approach understood.

81. *Commentaries on the Psalms* 141, 15.

82. *Against Julian* (incomplete work), IV, XX: "In short, it is human life, lived not according to God but according to man, which the Apostle here called 'the world.' "

83. *Commentaries on the Psalms* 141, 15.

also created by God. In the pure act of finding himself as part of God's creation, the creature is not yet at home in the world. Only by making himself at home in the world does man establish the world as such. Over against that "finding" or discovery (*invenire*), on which the creature remains dependent in all of its "making" (*facere*), stands the free creation and election of God.[84] Man's dependence as a creature on "finding" in his "making" expresses the particular strangeness in which the world as a "desert" (*eremus*) pre-exists for man.

Unlike God who "infused into the world, makes it"[85] and who thus has an original link with the product existing as his creation, man confronts his product as an outsider. Also, unlike God's creation, which is a continuous preservation, any product of man can be found as a thing in the world having no more to do with its maker.[86] Man can withdraw from it at any time, and its existence as a thing in the world will not cease for that reason. Man stands outside (*forinsecus*) his product and has no intrinsic power over it. Therefore, the world keeps its original strangeness, even as man by "making" suits the world to himself. Since his lack of power lets any product of his turn promptly into a thing he can find in existence and into a thing that confronts him as the "world," man has two choices. First, he can recall his own source and withdraw from this world which, by inhabiting it, he made habitable; or, second, he can once more expressly appropriate the world through desire. It is not "making" as such that ends the strangeness of the world and lets man belong to it, for making [A:033302] still leaves the essence of man outside his product. Rather, it is through love of the world that man explicitly makes himself at home in the world, and then desirously looks to it alone for his good and evil. Not until then do the world and man grow "worldly." In an-

84. *Against Felix the Manichaean* II, 18: "Whatever is made, whatever anyone makes, is made either out of himself, or out of something else, or out of nothing. Since man is not almighty, he makes his son out of himself; and since whatever he made out of himself [is made] out of something else, as a craftsman carves a bow out of wood, he should be said to have 'begotten' rather than 'made.'" *Against Two Letters of the Pelagians* II, 15: "Since he said 'the election' and in this God does not find made by someone else what he may choose, but himself makes what He may find."

85. *Tractates on John's gospel* II, 10: "For He did not make the world as a carpenter makes a chest. The chest which the carpenter makes is outside of him and so is in another place while it is being made. And although the carpenter is nearby, he occupies another place and is external to that which he makes. But God, infused into the world, fashions it. He makes it, being present everywhere and he does not withdraw to some other place, nor does He, as it were, handle the matter which he makes from the outside."

86. *Literal Commentary on Genesis* V, 20, 40: "Let us, therefore, believe and, if possible, also understand that God is working even now, so that if His action should be withdrawn from His creatures they would perish."

other sense, man also finds himself belonging to the world without any such expressions of love of the world as "making from something else" (*fabricare ex aliquo*) and "dwelling in the fabric" (*habitare in fabrica*). Man is "of the world" but only as one who has been created with it and in it.[87] The world cannot be worldly until man's making and loving occur independently of pure createdness.

Only insofar as there is a world at all can man be in the necessary state of being of the world. "All that are of the world are after the world, for the world came first; and so, man is of the world. But Christ was first, and then the world."[88] The finding includes the "after." Inasmuch as man does not create himself into the world, but finds himself in it, he is fundamentally "after"—after the world he lives in, and also, in this specific sense, after his own being.[89] However, since he is born into the world and is thereby of the world, this pre-existing world is for him a present and accessible one. Moreover his own being, the "eternal reason" that made him what he is, antedates even the world to which, as being "of the world," he belongs.[90] His own being lies before him and is accessible to him only as presented past, that is, in memory. His every search for himself, his every possible discovery of himself rests on this fact of being created. Thus, man is "later" than his own being. As a matter of principle, man's being is "prior" to his creation. It is from this "prior" being that the [A:033303] creature is what he is, and he seeks himself in seeking this "before." Thus being "of the world" precedes any explicit love of the world, and it means belonging to the realm of created things.

The createdness of the world has a twofold meaning for the creature. First, the creature has been created into the world and is thus "after the world" (*post mundum*). On this "after" rests his dependence on the world, that is, the possibility of growing worldly. The world, in a sense, is the wrong "before" (we shall elucidate this point later, see below, Part II, chapter 2). Second, the creature is of the world inasmuch as the world, by being part of creation, points back in its turn to its true source. We can see clearly that the "before" is derived from this creature-world context. Since the creature is created into the world, he seeks himself as the sole source of his "being in the world," which is later than his own being. This searching in-

87. Ibid., V, 23, 45: "So the world, since God created all things simultaneously, should be regarded as simultaneously containing all that was made in and with it."

88. *Tractates on John's Gospel* XXXVIII, 4.

89. The fact that man finds himself is evident, too, in the sense that in begetting (which is a "making out of himself," not "out of something else") man becomes such a pre-existing thing.

90. *Confessions* I, 2, 2, and I, 6, 9.

quiry into his own being is specific to human existence, but not for the divine fabric of the world. The inquiry rests on the wish to be happy, which in turn, referring back in memory, points to the Creator, in whose being the world as fabric is wholly unquestionable.[91] This world alone exists before and after man; and, though created, this world provokes no searching inquiry after its being. The fabric of the world knows no such inquiry because, while changeable, it is not perishable.

In asking about his own being, man who is guided by the Greek concept of being, asks about imperishable being, and he does so precisely out of his experiences of the world as heaven and earth. The primary experience is not that God is imperishable, but that the world is. We see this from the very phrase [A:033304] "after the world" *(post mundum)*. For, as we have seen above, that which is "after" is always distinguished by its determinant origin *(fieri)* from that which is "before." When Augustine speaks of the transiency of the world, he is always thinking of the world constituted by men and never the world as heaven and earth. He shows this most clearly by referring to this constituted world as *saeculum* (e.g., in *hoc saeculo*)[92] in order to express its temporalization.[93] However, it is not the temporalization of the world in the sense of the world that the creature is "after," but the world that man himself establishes in "being of the world." (For the inclusion of the world in the transiency of man, see above Part I, chapter 1.) The end of this world *(terminus saeculi)* coincides with the end of the human race.[94] In its search for its own being, the creature encounters the "before"—the Creator.

However, in order to understand this twofold "before," we must inquire further, and more concretely, into the creature's mode of life. For the moment, this explication allows us to make only the following statement: the world concept discussed above (in which the world meant "the whole" or "the universe"), which owed its eternity to the immutability of its structural context and in which man is not a creature but a part, touches on the

91. *The City of God* XII, 1: "Not every creature has the capacity for happiness. Beasts, trees, stones, and such things neither acquire nor have the capacity for this gift."

92. *Homilies on the First Epistle of John* I, 5: "to live in this world among temptations" *("vivere in hoc saeculo inter tentationes")*.

93. *Sermon* 76, 9: "The world only knows how to devour its lovers, not to carry them." See also *Confessions* IX, 4, 10: "Devouring temporal things and being devoured by them." Also, *Literal Commentary on Genesis* V, 19, 38: "Every creature came from the world, not before it *(Omnia creatura non ante saecula sed a saeculis)*. For the world originated from the creature, and the creature from the world, since its beginning is the beginning of the world. But the Only-Begotten, through whom the world came to be, was before the world."

94. *The Goodness of Marriage* 10, 10: "'What if,' they ask 'all men wished to refrain from intercourse, how would the human race survive?' . . . Much more quickly would the City of God be filled, and the end of the world be hastened."

sense of the world as constituted by man we are now discussing. It does so, first, since it deflects the original assumption from which "of the world" is to be understood, that is, the understanding of man as created simultaneously with and in the world, and, second, since the "world" is understood as the immutable "before" *(prius)*. With that, human [A:033305] life is viewed again as enclosed by the world rather than simultaneous with it. For continued life after death corresponds to birth "after the world."

The fact of being created has the structure of *fieri*, of having come to be, and thus has the structure of transience as such. Every creature comes from "not yet" *(nondum)* and heads for "no more" *(iam non)*. If man, coming from the "not yet," were to venture at all on the search for his own being, he would make the question about "before" an expression of referring back to his own source on the basis of this pre-existing relation. Heading for "no more," the creature refers forward to death *(se refert ad finem)*.[95] From the "not yet" to the "no more," life runs its course in the world. Hence, in inquiring backward and forward, man inquires beyond the world, provided that the world is seen as partly established by man, and thus in its character as a twofold product. As a questioning creature, man asks about the very thing that is not of himself, that is, about what precedes any createdness. This questioning beyond the world rests on the double negative into which life is placed. And this double negative (the "not yet" and the "no more") means exactly the same as "before" and "after" in the world. We are born into the world and in death we depart from the world in which we lived. Self-questioning *(se quaerere)* can thus be doubly guided: man can ask himself both about the "whence" and the "whither" of his existence.[96] Although both questions ask about negations of life, the negations differ in kind.[97] The negation "not yet" denotes the source of life and the "no more" denotes death.[98] Despite their seemingly identical negativity, the past and future negations are not the same.

For since the creature is made out of nothing, the final limit of the past is indeed non-being.[99] [A:033306] However, it is precisely at this final limit that the creature meets its proper being because it has been called into be-

95. *The City of God* XIX, 10: "[Virtue] itself refers to that end where our peace shall be so perfect and so great as to admit of neither improvement nor increase."

96. At one time life refers back to the Creator; at the other it sees itself determined by death.

97. *Confessions* XI, 21, 27, and XI, 14, 17.

98. Ibid., XI, 14, 17: "How can we say that time is, since the cause of its being is the fact that it will cease to be?" The negation of "not yet" is the "being made out of nothing." See also ibid., XI, 13, 15–16.

99. *The City of God* XII, 8.

ing. Thus it comes not exactly from nothing but from the Supreme Being in its attribute as First Principle *(summe esse qua principium)*.[100] Therefore, before the creature existed, there was the Supreme Being as well as absolute nothingness.[101] God is the "before" as such only for that creature that was made out of nothing. Any "before" other than God would only point further back, as the "before" of the world. The alternative is that the creature would be begotten of God, like the Only-Begotten Son, and would not be essentially different from God, but would be alike in substance.[102] The Only-Begotten is also "of God," but with regard to the Only-Begotten, God has no priority. The Only-Begotten has no beginning, because he was never nothing. The First Principle is permanent and it existed before the creature. However, the creature's relation to this permanence is definitely one of "coming from."

The negation of life through the "not yet" has a positive meaning: it has to do with what followed upon the "not yet." The positive meaning of the "not yet" is creation and creation only exists because this link with its own "not yet" assures it of the eternity of its "whence." Coming from "not yet," life "tends" to be.[103] This tendency lies in the mere fact that it has come from nothing into being. Yet life, in which the "tending to be" *(tendere esse)* takes place, has an end because it had a beginning. In other words, life "is not wholly, nor is it wholly nothing."[104] Thus, in living toward its end through the very tendency to be, life lives toward another non-being that is different from the first. This "tending to be" occurs in referring back to [A:033307] its own "not yet," because life's origin, too, lies in the original negation. Therefore, the "not yet" of life is not nothing, but the very source that determines life in the positiveness of its being. Life must refer back to its own "not yet," because life in the world will end.

100. *Tractates on John's Gospel* XXXVIII, 11: "Behold what Being is! The First Principle cannot change. The First Principle abides in itself and makes all things new."

101. *The Nature of Good* XXVI: "Therefore, since God made all things which he did not beget of himself, not of those things that already existed, but of those things that did not exist at all, that is, of nothing, [the Apostle Paul says, 'He calls into existence the things that do not exist' (Rom. 4:17)]."

102. *Against Julian* (incomplete work) V, 31: "In this, being of Him, they are what He is— [Christ] in being born, [the Spirit] in going forth; and in such a way they are of Him that He has never been prior to them."

103. *Confessions* IV, 10, 15: "So, when they arise and tend toward being, the more quickly they grow, in order to be, the more speedily do they hasten toward non-being. Such is their mode." See also *The Way of Life of the Manichaeans* II, 6, 8.

104. *Confessions* VII, 11, 17: "I beheld other things below you and I saw that they are not completely existing and not completely nothing. They are because they are from you; they are not since they are not what you are."

The beginning of life meant our entrance into the world and its end means that we must leave the world. The reference goes back before the world and before life in the world. Hence, what the "referring back" conveys is independent of the absolute "no more" of death. Since the "no more" of death is originally uninterpreted by any specifically Christian theology, this "no more" does not point to a being that would place the creature in a pre-existing relationship. The "no more" of death simply means the final "no more" of everything that the living in their condition of impermanence have or are.[105] Nonetheless, there would be no "referring back" if life were not transient. Only because our life has an end (which is already given with its beginning) does the search for our own being require us to refer back. Death is the utmost removal from our source, that is, from the Creator. Life loses its being to death if life has moved away from the source of its being.[106] The peril of man is ignoring this necessary "tending to be," and failing to refer back in reality; and thus falling prey to a kind of death that is the absolute and eternal estrangement from God (alienatio a Deo).

It takes death to direct man's attention to the source of his life. This is the meaning of his transience and the meaning of being a creature in the sense discussed earlier in this chapter. Life is thrown back upon the source of its own being by death. Now we can understand the full significance of "returning." It [A:033308] does not mean a relation to be established at will, in every case and for every creature. Through death-oriented questioning, which allows us to meet the Creator qua Being, we return from death. In this inquiry, life understands itself as having come from being and racing toward nothingness. From the perspective of death, the source, which is initially understood negatively as "not yet," turns about to become wholly positive as absolute Being. At the same time death, which was initially posited as the "no more" of the creature coming from the "not yet," turns about and becomes absolute nothingness.[107]

This in-between position of man, between being and non-being, [A:033309] is now viewed essentially as a matter of time. Indeed, it is time

105. This is precisely the point of the constant "losing" (amittere) that was shown in Part I to be the basic structure of life in Augustine's sense.

106. This is the basis of the conviction that keeps appearing in Augustine's interpretation of Paul's notion of death as the wages of sin: death is man's own fault, the punishment for his sins rather than a fact of nature; e.g., in Sermon 231, 2. See also The City of God VI, 12: "The greatest and worst of all deaths is where death itself does not die. Now since the soul, being created immortal, cannot be deprived of every kind of life, the supreme death of the soul is alienation from the life of God in an eternity of punishment."

107. The City of God VI, 12.

itself.[108] Time is not only the index of transience—time itself is transience. Insofar as human life owes its possibly positive aspect to its past alone, memory becomes the real possibility of holding on to the past and of arresting transience. This is because in memory the past is not pure past (not just "no longer being"), but the past is "presented" as present.[109] Death throws the living back upon their own source. It throws them back before the world and their entrance into the world, and thus on their own "not yet." In this "not yet"—which is the real "before"—all individual differences vanish. In the throwback death renders them all the same *(idem)*.[110] It manifests the two-fold negation of the "no more" and the "not yet." Together with the final "no more," it shows that all of us at some time did not exist. What is also manifest is that the truly positive aspect of our essentially death-determined existence lies in this "not yet" of our being, that is, in that which antedates us. We exist only insofar as we relate directly to the "before" and "not yet" of our existence.

The end of life, to which life relates and which throws life back, is an end in a twofold sense. It is *finis vitae*, the end to which life inherently comes. As such it is the end as the last and most radical indication of life's transience.[111] However, "end" is also understood as the end by which life ceases to be and for whose sake life is lived.[112] In this sense, "end" may be defined as the point where life meets eternity or even as eternity itself. Eternity is then the end achieved by life. In the first sense, the end (as *finis vitae*) confronts life with its own "before" and has only this somewhat provocative meaning. The end itself is understood as sheer, irrevocable nothingness to which life keeps heading and from which life can only save itself by "returning." In the second meaning, the end becomes eternity as the point of cessation in a radically positive sense and a bid for a lingering gaze and reflective calm. Hence, while life once saw its being in a "throwback" to its source, it now understands itself as racing toward its being. Indeed this is the meaning that appears constantly and exclusively whenever Augustine speaks of *se re-*

108. Since time comes from the "not yet" and rushes toward the "no more," it is understood as time "tending not to be" (*Confessions* XI, 14, 17).

109. Ibid., XI, 27, 35: "Therefore, I do not measure these syllables which no longer exist, but something in my memory which remains as a fixed impression."

110. *The City of God* I, 11: "Moreover, life's ending abolishes all difference between a long and a short life. For of two things that no longer exist, one can hardly be said to be better and the other worse, or one longer and the other shorter."

111. For this notion of the "end of life," see *Sermon* 306, 7, and *The City of God* I, 11.

112. *Homilies on the First Epistle of John* X, 5: "Whatever is loved for its own sake and freely, the end is there."

ferre ad finem. Therefore, this ambiguity of "end" does not correspond to two different contexts, but must rest on our context of "referring" (or "returning") itself.

In "referring itself to the end," we put being "before" us again. As to content, this "future before" is characterized exactly as the "before" of the most distant past, as immutability. However, our reflection on ourselves as creatures and on God as the Creator does not enter into this context. What this ambiguity reveals once more is [A:033310] our guiding phenomenon, that is, the interchangeability of beginning and end (see above in this chapter), which life apprehends in the dubiousness of an existence enclosed by the twofold negation and the relevance of this interchangeability for this life. An insight into this phenomenon is possible on the basis of an explication of the world, beyond which life inquires, and on the basis of an illumination of the meanings of beginning and end as creation into the world and removal from it.

We have seen at the beginning of this chapter that Augustine operates with a conception of the "world" that is twofold and factually heterogeneous. When life is viewed in its concrete mortality and createdness, it is understood as life with and in the world. To begin with, life is neither independent of the world (as in "returning" or going back from the world to the source) nor is the world independent of life. Instead, life has a hand in founding the world in which it lives. This life knows a beginning and an end, as being called into the world and into existence and being taken out of or losing them. According to this view it does not matter whether we mean by "world" the lovers of the world or the divine fabric of the world. For even if the man has a hand in founding the world, this foundation always takes place on the ground of the divine fabric, that is, on the ground of the world found in existence as God's creation. This alone makes it possible to establish the world once more in a more explicit sense. Death removes us from both the humanly constituted world and the divine fabric. Since man is transitory, he loses both the world into which he is created as well as the world he created for himself by his love of the world.

The part as part of the whole is changeable and interchangeable. [A:033311] The whole includes the part and yet is indifferent to the part. Still, the whole in its simultaneity and universality is an immutable being to which man relates. Yet this being itself allows two interpretations. In line with the Greek tradition, being is not properly the Creator but the eternal structure of the cosmos, and by imitation *(mimesis)* the man's essence comes to share in eternal being. Accordingly, the return to oneself would no longer mean a departure from the world. Instead, the imitation of God would be accomplished through proper integration into the world by the "well-ordered man" (see above notes 61 and 77), who fits himself into the encompassing; that is, into the whole that makes him the part that he is. However, if immutable being is separated essentially from the "being of the world" as being "before" the world (that is, if immutable being has not entered into the conception of the world, but transcends the world as its source), then the "return" is seen again in its original meaning of "going back." But since man's own being as the point of reference continues to be understood as absolute immutability, being also continues to be encompassing because its eternity includes temporality as well. It is at the end what it was at the beginning. The direction or goal of life is identical to its source.

Now we understand the meaning of the ambiguity of "end." "To refer oneself to the end" *(se referre ad finem)* makes sense only if Augustine's point is the "tending to be" in which "end" is simultaneously the source, the encompassing being, and eternity as such. The usual sense of end as *finis vitae* can assume this second meaning only on the basis of a concept of being in which being is conceived as [A:033312] transcendent and yet, at the same time, as encompassing life and the world. Death shows man that he is nothing if man does not understand himself as a part of the whole. By showing man his nothingness, however, death also points out both his source and a possible escape from nothingness—from death. The escape is the concept of immutable being that death itself becomes. Life, encompassed by eternity, borders upon eternity at the beginning as well as at the end. The original boundary character of beginning and end (as limits against the "not yet" and the "no more") gave rise to the impulse of self-questioning. Now, in the course of man's search for his own being, it has turned around and the boundaries themselves come to be bounded by eternity. Their very character as boundaries is voided by this twofold delimitation and envelopment of life. There is no longer any meaning to "coming from nothing" and "racing toward nothing." Death itself has lost its meaning. This is the specifically confined character that life assumes when it is seen from the perspective of the being that surrounds it.

Thus the twofold "before" is to be understood from the ambiguity of "end" and also according to the original assumption of being as being forever. Yet for death to come "before," it must first be shown to the living in its function of revealing the nullity of life, which at the same time points back to the source. In this role, death detaches the living from the world by making them see the nullity of "being in the world." This nullity lies precisely in the change from being to non-being. The specific nullity of life itself is avoided if death becomes the beginning of eternity in which life is embedded. Death [A:033313] is then the end to be achieved as the positive point of cessation.

However, with this redefinition, life's factual course ceases to be the singular, invariable, and irreversible one of being toward non-being. Life now runs from being to being, from eternity to eternity. Together with this devaluation of the end, the course of life itself is leveled out, since beginning and end are no longer absolutely separated but have become identical in the concept of the encompassing. The question about man's own being, in which the specific being in life assumes such decisive importance even if it is seen as a nullity, becomes a moot question. The concrete course of life is no longer important. If death only brings us a new being (which in fact is our original being), existence has been leveled out, and it does not matter whether human life is long or short.

> Thus the course of life is nothing but a race toward death, a race in which no one may stand still or slow down even for a moment, but all must run with equal speed and never-changing stride. For to the short-lived as to the long-lived, each day passes with unchanging pace. . . . On the way to death the man who takes more time travels no more slowly, even though he covers much more ground.[113]

The interchangeability of life's beginning and end lets life itself appear to be no more than a mere distance stripped of any qualitative significance. Existence itself loses its autonomous meaning, which can only be extension in time. Once we assume the perspective that we no longer view life as "before death" but as "after death," death equalizes by devaluing life as such.

113. *The City of God* XIII, 10.

PART II
CREATOR AND CREATURE:
THE REMEMBERED PAST

2 / Caritas and Cupiditas

[A:033314] We have seen that the return to the Creator is the original structural definition of the creature's being. Yet the return is not an issue until man has the structural connection pointed out to him by the awareness of death. There is no "before" as "before" until man positively takes it up. This positive turn to his own reality in his relation to God is achieved in *caritas*. The missing of the turn—a mistaking of the world that exists before and after man for eternity—is a turn to the wrong "before." It is characterized as covetousness (*concupiscentia*), or *cupiditas*. Both *caritas* and *cupiditas* depend on man's search for his own being as perpetual being, and each time this perpetual being is conceived as the encompassing of his concrete, temporal existence.

"There is no one who does not love; but he asks what he should love. Therefore I do not exhort you not to love, but to choose what we should love."[1] It is not only the object of love that distinguishes *caritas* from *cupiditas*, but the choice itself. Love of the world is never a choice, for the world is always there and it is natural to love it. In referring back, we reach beyond the world, and we take up and choose precisely what the world does not offer on its own. In this selective love the Creator is personally approached. Man knows himself as a creature when he chooses the Creator in *caritas*. His existence wholly depends on the Creator who antedates man's choice. In other words, man's choice still depends on the priority of what he chooses, [A:033315] but this choice can only be made on the ground of a preceding choice by the Creator himself. As Augustine writes, "If we were slow to love, let us not be slow to love in return. He loved us first; not so do we love."[2] Even the choice of *caritas*, in which the referring back becomes reality, requires something prior. If the Creator himself does not make man's dependent relationship an actuality, man is unable to undertake his part of this

---

1. *Sermon* 34, 2.
2. *Homilies on the First Epistle of John* VII, 7.

process of actualization in *caritas*.[3] This divine actualization of the man's relationship is the "choice out of the world" *(electio ex mundo)*.[4] It is the true "grace of God." The grace of God enables man to turn to his own being, prescribed in the "return," and if this being is from God (if indeed it is God), it is the ability to "live in accord with God" *(secundum Deum vivere)*.[5] By the explicit acceptance of divine grace we accept ourselves as creatures and realize our pre-existing dependence on the Being that has made our own existence what it is. Since this existence is lived in the world, it is still determined by what is wholly outside and before the world. However, divine grace takes man out of the world; it is the choice out of the world.[6] Man comprehends himself as belonging not to the world but to God through this choice.[7]

In this act of love we understand once again, and more fully, the decisive role that death played in the disclosure of man's being. Since death is the only power except for God that is capable of removing man from the world, it thereby points to the choice out of the world. The horror of death rests on love of the world. Death destroys not only all possession of the world, but all possible loving desire for any future thing we may [A:033316] expect from the world.[8] Death is the destruction of our natural relation to the world, whose expression is love of the world. In a purely negative sense, death is thus as powerful in separating us from the world as love, which chooses its own being in God. Augustine writes:

> Love itself is our death to the world, and our life with God. For if it is death when the soul leaves the body, how is it not death when our love goes forth from the world? Therefore, love is as strong as death.[9]

The choice out of the world makes it possible to live in accord with God. In taking up *caritas*, the necessary and ontologically based imitation of every man becomes an explicit assimilation to God *(sicut Deus)*. At the same time, this "being out of the world" destroys the individualization and isola-

---

3. Ibid., IX, 9.

4. *Tractates on John's Gospel* CVII, 1: "By the world he now means those who live after the lust of the world and are not in that state of grace of those that have been chosen by him out of the world."

5. *Against Julian* (incomplete work) IV, 20.

6. *Tractates on John's Gospel* LXXVI, 2: "For those who love are chosen because they love. . . . The holy ones are distinguished from the world by that love which makes the single-minded to dwell together in a house."

7. *Confessions* I, 13, 21: "For the friendship of this world is unfaithfulness to You."

8. See above Part I, chapter 1.

9. *Tractates on John's Gospel* LXV, 1.

tion of man that are derived from the world. This "being out of the world," like death, makes everyone the same, because the disappearance of the world removes the possibility of boasting, which came precisely from the individual's worldliness in comparing himself with others.[10] As man advances in *caritas* to Being as such, which at the same time and with the same absolute generality and omnipotence is his own being, he casts off all that belonged to him as a specific individual. And so, Augustine prays "that I may reject myself and choose You."[11]

It is true that imitation as a basic ontological structure governed the entire context of life, regardless of whether it was correct or perverse imitation. Nonetheless, imitation left each single act of this life entirely free and independent of the human will that performs it. Man's life and actions in the world were functions of this imitation, but he himself did not submit to its rule in explicit dependence. [A:033317] As an ontological structure, imitation is independent of man's attitude toward it, and it leaves man in his inherent freedom as long as this function (which he is himself) has not been expressly taken up by him, through not subjecting himself to its judgment on the right and wrong of his actions. Within imitation he is free, though only for himself and not for God. As the determinant of all man's actions and omissions, God cannot even be discovered as long as man leaves imitation objective, that is, as long as he does not expressly take up imitation and thereby once more seal his dependence on something outside him.[12] It is only when imitation is taken up explicitly that the demand of "being as God" appears.[13]

The eternal limit to this assimilation process is equality.[14] It is the limit of the creature a such. In his advance to his own being, he always remains en

10. *The City of God* V, 17: "When all the boasting is over, what is any man but just another man?" *Sermon* 142, 3: "It was pride that hindered the soul's return."

11. *Confessions* X, 2, 2.

12. The equivalent of this "being discovered" in the Augustinian construction of history is "being prior to the law." See *Propositions from Paul's Epistle to the Romans* 13–18: "We thus distinguish these four classes of men: prior to law, subject to law, subject to grace, and in peace. . . . Prior to law, therefore, we do not struggle, because we not only covet and sin, but also approve of sin; subject to law, we struggle, but are conquered."

13. *Homilies on the First Epistle of John* IV, 9: "He purifies us, then, even as he is pure." Ibid., IX, 3: "If this then is the perfection to which God invites us, that we love our enemies as he loved his; this is our boldness in the day of judgment, that 'as he is, so we are also in this world.' And so, since he loves his enemies in making his sun to rise on the good and the bad and in sending the rain upon the just and the unjust, so we, since we cannot bestow upon them the sun and rain, bestow upon them our tears when we pray for them."

14. *Tractates on John's Gospel* XLII, 10: "Clearly, Creator is Creator, creature is creature; and the creature cannot be made equal to the Creator." *Homilies on the First Epistle of John* IX, 3: "For is it possible for man to be as God? I have already explained to you that 'as' is not always said of equality, but is said of a certain resemblance."

route. Though chosen out of the world, he is still of the world. Man was originally created into the world and, in spite of his election, this fact of being in the world separates him from God, that is, from pure Being. This is why man can never have himself as a whole *(totum)*. If he had himself as a whole, he would have his being, as the concept is here understood. However, since he was created so that his being exists for him only as a source, man's concrete existence is governed by temporality in which he can never fully grasp himself.[15] At the same time, however, equality is the goal, the perfection that can never be attained. What remains possible for man is ever-increasing resemblance.[16] The object of this assimilation is God as the Supreme Being, as Being pure and simple, which makes all individual distinctions vanish [A:033318] because they pertain to createdness. Self-rejection is the same as being more like God. In performing this imitation, the reality of which is the absolute denial of the self found in the world, man comprehends his existence as the outright opposite of God, expressed in the impossibility of equality between him and God. Man grasps this opposition in a far more radical sense than was the case in pointing out the connection between the Creator (as Being) and creature, where the world and man constituted an eternal imitation of the divine. It is only here, in his chosen love of the Creator, that the creature sees his limitations and his utter inadequacy to the demand that lies in being created by God, which also must mean "to God" as well. This demand, along with the impossibility of its fulfillment, indicates man's dependence on God and finds concrete expression in the law and the impossibility of compliance *(implere)*.

"The law is written in the hearts of men, which even iniquity itself does not erase."[17] The law is the ever-present demand that God as the Creator makes of his creature. The law demands what man is not willing to do on his own, that is, to advance to his own being and recognize his own createdness. This entails recognizing himself as one who does not simply exist, but who has been created into the world, thereby living amid specific doubts about his own being.[18] The law gives knowledge of sin *(cognitio peccati)*.[19] The

15. *Confessions* X, 8, 15: "Yet memory is a power of my mind and it belongs to my nature; I myself do not grasp all that I am. Thus the mind is too narrow to hold itself."

16. Ibid., VII, 16, 22: "For they [the wicked] are in harmony with those lower things of creation insofar as they are unlike you [God], but they are in harmony with higher things, insofar as they become more like you."

17. Ibid., II, 4, 9.

18. Ibid., X, 16, 25: "But what is nearer to me than I am to myself? Consider: the power of my memory is not understood by me, and yet apart from it I cannot even name myself."

19. *The Spirit and the Letter* 52: "But knowledge of sin [comes] through the law." There are many other texts in which Augustine states this same point.

law's concrete demand asserts, "Thou shalt not covet."[20] The knowledge we get from the law is the knowledge of covetousness *(cognitio concupiscentiae)*. Covetousness is the turn to the wrong "before." Since the world antedates man, having been [A:033319] created into the world, he came after it. The world has for him an imperishable quality. Though death removes him from the world, it leaves the world intact. In covetousness he turns to this world and desires it, and in loving the world for its own sake, he loves the creation rather than the Creator.[21] Through inquiring back and seeking his own perpetuity, covetous man meets the world, and over the world's priority he forgets the absolute priority of God.[22] In this process man sees that his own existence—death-determined, and thus obviously powerless over its own being—points backwards. However, he does not see that all creation, that is, all existence that is not absolute Being, points backwards even when it is not mortal and transient.

Everything created is good when viewed and taken in the original relation to its Creator.[23] Yet if we love the creature in the Creator's place, the creature is detached and taken for an independent being, as though it had made itself. It is the lovers of the world who turn the world that God created into one that can be coveted. Covetousness loves what was first made by man, and that is his real sin. When man sets up the world anew by his love of the world, he simultaneously sets himself up as one who belongs to the world. Similarly, by loving God man belongs to God, his creator. However, in his love of the world man belongs solely to what he made himself, while in the love of God he belongs to him who first made him. That is why pride is the perverse imitation of God's grandeur, because it lets man imagine himself a creator.[24] The basis of covetousness is man's own will, that is, the very possibility of doing anything on his own.[25] If man loves himself according to his own will, he does not love what he finds created by [A:033320] God, but what he makes of himself on his own. Man cannot call himself into existence and cannot make anything out of nothing; in other words, he lacks true cre-

20. *Tractates on John's Gospel* XLI, 12: "For what is the perfecting of good, but the elimination and end of evil? And what is the elimination of evil, but what the law says, 'Thou shalt not covet'? Not to lust at all is the perfecting of good, because it is the elimination of evil."

21. *The Trinity* IX, 8, 13: "For it is *cupiditas* when the creature is loved for its own sake."

22. *Confessions* II, 3, 6: "He [Augustine's father] rejoiced over it with that intoxication whereby the world . . . forgets you, its Creator, and loves your creature more than yourself."

23. Ibid., VII, 14, 20: "There is no health in them to whom any part of your creation is displeasing."

24. Ibid., II, 6, 13: "Pride imitates loftiness of mind"; also ibid., II, 6, 14: "In a perverse way, men imitate you who put themselves far from you, and rise up in rebellion against you."

25. *The Free Choice of the Will* I, 11, 21: "Nothing makes the mind give way to desire except its own will and free choice."

ative power, which is at the same time pure Being. As a result he can only proceed from the fact that he is "of the world" and make himself a lover of the world by turning it into "his own country" *(patria)* and denying that it is a desert.[26] In so doing, he has perverted the original point of his created-ness, which was precisely to show him the way beyond the world and to his proper source.

The temptation to miss this way lies in habit *(consuetudo)*, according to Augustine: "For the law of sin is the force of habit, by which the mind is dragged along and held fast, even against its will, but still deservedly so, since it was by its will that it slipped into the habit."[27] Time and again, habit is what puts sin in control of life. Insofar as the man is of the world, habit has already delivered him to the world. In other words, through habit the man has already yielded to the temptation of turning the world into one defined by those who love it. Hence, habit is the realization of that "second nature" from which man can estrange himself only if he recollects his real source.[28] Through habit, covetousness constantly seeks to cover this real source by insisting that man is "of the world," thereby turning the world itself into the source. Thus man's own nature lures him into the service of "things made" instead of to the service of their Maker.[29] The turn to his own source is tied to death, whose function is the indication of transience. Habit stands in op-position to this view of transience and death, which it dreads as much as death.[30] In blocking the view [A:033321] of death and dragging us down into the world, habit leads even more surely to death.

The actualization of the return in *caritas* is a choice tied to free will. In this act of willing, man simultaneously wills his very own source, which is the utmost limit of the past and the future. For him past and future coincide in reference to eternity. Habit opposes both past and future by making man

26. *Tractates on John's Gospel* XXVIII, 9: "For that man, who understands that he is a so-journer in this world, is in tabernacles. That man understands that he is traveling in a foreign land, when he sees himself sighing for his native land. . . . What is it to be in the wilderness? In the desert waste. Why in the desert waste? Because in this world, where we thirst in a way in which is no water." See also *Homilies on the First Epistle of John* X, 5: "Have you firmly grasped hold of God? You have finished the way. You shall abide in your own country." Further, *Com-mentaries on the Psalms* 141, 15: "Do not love to dwell in the building, but dwell in the Builder."

27. *Confessions* VIII, 5, 12.

28. *On Music* VI, 19: "For not for nothing is habit called a second and a kind of manufac-tured nature."

29. *Homilies on the First Epistle of John* II, 11: "But woe to you if you love the things made and forsake the Maker of them."

30. *Confessions* VIII, 7, 18: "There remained only speechless dread and my soul was fear-ful, as if of death itself, of being kept back from that flow of habit by which it was wasting away to death."

cling to the wrong "before," once he has taken it up. Habit is the eternal yesterday and has no future. Its tomorrow is identical with today. At the bottom of this leveling of temporal, transient existence lies the fear of the most distant future, of death. Death destroys the existence that man has built on his own will. As the utmost limit of the future, death is simultaneously the utmost limit of life's power over itself. Once human life has turned to the world and once it has denied its own createdness as determined by God, it clings to habit. Habit can only justify having once loved the world. Habit shrouds the dangers that this past turn to the world necessarily involves, since it contravenes the meaning of the creature as such. Death is a peril only where man's dependence on his source has not been uncovered. To uncover this dependence is the function of death.

In habit's attachment to the wrong "before" of the world, it would make something imperishable out of life itself, a life that surrenders to this world and its imperishableness as if it were its antecedent. In habit, life always belongs only to what it has once taken up; it has bound itself over to its own past, which is precisely its sin.[31] Against this law of sin, however, stands the fact [A:033322] that sin springs from insistence on our own will. Augustine argues that "humankind's inclination to value its sins is not so much due to passion itself as to habit."[32] The inclination to sin springs more from habit than from passion itself, because the world man has founded in covetousness is consolidated in habit. The creature, in the search for its own being, seeks security for its existence, and habit, by covering the utmost limit of existence itself and making today and tomorrow the same as yesterday, makes it cling to the wrong past and thus gives it the wrong security.[33] This inclination itself rests on the fact that life is "after the world." Shown its own source, which is the utmost limit of its own past, humankind tends to adopt the wrong "before," the wrong past—wrong because it is not the "whence" of its existence. It is precisely by clinging always to the past that habit demostrates the original sinfulness of man's own will, since this will alone established habit as a haven where death would not remind him of the dependence of created human life.[34]

31. *Against Julian* (incomplete work) IV, 103: "That by force of habit it be done without willing."

32. *Christian Doctrine* III, 10, 15.

33. *Homilies on the First Epistle of John* I, 7.

34. *Against Julian* (incomplete work) IV, 103: "Does he not lose his work by his work, being deprived of his will by force of habit, when there would be no habit without his will? . . . Indeed, you have said that there cannot be will and necessity at the same time when they agree, and also when they conflict."

Against the security of habit, the law calls on conscience.[35] Conscience is "of God" and has the function of pointing to the Creator rather than to the creature.[36] Since conscience is of God, it lets us refer back directly to the Creator. The law's command, "Thou shalt not covet," demands man's detachment from all created things—from the world in the broadest sense. Coveting entails the man-made, habitual world that has become independent of the Creator. In the human world established by man, the individual no longer stands in isolated relation to his very own "whence"; [A:033323] rather, he lives in a world he has made jointly with other men. He no longer hears what he is from conscience, which is of God, but from "another's tongue" (aliena lingua).[37] He has turned himself into a resident of this world, one who is no longer of God alone but owes what he is to this world which he helped to establish. This alien tongue determines man's being, whether good or evil, from outside and from what man has founded. Conscience speaks in ourselves against this alien tongue,[38] and it speaks so that the one addressed cannot escape: "An evil conscience cannot flee from itself; it has no place to which it may go; it pursues itself."[39] For the world to which we could flee and our habituation to it are the very things of which we are accused by conscience. To conscience, the world is again a desert. Conscience directs man beyond this world and away from habituation. As the voice of the Creator, conscience makes man's dependence on God clear to him. What the law commands, conscience addresses to the one who has already succumbed to the world in habit. The voice of the law summons him against what "habit previously entangled him in."[40] The estrangement from the world is essentially an estrangement from habit. While man lives in habit, he lives in view of the world and is subject to its judgment. Conscience puts him coram Deo, into the presence of God.[41] In the testimony of conscience, God is the only possible judge of good and evil. This testimony bears witness to man's de-

---

35. Confessions III, 7, 13: "Nor did I know the true, inner justice which does not base its judgments on custom, but on the supremely right law of the all-powerful God."

36. Homilies on the First Epistle of John VI, 3: "Let your conscience bear you witness, for it is of God."

37. Ibid., VI, 2: "Not when another's tongue bears witness to him, but when his own conscience bears witness."

38. Tractates on John's Gospel LXXIV, 5: "Therefore, God is seen in an invisible way. Nor can we have any knowledge of Him unless He is in us. For it is in a similar way that we come to see our conscience within us."

39. Ibid., XLI, 4.

40. Seventeen Questions on the Gospel of Matthew III.

41. Commentary on Paul's Epistle to the Galatians 57: "The job of reproving another's faults should never be undertaken unless we have examined our souls, searched our consciences, and clearly replied to ourselves in God's presence that we are doing it out of love."

pendence on God, which he finds in himself.[42] The world and its judgments crumble before this inner testimony. There is no fleeing from conscience. There is no togetherness and no being at home in the world that can lessen the burdens of conscience.[43]

Driven [A:033324] by the divine law, conscience speaks into the world-entangled life of man and puts him into God's presence to face his source. In man's relationship, independent of its actualization, he refers to what was conceived as the twofold "before" in which the beginning and the end of life were leveled. Here man is called upon to realize this relationship for the first time, and this realization is possible only on the ground of testimony derived from God himself. Furthermore, this realization is to be performed in *caritas* over the concrete course of a life that is a prey to habit and inevitably leads to death.[44] Here the "before," in its twofold meaning of returning to the Creator who precedes all things and of referring to the end, is set aside in favor of God's immediate presence. Thus *coram Deo* is possible only on the ground of man's structural link with his "before."

However, in the actualization of the return, the source itself is no longer characterized as eternity and the encompassing, but as the Creator who makes demands on the creature. The imitation of God is no longer the determining factor of the man's being. It is, instead, God's bidding expressed by the law in conscience and confronting man at every moment. The Creator, as encompassing eternal Being, no longer determines only the beginning and the end of the creature's life. If man tears himself loose from his mundane moorings and from making his home in the world, this possible turn to his own being occurs in God's commanding presence. Only in this context does the purely ontological concept of God as Creator and Supreme Being grow specifically Christian and theological. The [A:033325] ontological substance of the concept of God is forgotten, so to speak, over the divine command that enters into the man's concrete, transient life. The Creator is now understood solely as the almighty and personal God who (because he is the Creator) has a claim upon his creature against all the existential possibilities offered by its own will.

Yet how is this about-face, from *ante* to *coram*, that is, from "before" to

---

42. *The City of God* XII, 8: "Boasting is not something wrong in human praise; the fault is in a soul which perversely loves the praise of others and cares nothing for the witness of conscience." Ibid., XIV, 28: "The city of man seeks the praise of men, whereas the height of glory for the other is to hear God in the witness of conscience."

43. *Commentary on Paul's Epistle to the Galatians* 59: "Those who praise do not lessen the burdens of our conscience."

44. See above, notes 30 and 31.

"in the presence of," possible?[45] In the actual referring back that brings the man to his own being as eternity, he finds himself face to face with being in a previously unknown sense, namely, as incapable of turning to being, as eternity, on his own. Indeed, this incapacity is only possible on the ground of the dependence that had always existed and is expressed in imitation. However, imitation as such did not yet mean our inability to realize our dependence in a positive sense, that is, an inability to ascertain explicitly and to appropriate what we depend upon. Imitation simply meant that man has not called himself into being. It did not mean that on his own man was unable to find the "whence" of his createdness. It does mean that to effect his relation to being is a demand inherent in man.[46] But only if man submits to the world in habit does this demand confront him from without.[47] The individual commandments of the law, one of which is "Thou shalt not covet," are expressions of that basic demand inherent in man. Thus the fulfillment of the law is the "perfecting of good" and the "consuming of evil."[48]

The perfection of good is negatively defined because [A:033326] self-deliverance from the world already amounts to a choice of the Creator. This negative definition means nothing else than that: in the search for his own being, man does not have all possibilities open to him but is subject to the alternative outlined in createdness and being of the world. Man is unable to fulfill this law, that is, to keep himself pure from the temptations that lie in "being of the world," which is necessarily "being after the world." Even if man could fulfill the law, he would still be living according to his own righteousness. God's law is given with the creature's "being of God." In this "of God," God is the Supreme Being and the man's own proper being. This is not the being diametrically opposed to him, but one whose demand, as the

45. Augustine uses "in God's presence" (coram Deo) and "before God" (ante Deum) interchangeably. I chose the phrase "in God's presence" first because I needed to distinguish it from "before" in quite a different [temporal] sense, and second, because "in God's presence" is the traditional translation from Greek as well as Hebrew. See note 57 below.

46. Confessions II, 4, 9: "Surely, Lord, your law punishes theft, as does that law written on the hearts of men, which not even wickedness itself blots out." See also The Free Choice of the Will I, 15, 32: "So the eternal law bids us turn away our love from temporal things, and turn it back, when purified, toward the things that are eternal."

47. Commentaries on the Psalms 57, 1: "'Do not do to another what you would not have done to yourself.' No one was suffered to be ignorant of this truth, even before the Law was given, in order that there might be some rule whereby even those to whom the Law had not been given might be judged. . . . However, because men desired external things and became exiles even from themselves, a written law had also been given; not because it had not been given in our hearts, but because you were a deserter from your heart."

48. Tractates on John's Gospel XLI, 12.

man's very own, renders him helpless.[49] What becomes sinful here is independence as such, not as a revolt of the part against the whole, but as an independent performance of submission. God is no longer understood as the Supreme Being, which as eternity presents the eternal law simultaneously in its several parts, but as the ever-present authority that man keeps confronting on his way through life.

Man's inability to comply with the law does not consist in a lack of will but a lack of power, since in seeking the Creator rather than the world he has already made his law-bidden choice not to covet. To experience this inadequacy is to experience the gulf between "to will" and "to be able."[50] In God's case, will and power coincide.[51] The gulf between "to will" and "to be able" marks the creature that has no power over its own being. Its lack of power makes the creature depend on the Creator once again and more decisively. It is up to [A:033327] God whether man who has already set out on the searching quest for his own being, that is, has already turned away from the world, will ever reach this self-demanded goal and whether his isolation from the world will be successful.[52] Even in conscious acknowledgment of the law (sub lege), man gains nothing but a knowledge of sin.[53] His sin as such remains in the discrepancy between will and power. Thus the law accomplishes the humbling that enables the creature to experience the Cre-

---

49. *Grace and Free Choice* 24: "[Saint Paul] says that they wished to establish their own righteousness. This righteousness is of the Law, not that the Law was established by them, but that they had constituted their righteousness in the Law which is of God. They did this when they supposed themselves able to fulfill the Law by their own strength, ignorant of God's righteousness, but not that righteousness by which God himself is righteous, but that which man has of God."

50. *The City of God* V, 10: "For wherever there is a mere will without power to carry out what it chooses, it would be impeded by a stronger will. Even so, there would be no will in such a condition unless there were a will, and not merely the will of another but the will of the one choosing, even though he is unable to carry out his choice."

51. *Confessions* VII, 4, 6: "God's will and God's power are God himself."

52. *Propositions from Paul's Epistle to the Romans* 40: "For each man, when he cannot fulfill a precept he recognizes as just, acknowledges that he is dead." Ibid., 61: "It is we who believe and will, but he who gives to those believing and willing the ability to perform good works through the Holy Spirit, through which the love of God is poured forth in our hearts, thus making us compassionate." *Letter* 177, 5: "There has to be a distinction between the Law and grace. The Law knows how to command, grace how to help. The Law would not command if there were no free will, nor would grace help if the will were sufficient."

53. *Propositions from Paul's Epistle to the Romans* 13–18; see also ibid., 30: "But the Law is given to show how tight are the sinful chains binding those who presumed to do justice of their own power." See also *Commentary on Paul's Epistle to the Galatians* 26: "For the knowledge of being more seriously ill intensifies the desire for the physician."

ator once again, and anew, in keeping with its newly felt dependence.[54] If its attempted actualization of the return in conscience had made the creature feel the demand inherent in itself as a law given by the Creator (a demand concretely met by that very actualization), its inadequacy to comply with that law makes it feel the Creator once more as bestowing the power. In this process man experiences grace.

> As God is the Creator of all natures, so is He the giver of all
> powers, though not the maker of all choices. . . . Therefore,
> our wills are capable of as much as God willed them to be cap-
> able of.[55]

This power is given to the willing only, just as the Being from which we spring is outside ourselves.[56] Though the command to return to Being as our source is within ourselves as conscience, the granting of the power to do so, which is divine grace, comes from outside ourselves. We defined the "outside ourselves" of the Being that makes us what we are as the twofold "before" of eternity. Even though the law is of God, it is also in ourselves as the command inherent in our existence. It lays bare man's inadequacy and redirects him toward the Creator. This new direction uncovers the sinfulness of man, [A:033328] which is inevitable and ingrained in one who is "of the world" and thus has already chosen the wrong "before" through habit. The discovery of sinfulness does not lie as yet in createdness by God and the resulting return. Rather, this discovery newly subordinates man to God, this time as a sinner. This sinful confrontation with God corresponds to being in God's presence. The "return to Him who was before all things" turns into the *coram Deo* at the moment when man's inadequacy to comply with the inevitable demand inherent in him has been laid bare.[57] And this inadequacy in God's presence lies in the mere fact of the law, which demands and commands as law. The gulf between will and power corresponds to the uncertainty of "to will" and "to nill" *(partim velle, partim nolle).*[58] What com-

---

54. *Commentary on Paul's Epistle to the Galatians* 24: "Because then only the humbled can accept the grace of *caritas*, and without this grace there is no way to fulfill the commands of the Law. Man is humbled by sin in order to seek grace."

55. *The City of God* V, 9.

56. Ibid., V, 10.

57. This can be seen in Augustine. The Septuagint text (the translation of the Hebrew) shows that the divine presence and the consistently present authority of God can already exist in the human condition, which Augustine characterizes as "being subject to the Law."

58. *Confessions* VIII, 9, 21.

mands in the law is our conscience, which at the same time is our will.[59] If the will were entire, it would not need to command.

> For the will commands that there be a will, and that this be itself, and not something else. But the complete will does not give the command, and therefore what it commands is not in being. For if the will were complete, it would not command itself to be; it would already be. Hence, it is not monstrous partly to will a thing and partly to nill it, but it is a sickness of the mind. Although the mind is supported by truth, it does not wholly rise up, since it is heavily weighed down by habit.[60]

This discrepancy in the will itself, which stems from habit, permits us to understand the law both as a commandment from outside and as the will's simultaneous inability to comply with the law.[61] The will is not sufficient.[62]

By pointing out a sinfulness it cannot remove, the law accomplishes the renewed turn to the Creator.[63] This turn is no longer [A:033329] a simple relation to God, but a direct plea for his help. God's function is changed from that of a Creator to a giver and helper. God's help is grace, and this can be attained and accepted only by one who has been humbled (*humiliatus*), that is, by one who has recognized the sinfulness of his own incapacity and inferiority to the command.[64] Grace is God's renewed acceptance of the creature He has made and corresponds to the plea for help in the renewed turn to God. This acceptance is the love by which God acknowledges the creature and is tantamount to a new creation.[65] It is a love (*dilectio*) only the humbled [A:033329] can know and accept. In this love the reconciliation with God takes place, and it is always a reconciliation with the creature's

---

59. *The City of God* XIV, 6: "The will is in all of these affections; indeed, they are nothing else but the inclinations of the will."

60. *Confessions* VIII, 9, 21.

61. Ibid., X, 40, 65: "Such is the weight of habit! Here I abide, although I would not; there I wish to be, but cannot. In both ways I am unhappy."

62. *Letter* 177, 5.

63. *Propositions from Paul's Epistle to the Romans* 37: "For the Law is good; but without grace it only shows that it does not take away sins."

64. *Letter* 217, 12: "Therefore, the grace of God is not found in the nature of free will, or in the law, or in doctrine, as the Pelagian aberration falsely claims, but it is given to separate acts of the will."

65. *Enchridion* 31: "We shall be made truly free, then, when God fashions us, that is, forms and creates us anew, not as men (for he has done that already), but as good men, which his grace is now doing, that we may be a new creation in Christ."

own God-derived and inherent demand.[66] Man is re-created by being delivered from his sinfulness and thus from being of the world.[67]

Even though man's deliverance permits him fully to understand the world as a desert again, he is no longer lost in this desert. He can live in the world, because in *caritas* he now has the "whence," and thereby the meaning of this life.[68] This in turn means that in the law God shows himself from afar and through grace as nearby.[69] This proximity is the meaning of Christ's earthly life and Incarnation. Thus *caritas* accomplishes the "tending to be," as *cupiditas* accomplishes the "approach to nothingness." However, this approach depends on God's own previous inclination to the creature, who is re-created *(nova creatura)* as one who has been reconciled with God and at the same time with its own createdness. Man the creature has renounced himself. Now the creature is only the object of God's love, [A:033330] which is extended to him as a creature and is not extended to what he could be on his own. Man on his own is always sinful in God's presence, whether steeped in covetousness or trying by his own will to surmount his nature as a creature in the searching quest of his own source. Each time the Creator has really been forgotten, in the first instance over the world, and in the second, over man's own possible independence. In this independence, or pride, man misses the very chance of actualization. He forgets the "whence" over himself.[70] "It was pride, then, that hindered the soul's return."[71]

The comprehension and choice of divine grace happens in *caritas*. Corresponding to the necessity of referring back, *caritas* is also defined as "loving back" *(redamare)*. Only in this return of love can man refer back so as to come to the truth of his existence ("uplifted by truth, weighed down by habit"). *Caritas* alone lets him fulfill the law in accepting the help of the Creator, the "giver of all powers," for only in the accepted grace of God is the

66. *Tractates on John's Gospel* CX, 6: "We were reconciled to one who already loved us, but we had enmity against him because of sin." See also CXI, 1: "So shall the world reconciled be delivered out of the world at enmity."

67. Ibid., CVIII, 1: "This was conferred upon them by regeneration; for by natural generation they were of the world." See also CXI, 1: "So shall the world be delivered out of the world."

68. *Homilies on the First Epistle of John* VII, 1: "And so, if you would not die of thirst in this wilderness, drink *caritas*."

69. *Sermon* 171, 3: "Even though the immortal and just one was so far from us, since we are mortals and sinners, he descended to us so that the one who was very far might become very close to us. . . . In order for him to become very close, he took our penalty, but he did not take our guilt."

70. *The City of God* XIX, 25: "The virtues on which the mind prides itself, as giving control over the body and its urges and which aim at some other purpose of possession than God, are in point of fact vices rather than virtues . . . they are spoiled and puffed up by pride."

71. *Sermon* 142, 3.

world truly renounced. Augustine cites Paul's first epistle to the Corinthians 1:27–28: "And you have chosen the ignoble things of this world, and the despised things, and those which are not, as if they were, to bring to naught the things that are."[72] Only in the election of God, which is later than, but not independent of, the creation does the world turn back into what it had been at creation, and what man had made of it is brought to naught. *Caritas* fulfills the law, because to *caritas* the law is no longer a command; it is grace itself.[73] In loving God, which is the new turn to him, the law has ceased to be demanding and fearsome. [A:033331] the world has become a desert, and covetousness has lost its meaning. This loving acceptance reconciles the creature with its Creator. Man has returned to God from the world; he has denied the world as well as himself, insofar as he is of the world. In this self-denial man achieves the real truth and meaning of his createdness.

> When man lives according to himself, that is, according to human ways and not according to God's will, then surely he lives according to falsehood. Man himself, of course, is not a lie, since God who is his Author and Creator could not be the author and creator of a lie. Rather, man has been so constituted in truth that he was meant to live not according to himself but to him who made him, that is, he was meant to do the will of God rather than his own. It is a lie not to live as man was created to live.[74]

This self-denial can only be achieved in *caritas*, because nothing else provides a reason for the sacrifice. Only through love can man renounce his own will, and this renunciation born of love is the prerequisite for choosing grace. This is why, compared to "the will which nature has implanted in us," love is "the stronger will."[75] In self-denial, man acts "as God" toward himself. He loves himself as God loves him, hating everything he has made in himself, and loving himself only insofar as he is God's creation. What he loves in himself is exclusively God's goodness, the Creator.[76] Man hates

---

72. *Confessions* VIII, 4, 9. Even in primitive Christianity (e.g., in the Pauline epistle cited), this "bringing to nothing" is the only ground of the election of the lowly and the despised. It means the annihilation, but not the reversal, of all human conduct. This point is relevant especially against Nietzsche's psychological derivation from resentment (however valid this may have been in each individual case). This point is also relevant in opposition to Scheler's theory of the nobility's inclination toward ignobility. (See "Das Ressentiment in Aufbau der Moralen," in *Gesammelte Aufsätze und Vorträge*, vol. 2).

73. *Various Questions for Simplicianus* I, 17: "Thus the Law is at once a command for those who fear and grace for those who love."

74. *The City of God* XIV, 4.

75. *The Trinity* XV, 21, 41.

76. *Tractates on John's Gospel* LXXXVII, 4.

himself insofar as free will enables him to give his being of the world an independent significance:

> For he hated us as being such as he had not made us; and because our iniquity had not consumed his work in every part. He knew how at once to hate in each one [A:033332] of us what we had made, and to love what he himself had made.[77]

77. Ibid., CX, 6.

PART II
CREATOR AND CREATURE:
THE REMEMBERED PAST

3 / Love of Neighbor

[A:033340] In Augustine's view, self-denial is expressed in man's attitude toward the world. Man loves the world as God's creation; in the world the creature loves the world as God does. This is the realization of a self-denial in which everyone, including oneself, simultaneously regains his own God-given importance. This realization is neighborly love.[1] Let us try to see how the "neighbor" is understood in this love which is both God-given and self-denying.

Love of neighbor is man's attitude toward his neighbor, which springs from *caritas*. It goes back to two basic relations: first, a person is to love his neighbor as God does *(sicut Deus)*; and second, he is to love his neighbor as he loves himself *(tamquam se ipsum)*. In line with these basic relations, we propose two questions: first, how does the self-denying person meet his neighbor; and second, in this encounter what is the neighbor's role?

The law bids us love one another. This is the essence of the law and that toward which all the other laws aim.[2] The law regulates and determines what is done in the world by man who regards the world as a desert and lives in relation to his own source. Since this world has always been constituted by men, it defines how men act toward each other. Love is the essence of all

1. There is certainly no denying the statements by Karl Holl (in "Augustins innere Entwicklung," *Preussische Akademie der Wissenschaften* [1928]: 47) that "this brief outline confirms, to begin with, that the influence of Saint Paul did not extend into Augustine's ultimate depths. It did not touch the basic eudaimonistic trait of his ethics, nor, for all the talk about *caritas*, the endeavor's concentration upon the self." Holl claims that "this has to do with the fact that Augustine knows how to grasp the commandments of the Sermon on the Mount from their negative side only. The innermost essence of neighborly love, its meaning as a will to self-sacrificing community, remained hidden from him" (ibid., 29). However, it can be shown that even in Saint Paul's case (though not in Jesus' own words), love of neighbor remains consistently tied to the individual, i.e., that the fundamental question for an understanding of neighborly love, as commanded by Jesus, reads as follows: As one seized by God and detached from the world, how can I still live in the world?

2. *Enchiridion* XXXII, 121: "Thus the end of every commandment is *caritas*, that is, every commandment has love for its aim."

the several commandments. According to its own meaning, each possible commandment is fulfilled by love. The fulfillment of love depends on God's grace and the power to love one's neighbor depends on the love of God.[3] In [A:033341] accepting God's love man has denied himself. Now he loves and hates as God does. By renouncing himself man at the same time renounces all worldly relations. He then views himself solely as created by God, rejecting whatever he himself has made and whatever relations he has established. In this way the neighbor loses the meaning of his concrete worldly existence, for example, as a friend or enemy. For the lover who loves as God loves, the neighbor ceases to be anything but a creature of God. The lover meets a man defined by God's love simply as God's creation. All meet in this love, denying themselves and their mutual ties. In this meeting all people have an equal, though very minor, relevance to their own being. Because man is tied to his own source, he loves his neighbor neither for his neighbor's sake nor for his own sake. Love of neighbor leaves the lover himself in absolute isolation and the world remains a desert for man's isolated existence. It is in compliance with the commandment to love one's neighbor that this isolation is realized and not destroyed, in regard to the world in which the creature also lives in isolation. Since man is not God and never attains equality with God, the "as God" deprives him of any chance to choose his neighbor.[4] And this "as God" destroys every human standard and separates love of neighbor from any carnal love.[5]

However, this view of neighborly love as the commandment of self-denial fails to explain how the absolutely isolated person can have a neighbor at all. We have seen that in the search for his own source, man inquires beyond the world. In this process man meets the absolute "before," the Creator, and concretely turns to him in the [A:033342] actualized "presence of God." Yet in asking "beyond the world," the quest for the source also exceeds every source that is historical and immanent in the world. The historical source of man would be the very token of his worldliness and would accord with his being of the world. Even in the most far-reaching sublima-

---

3. *Commentary on Paul's Epistle to the Galatians* 45: "Who can love his neighbor, that is, everyone, as himself, if he does not love God whose command and gift enable him to love his neighbor?"

4. *Commentaries on the Psalms* 25, ii, 2: "You should consider every person your neighbor, even before he is a Christian. For you do not know how he stands with God; furthermore, you do not know how God may have foreknown him."

5. *Tractates on John's Gospel* LXV, 1: "For it is not indeed every kind of love that renews him who listens to it or rather yields to it in obedience, but love regarding which the Lord, in order to distinguish it from all carnal love, added 'As I have loved you.'"

tion, it would only be the choice of *cupiditas*, the wrong "before." This may be the wrong "before," but it is not pointless since the very point of *cupiditas* lies in the fact of being "after the world." Man's absolute isolation in God's presence, which actualizes the return, explains how divinely ordained love serves to realize self-denial. The reason is that love amounts to renouncing any independent choice and any originally established relation with the world.

However, what we cannot understand is how, through this love by which we deny both ourselves and the world, another person can still be considered our neighbor, that is, as someone specifically connected to us. In Part III we shall see that we meet the other person as our neighbor in "social" *caritas*, because human beings belong together due to their common historic descent from Adam. Even though this belonging is of the world, it gives the neighbor a definite relevance even in self-denying love. But at this point we shall ignore the discrepancy arising from man's absolute isolation in God's presence. We shall ignore it because, from Augustine's perspective, we would be able to understand the neighbor's relevance only as "of the world," and so would be unable to do justice to the real source of the neighbor's relevance in Augustine's thinking.

Self-denying love means loving by renouncing oneself; and this [A:033343] in turn means to love all people so completely without distinctions that the world becomes a desert to the lover. Moreover, it means to love them "as oneself." By the fact of referring back, man as creature gains his own being. Since man is both "from God" and "to God," he grasps his own being in God's presence. This return through recapturing his own being, and the isolation achieved in it, is the sole source of neighborly love. The prerequisite of the right comprehension of my neighbor is the right comprehension of myself. It is only where I have made sure of the truth of my own being that I can love my neighbor in his true being, which is in his createdness. And just as I do not love the self I made in belonging to the world, I also do not love my neighbor in the concrete and worldly encounter with him. Rather, I love him in his createdness. I love something in him, that is, the very thing which, of himself, he is not: "For you love in him not what he is, but what you wish that he may be."[6] This not only preserves the isolation of the lover who is concerned about even those nearest to him only insofar as he loves God in them.[7] It also means that for the neighbor as well

---

6. *Homilies on the First Epistle of John* VII, 10.

7. *Sermon* 336, 2: "For he truly loves a friend who loves God in his friend, either because God is in him or so that God may be in him."

love is merely a call to isolation, a summons into God's presence.[8] The lover turns the beloved into his equal.[9] He loves this equality in the other whether or not the beloved understands it.[10] In self-denying love I deny the other person as well as myself, but I do not forget him (see above Part I, chapter 3). This denial corresponds to "willing that you may be" and "carrying off to God." I deny the other person so as to break through to his real being, just as in searching for myself I deny myself.

It should be noted here that the adequate experience [A:033344] of my own source lies in self-denial, which is the understanding of my own existence as originally fraught and weighted with meaning. Yet the denial of the other person is not the end of the process of searching back; it is the beginning. The denial is intended to provide the impetus for self-denial. Moreover, the neighbor's original being is pointed out in the denial that is a comprehension of his being. Thus, love of neighbor is the concrete realization of referring back beyond the world, and in so doing it thrusts the other out of the world that he considers the point of his being. In accordance with the meaning of being as being-forever, love of neighbor does not mean to love the other in his mortality, but to love what is eternal in him, his very own "whence."[11] "If souls are pleasing, let them be loved in God, for they too are mutable, but when fixed on God they become stable; otherwise they would pass and perish."[12] In this stabilization lies the original meaning of what we love. The lover reaches beyond the beloved to God in whom alone both his existence and his love have meaning. Death is meaningless to love of neighbor, because in removing my neighbor from the world death only does what love has already accomplished; that is, I love in him the being that lives in him as his source. Death is irrelevant to this love, because every beloved is only an occasion to love God. The same source is loved in each indi-

8. *Letter* 130, 14. ["For, our temporal life is lived profitably only when it is used to gain merit whereby eternal life is attained. Therefore, all other things which are profitable and properly desired are unquestionably to be referred to that one life by which we live with God and by His life. Inasmuch as we love ourselves in God, if we really love Him, so also, according to another commandment, we truly love our neighbors as ourselves, if, as far as we are able, we lead them to a similar love of God. Therefore, we love God for Himself, but ourselves and our neighbor for His sake. But, even when we live thus, let us not think that we are established in happiness, as if we had nothing left to pray for. How can we find happiness in life when the one incentive to a good life is still lacking to us?"]

9. *Homilies on the First Epistle of John* VIII, 8: "You ought to wish all men to be your equals."

10. *Tractates on John's Gospel* LXXXVII, 4: "Therefore, we are forbidden to love in it [the world] what it loves in itself, and bidden to love in it what it hates in itself, namely the workmanship of God and the various consolations of his goodness."

11. *Confessions* IV, 4, 7–9, 14.

12. Ibid., IV, 12, 18.

vidual human being. No individual means anything in comparison with this identical source. The Christian can thus love all people because each one is only an occasion, and that occasion can be everyone. Love proves its strength precisely in considering even the enemy and even the sinner [A:033345] as mere occasions for love. It is not really the neighbor who is loved in this love of neighbor—it is love itself.[13] Thus the neighbor's relevance as a neighbor (which was previously described as a discrepancy) is overcome and the individual is left in isolation.

13. *Homilies on the First Epistle John* IX, 10: "Can one love his brother and not love Love? Of necessity he must love Love. . . . In loving Love, he loves God." See also *The City of God* XI, 27.

PART III
SOCIAL LIFE

[A:033348] Beginning from the fact that in this world Christian *caritas* is tied to the love of God, we have pursued two different trains in Augustine's thought that showed the human ties to God as different in each case. The negative result has been to leave love of neighbor incomprehensible in its true relevance. According to the traditional commandment, love of neighbor is tied to God's love as well as to loving the other "as oneself." Whenever Augustine speaks about love of neighbor, he is particularly explicit about the phrase "as oneself." Thus, in the return from eternity, the self-oblivion of craving would let man see his neighbor as well as himself only from an absolute distance, since every original relationship had been forgotten along with the self. In the self-denial of referring back, in which the creature finds his sole meaning in the total isolation which is the beginning of self-denial, the other had to be denied along with the self. The question remains: why does love of neighbor, despite the repeated discrepancies, play so large a role even in these originally alien contexts of Augustine's work? Is there, perhaps, another empirical context, different in origin, that would give the neighbor a specific relevance, apparently voided in theory by what we said before, but with a de facto impact on Augustine that might explain his concern with this aspect of Christian tradition?

Referring [A:033349] to the early followers of Christ, Augustine writes, "Those saw; we have not seen and yet we are fellows because we hold the faith in common."[1] True fellowship rests on the fact of the common faith. Therefore, by observation we can define the society of believers by two distinguishing marks. First, since the society of believers is established by what in principle is not mundane, it is a community with others grounded not in a pre-existing reality in the world, but in a specific possibility. Second, because this possibility is the most radical of all possibilities available to human existence, the community of faith that is realized in loving each

1. *Homilies on the First Epistle of John* I, 3.

other calls for and demands a total response from each person. In contrast to all worldly communities, which always isolate only one definition of being in regard to which the community is a community, the community of faith demands the whole man, as God also demands him.[2] Thus, at the same time the faith of which it is said that "each has his own" is at the same time so radically the common faith that every other individual is viewed only from the perspective of the potential faith that would make him a fellow believer.[3] And at the same time (as was shown in Part II, chapter 2), this faith is understood as a last and most radical possibility of being human.

However, we have seen that this very faith will thrust the individual into isolation from his fellows in the divine presence. Even if all do believe the same, this concurrence is irrelevant to the being of the individual ("each has his own"). The simple sameness of the God in whom they all believe does not as yet bring about a community of the faithful. How does the mere concurrence of believers turn into a common faith, that is, into a community of faith itself that regards all people, even [A:033350] unbelievers, as brothers, since everyone is my neighbor? It is only by posing the question in this way that we obtain the common ground of experience on which the Christian community becomes decisive for the individual believer. And we continue to ask: where does this experiential ground come from that can no longer be traced by the inner dialectics of faith?

Both craving and referring back are mere ways of conduct and choices of a human possibility whose realization remains dependent on divine grace alone. Here, however, faith as faith is tied to a distinct and concretely historical fact. What makes my neighbor appear in the relevance required for a commandment of love is not the fact that "I have become a question to myself."[4] Rather, it is a historically pre-existing reality, obliging as such even for the redeeming death of Christ and essential for turning it into a similar reality. Therefore, for the moment the difference in viewpoint is evident from two possible concepts of faith. First, faith is the individual's approach to the question of his own being. And second, faith is tied to the factuality of history and to the past as such.

The redeeming death of Christ did not redeem an individual but the whole world (*mundus*), understood as the man-made world. However faith may isolate the individual, the object of faith (redemption by Christ) has come into a given world and thus into a given community. Faith takes man

2. *Sermon* 34, 7: "He who made you demands the whole you."

3. *The Trinity* XIII, 2, 5: "Therefore this faith is common to all . . . as the human countenance is said to be common to all, for this is so said that yet each one certainly has his own."

4. *Confessions* X, 33, 50.

out of the world, that is, out of a certain community with men, the *civitas terrena*. This earthly city is always a society as well, that is, a social organism defined by people's living with and for each other and not just alongside each other.[5] This *civitas terrena* is [A:033351] not arbitrarily founded and not arbitrarily dissolved. Rather, it is founded on a second historical fact. In God's plan for salvation, this historical fact alone could make Christ a historical and effective reality.[6] This second fact is the common descent from Adam, the foundation of a definite and obligatory equality among all people.[7] This equality exists because, as Augustine writes, "the human race was instituted, as if rooted *[tamquam radicaliter]*, in Adam."[8] "Rooted" means that no one can escape from this descent, and in this descent the most crucial determinant of human existence has been instituted once for all.[9] Thus, what unites all people is not an accidental likeness *(simultudo)*. Rather, their likeness is necessarily founded and historically fixed in their common descent from Adam and in a kinship beyond any mere likeness.[10] This kinship creates an equality neither of traits nor of talents, but of situation. All share the same fate. The individual is not alone in this world. He has companions-in-fate *(consortes)*, not merely in this situation or that, but for a lifetime. His entire life is regarded as a distinct fateful situation, the situation of mortality.[11] Therein lies the kinship of all people and at the same time their fellowship *(societas)*.

5. *The City of God* XIX, 17: "Because, of course, any community life must emphasize social relationships."

6. See Paul's Epistle to the Romans 5:12–21 for the correspondences between Christ and Adam; also, *On the Merits and Remission of Sins* I, 16–19.

7. *Homilies on the First Epistle of John* VIII, 8: "You ought to wish all men to be your equals."

8. *Literal Commentary on Genesis* VI, 9, 14.

9. *Sermon* 96, 6: "If you take the world for men, he who first sinned made the whole world evil."

10. *The City of God* XIV, 1: "I have already said in previous books that God had two purposes in deriving all people from one man. His first purpose was to give unity to the human race by the likeness of nature. His second purpose was to bind all humanity by the bond of peace, through blood relationship, into one harmonious whole. . . . The sin which they committed was so great that it impaired all human nature, in this sense, that human nature has been transmitted to posterity with a propensity to sin and the necessity to die." See also ibid., XII, 22: "God created one sole individual, not that he was meant to remain alone deprived of human companionship, but in order that the unity of society and the bond of harmony might mean more to man, since all people were to be united not only by the likeness of nature, but also by the affection of kinship."

11. *Confessions* X, 4, 6: "Such is the benefit of my confessions, not of what I have been, but of what I am, that I may confess this not only before you in secret exultation with trembling and in secret sorrow with hope, but also in the ears of believing sons of men, partakers of my joy and sharers in my mortality, my fellow citizens and pilgrims with me, those who go before me and those who follow me, and those who are my companions on my journey."

Though this equality is only implicit in the earthly city it permits us
to understand interdependence, which essentially defines social life in the
worldly community. This interdependence shows in the mutual give and
take in which people live together.[12] The attitude of individuals toward each
other is characterized here by belief *(credere)*, as distinguished from all real
or potential knowledge.[13] We comprehend all history, that is, all human
and temporal acts, [A:033352] by believing—which means by trusting, but
never by understanding *(intelligere)*. This belief in the other is the belief that
he will prove himself in our common future. Every earthly city depends
upon this proof. Yet this belief that arises from our mutual interdependence
precedes any possible proof.[14] The continued existence of humankind does
not rest on the proof. Rather, it rests on necessary belief, without which social life would become impossible.[15]

Equality had always been the prerequisite of worldly interdependence,
but it was never grasped thematically in establishing society on earth. The
situation of men is not explicitly equal as long as death is a mere fact of
nature rather than the indication of sinfulness, that is, as long as the individual does not know what equality really means. Until its relevance is known,
men's mutual interdependence cannot be replaced by the isolation in which
the individual searches for his being. The concealment of equality leads
Augustine to the question: "Tell me, I ask you, with what eyes do you see
your friend's will toward you? For no will can be seen with bodily eyes."[16]
Here the equivalent of mutual trust is an inability to see (note 14 above) as
elsewhere it is the inability to understand (note 12 above). Seeing is a possibility of knowledge and an evident one at that. However, knowing another's
will toward me is relevant only in mutual interdependence. In the equality
of all people before God, which love of neighbor makes thematic, this "will
toward myself" (which can be friendly or hostile) is a matter of the same
indifference as my concretely temporal [A:033353] encounter with the

12. *On Various Questions to Simplicianus* I, 16: "Since it is by mutual give and take that
human society is bound together."

13. *Eighty-Three Different Questions* 48: "There are three kinds of objects of belief. Some
are always believed and never understood, such as all history, which runs through temporal and
human acts. Other must be understood to be believed, such as all human reasonings. Thirdly,
there are those which are believed first and understood later, like divine matters."

14. *Faith in Things Unseen* 2, 3: "But surely, to test your friend you would not submit yourself to dangers if you did not believe. And since you thus submit yourself that you may prove
him, you believe before you prove."

15. Ibid., 2, 4–3, 4: "If this faith in human affairs is removed, who will not mark how great
will be their disorder and what dreadful confusion will follow? Therefore, when we do not
believe what we cannot see, concord will perish and human society itself will not stand firm."

16. Ibid., 1, 2.

other as friend or foe. It is precisely not the other person's worldly significance to which my every question about him is directed. It is his being before God. Yet in the being before God all people are equal, that is, equally
sinful.

Humanity's common descent is its common share in original sin. This
sinfulness, conferred with birth, necessarily attaches to everyone. There is
no escape from it. It is the same in all people. The equality of the situation
means that all are sinful. "The whole world was guilty from Adam."[17] This
equality is the predominant fact that wipes out all distinctions. Thus, even
though there may be several states and communities, there are always, in
fact, only the two cities—the good and the bad, the one based in Christ and
the one based in Adam.[18] In a similar sense, there are but two loves: love of
self (or the world) and the love of God.[19] Each individual already belongs to
Adam (that is, to the human race) by generation, not by imitation.[20] The
possibility of imitation, and thereby of freely choosing the grace of God (see
Part II, chapter 2), did not exist until Christ revealed this grace to all people
through his historic sojourn on earth. Though freedom of choice recalls the
individual from the world and severs his essential social ties with humankind, the equality of all people, once posited, cannot be canceled out. In this
process, equality receives a new meaning—love of neighbor. Yet the new
meaning denotes a change in the coexistence of people in their community,
from being inevitable and matter of course to being freely chosen and replete with obligations. The individual takes up these obligations on the
ground of the common trait, which is made explicit as a community-
in-sinfulness. This common situation makes each belong to everyone.

17. *Against Julian the Pelagian* VI, 5.
18. *The City of God* XIV, 1: "Now the reign of death has held mankind in such utter subjection that they would all be driven headlong into that second death, which has no end, as their
well-deserved punishment, if some were not rescued from it by the undeserved grace of God.
The result is that although there are many great peoples throughout the world, living under
different customs of religion and morality . . . it is still true that there have come into being
only two main divisions, as we may call them, in human society. And we are justified in following the lead of our Scriptures [see Eph. 2:19; Philip. 3:20] and calling them two cities."
19. Ibid., XIV, 28: "Thus the two cities were made by two kinds of love: the earthly city
was made by self-love reaching the point of contempt for God and the heavenly city by the love
of God carried as far as contempt for self."
20. *Against Julian* (incomplete work) II, 190: "The Apostle did not set imitation against
imitation, but regeneration against generation." See also II, 163: "Since all of us were in Adam
who did this (when he did it), and his offense was of such a manner and magnitude, all human
nature was corrupted by him which, by the way, sufficiently accounts for the misery of all humanity." And also *Marriage and Concupiscence* II, 45: "He used the phrase 'by one man'
[Rom. 5:12], from whom the generation of men, of course, had its beginning, in order to show
us that original sin had passed upon all human beings by generation."

[A:033354] The result is a sudden turn in the individual's attitude toward his environment and the new, crucial importance of equality, which extends even to the Christian isolated from the world. For a closer and more concrete understanding of this turn, we must examine the fellowship of the race established by Adam and the kind of social relations that are prescribed by the new law of Christ.

The community of all people among themselves goes back to Adam and constitutes the world;[21] it always precedes any city of God *(civitas Dei)*.[22] It is a pre-existing community into which the individual comes by birth. Therefore, by generation he becomes sinful as well. His being is sinful prior to any free choice. Human equality is not just an equality of those who happen to be living together. It goes back to the most distant historic past.[23] Just as the creature derives its true and God-given being from its origin in the most distant and unworldly past, so, too, historic man exists in this world and derives his being from the earliest past that is historically established— from the first man. This historic world, the *saeculum*, is the world in which all live together as a matter of course.

In the society founded on Adam man has made himself independent of the Creator. He depends on other persons and not on God. The human race as such originates in Adam and not in the Creator. It has come to be by generation and relates to its source only through all its generations. Based on kinship, the human community is thereby a society from and with the dead; in other words this community is historical. The world's independence from God rests on historicity, that is, on mankind's own origin, which possesses its own legitimacy. The world's [A:033355] sinfulness derives from its origin independent of God. Yet, this origin does not denote the direct extraction from the Being without which man, if he is at all, would not be. Rather, it is the origin of the whole race transmitted indirectly to the individual by generation. The first man, the source, hands down this indirectness by way of

21. In the following discussion we are deliberately ignoring Augustine's other theory of the two communities as going back to Cain and Abel. To consider this other theory would unnecessarily hamper the present interpretation. The good community, personified by Abel, is the harbinger of the city of God, which Christ will later found as a factually effective reality. What follows in our discussion must suffice for a philosophical interpretation. Augustine mainly discusses the Cain and Abel theory in *The City of God* XV, 1.

22. *The City of God* XV, 1: "Now the first man born of the two parents of the human race was Cain. He belonged to the earthly city. The next born was Abel and he was of the city of God." See also *Against Julian the Pelagian* VI, 4: "In Christ there was no sin, which is the reason every person is born first to the world, not to God."

23. *Against Julian* (incomplete work) II, 163: "Since all of us were in Adam who did this (when he did it) . . . it is clear that everyone born in the succession of his line belongs to him."

all men through the historically made world. Indirectness alone first establishes the equality of all people. For only in being handed down from one to
the other does the descent (and thus the share in original sin) exist for the
individual as his source. Indirectness through descent establishes the fateful kinship, and thus the interdependence of the whole human race on
which society rests. Therefore, this society is both a fact of nature and a
product of history. The fact that man is by nature a social being means at the
same time that, from the perspective of this distinctive human origin, he is
familiar with the world both by nature and by historical generation.[24] Man's
nature, qua nature, has its historical source in Adam. This twofold familiarity with the world is overcome in the heavenly city.

Thus we see that in Augustine's attempt to come to an original definition of man as a social being, the source of being itself is altogether different
from the one we presented and discussed in Part II. Augustine's question
about the being of man as a creature concerned the being of the individual,
and the very question itself was stated in complete isolation. The question
about the being of man among men [A:033356] concerns the being of the
human race as such. Each time the question about being points to the utmost limit of the past. However, while the individual feels that "all the way
back" he was "out of this world," as a member of human society he feels that
even all the way back he has been worldly. Man's origin is at the same time
both the beginning of the man-made world in Adam's original sin and the
origin of his separation from God. His descent is defined by generation and
not by creation. The world is no longer an utterly strange place into which
the individual has been created. Rather, by kinship in generation the world
has always been familiar and belongs to him. In this conception of the being
of man, we can understand the obligatory function of equality. "Thus there
is not one in the human race to whom love is not due, either as a return of
mutual affection or by virtue of his share in our common nature."[25] This
love is simply an expression of interdependence. Yet how is it possible for
their equality, based on the Christian sense of sin (that is, on the wrong "before" of Part II, chapter 2 of our analysis), to become obligatory for one
gripped by faith? The creature knows itself dependent on the source, the
epitome of being out of this world, that is, on the Creator. How can duties
be derived from a past that is to be totally eradicated?

24. *The City of God* XII, 28: "For there is nothing so social by nature, so anti-social by sin,
as man. And if anyone should ever need an argument against the evil of dissension . . . there is
nothing better than to recall that single father of all our human race whom God created as a
solitary individual."
25. *Letter* 130, 13.

What actually enables the person to relate to his source, as the creature to the Creator, is a historical fact: God's revelation in Christ. As a historical fact, this is revealed to human beings living together in a historical world. Just as faith, the being in God's [A:033357] presence *(coram Deo esse)*, recalls the individual from entanglements with the world, so, too, the message of salvation has come to all people into this world that they founded. Augustine writes, "He is your brother, alike you are bought; one is the price paid for you and you are both redeemed by the blood of Christ."[26] The "alike," that is, the share in being ransomed, points to the equal status in which Christ finds all people in the world.[27] This equality means participation in original sin. The world is truly redeemed from this participation, which is grounded in the common descent. However, redemption occurs without merit on the part of any individual; all are redeemed together, just as all were found together in the same situation. This equal situation first becomes manifest and transparent to people at the same time as redemption. The manifestation of equality in their new situation of having been redeemed is identical with the knowledge of their sinful past. Equality before God corresponds to actuality in sin and rests on the same sinful past, even in the midst of lives established in Christ.

The sinful past has established the earthly city and made the world the home of human interdependence. To be at home in the world is a matter of course. Being a stranger in the world, for the Christian, is only a possibility, for the matter of course is to be at home in the world.[28] Thus the sinful past is common to all, and nothing else could stabilize social life in a community.[29] Yet the past is not simply wiped out, as it had seemed. Rather, it is the absolute obligation because it is past sinfulness. It does not remain pure past, but is newly experienced and reinterpreted out of the new situation of man redeemed. Only in this reinterpretation can the pre-existing past continue independently, beside the newly [A:033358] experienced being. Thus, it is only from this pre-existence that the neighbor derives his specific relevance. The neighbor is the constant reminder of one's own sin, which does not cease to be sin because divine grace has made it a thing of the past. The neighbor is a living warning of pride, because he is never viewed as he hap-

26. *Homilies on the First Epistle of John* V, 12.

27. *The City of God* I, 9: "Both are scourged, not because both lead a bad life, but because both lead an earthly life; not indeed to the same extent, but yet both together."

28. Ibid., XV, 1: "The first to be born was a citizen of this world and only later came the one who was an alien in the earthly city. . . . This does not mean that everyone who is wicked is to become good, but that no one becomes good who was not once wicked."

29. Ibid, XV, 1: "Scripture tells us that Cain founded a city, while Abel, as though he were merely a pilgrim on earth, did not found one."

pens to be in the world. (see Part I, chapter 3, and Part II, chapter 3).[30] He appears either as one in whom God has already worked his grace and who is thus, for us, an occasion not only to love but to pay homage to grace; or he appears as one who is still entangled in sin, and so is nothing but what the Christian was and would still be but for the grace of God. In the second case, the neighbor is a sign of our own peril along with the reminder of our past.[31] Therefore, far from being voided by the message of salvation, equality is made explicit in a definite sense. The explicitness of equality is contained in the commandment of neighborly love. The reason one should love one's neighbor is that the neighbor is fundamentally one's equal and both share the same sinful past.[32] This is another way of saying that it takes the past to turn mere sameness of belief into the common faith *(communis fides)*.

Moreover, one should love one's neighbor not on account of his sin, which indeed was the source of equality, but on account of the grace that has revealed itself in him as well as in oneself *(tamquam te ipsum)*. By being made explicit, equality obtains a new meaning; it becomes an equality of grace. However, it is no longer the same equality. While the kinship of all people prior to Christ was acquired from Adam by generation, all are now made equal by [A:033359] the revealed grace of God that manifests everyone's equally sinful past. Thus, although it takes grace to make it visible, the equality itself rests on the past. It is only the fact of the past (which means "the world" in the broadest sense) that permits us to understand the binding equality of all people even in the presence of God.

However, there is another fact indicating that alienation from the world and its desires by means of faith does not simply cancel out the togetherness of men. This is the fact that the same sinful past remains a constitutive factor for the state of grace. The rights of the past are preserved in the continued existence of the world. It is against the world, not simply without it, that the message of salvation has come to all people: "For He would not have overcome the world if the world still could have overcome his members."[33] The

30. *Homilies on the First Epistle of John* VII, 8: "So then the Christian ought to be, that he glory not over other men. . . . I say then, man has past bounds; he is greedy for more than his due and wants to be above men, he that was made above the beasts; and this is pride."

31. *Commentary on Paul's Epistle to the Galatians* 56: "For nothing so moves one to pity as the thought of his own danger. . . . Peace and love are preserved, therefore, by reflecting in our hearts on our common danger." See also ibid., 57: "Love and say what you will. What might sound like a curse will in no way be a curse if you remember and feel yourself at the sword's point of the word of God."

32. *Christian Discipline* 3: "From your neighbor a rule has been found for you, because you yourself were found to be his *equal*."

33. *Tractates on John's Gospel* CIII, 3.

civitas terrena as such is abolished, but at the same time the believer is called upon to fight it. The past remains at work in the impossibility of complete isolation for the believer, who cannot act by himself *(separatus)*, only with others or against them. Even though the believer is estranged from the world, he continues to live in the world. Moreover, since Christ himself has come into the world, man's being with Christ depends on the world's transformation into the body of Christ, which expresses the believer's connection to Christ.[34] Salvation itself is made to depend on the conduct of the world, or rather, on its conquest. Thus the world is relevant, not because the Christian still lives in it, to a certain extent by mistake, but on the ground of his constant tie to the past and thereby to original kinship, which consists of an equal [A:033360] share in original sin and thus in death. Death is never conceived as a fact of nature, but as a fateful event coming from Adam as a punishment for sin.[35] Death shows that the past has not been eradicated by salvation. Mortality remains the common fate. However, as death does not prevail by the law of nature, it has a new meaning for the believer as well. As a comprehensible event it can be interpreted either way—it is good for the good and bad for the wicked.[36] Here the human world takes on the singular relevance of its own past. Its own past lives on in the world, and both the fight against the world and the concern with it are comprehensible only by this fact of belonging to the world.

The new life can only be won in fighting the old and through a constant struggle that will not end until death. As long as the person lives in the world, he is tied to it and its desires, whether yielding to them or combating them.[37] While the world exists, so does the past. And so Augustine writes, "Extend your love *[caritas]* over the whole earth if you will love Christ."[38] For the neighbor's relevance is not tied to Christianity. The binding power of the common faith in Christ is secondary. Faith in Christ redeems the past and only the common past can make the faith a common faith. This past alone is common to all. To the world the past is a matter of course, and only the

---

34. *Homilies on the First Epistle of John* X, 3: "And by loving he becomes himself a member, and comes through love to be in the frame of the body of Christ, so that there shall be one Christ loving himself."

35. *The City of God* XIII, 15: "Since God created for man an immortal nature, it is not by a law of nature that man is subject to bodily death, but as a just punishment for sin." See also *Sermon* 231, 2.

36. *The City of God* XIII, 2: "It can be said of the first death, the death of the body, that it is good for the holy and bad for the sinners."

37. *Sermon* 151, 7: "It does evil, since it excites evil desires. It does not accomplish evil, since it does not drag me into evil. And in this struggle lies the whole life of the holy."

38. *Homilies on the First Epistle of John* X, 8.

Christian experiences the past in this explicit way as sin. To bring one's neighbor to this explicitness of his own being, to "carry him off to God" *(rapere ad Deum)*, is the duty to his neighbor that the Christian assumes from his own past sin. "He is of the same substance as you are. . . . In all this he is as you were. Acknowledge him as your brother."[39] This is why a flight [A:033361] into solitude is sinful.[40] It robs the other of the opportunity to change.[41] Thus, is estrangement from the world, divine grace gives a new meaning to human togetherness—defense against the world. This defense is the foundation of the new city, the city of God. Estrangement itself gives rise to a new togetherness, that is, to a new being with and for each other that exists beside and against the old society.[42] This new social life, which is grounded in Christ, is defined by mutual love *(diligere invicem)*, which replaces mutual dependence. Faith dissolves the bonds that tied men to the world in the original sense of the earthly city, and so faith dissolves men's dependence on one another. Therefore, one individual's relationship to another also ceases to be a matter of course, as it was in interdependence. The fact that it is no longer a matter of course is expressed, on the one hand, by the commandment of love, and, on the other hand, by the specific indirectness of this love.

When I attain the explicitness of my own being by faith, the other person's being becomes explicit as well, in equality. Only then will the other become my brother ("brother" for neighbor and "brotherly love" are terms found throughout Augustine's writings). Out of this explicit tie of brotherliness grows *caritas*, which is at the same time a necessity.[43] It is a necessity because past sins prevent escape from the pre-existing world even in the isolation of faith. The community of Christ is understood as a body containing all individual members within itself.[44] Each suffers with the others.[45] Here

39. *Sermon* 56, 14.

40. *Confessions* X, 43, 70.

41. *Homilies on the First Epistle of John* VIII, 2: "Did he mean to say we should hide from people's eyes whatever good things we do, and fear to have them seen? If you fear observers, you will have no imitators; hence, you ought to be seen." See also VIII, 9: "For if you hide it from people's eyes, you also hide it from their imitation. In so doing you withdraw the praise from God."

42. *On Catechizing the Uninstructed* 19, 31: "Thus the two cities, one of the wicked, the other of the just, extending from the beginning of the human race to the end of time, are now intermingled in body."

43. *The City of God* XIX, 19: "However, once it is imposed [righteous engagement in activity], it should be undertaken because of the necessity of *caritas*." See also this entire chapter, which distinguishes the necessity of *caritas* from the voluntary practice of contemplation.

44. For these early Christian views of probable Stoic origin, see *Homilies on the First Epistle of John* X, 3 and 8; *Tractates on John's Gospel* CX, 5.

45. *Tractates on John's Gospel* LXV, 1: "And if one member suffers, all the members suffer with it."

lies the ultimate hyperbole of the idea that being is common to all. The individual is completely forgotten [A:033362] over this community. The individual has ceased to be anything but a member, and his entire being lies in the connection of all members in Christ.[46] Mutual love becomes self-love, since the being of one's own self is identified with the being of Christ, that is, with the being of the body in which it shares as a member.[47] Augustine rarely uses this hyperbole in which the ambiguity of the human being in the world, expressed by the intermingling of the two cities, is eliminated.[48] However, even if we disregard this hyperbole, the necessity of *caritas* is maintained against any tendency to isolate the believer altogether.[49] This necessity no longer concerns one man or another who as such, in his worldly significance for the lover, may be good or bad. This necessity of *caritas* is concerned, in the explicitness of man's own being, with the human being as a creature, that is, with the whole human race. Its sole determinant is what is common to all. This commonality alone is taken up in faith. What is common to all, as the common past of the human race, is sin. And it is only as sin that the past concerns the believer. However, the common past determines *caritas* at the same time. And in general, one's obligation toward another arises from this common past of sin, the concrete impulse of neighborly love arises from the thought of one's own peril. This thought is constantly awake from the past, from the descent from Adam, in this life which is seen as an enduring trial.[50] Augustine writes, "For nothing so moves one to pity as the

46. *Sermon* 24, 5: "So that there be no discord among the members of Christ, let his duties fill all those who are in his body: let the eye, in its high place, do that which pertains to the eye." See also *Tractates on John's Gospel* XVIII, 9; *Sermon* 267, 4: "Tasks differ; life is in common. Thus it is with God's church. . . . One is engaged in some things, another in others; individually they carry out their private concerns, but they live as equals." *Commentaries on the Psalms* 32, 21.

47. *Homilies on the First Epistle of John* X, 3: "For when the members love one another, the body loves itself."

48. *The City of God* XI, 1: "The respective cities, earthly and heavenly, are at present, as I have said, inextricably intermingled one with the other."

49. Ibid., XIX, 19. ["As for the three kinds of life, the life of leisure, the life of action, and the combination of the two, anyone, to be sure, might spend his life in any of these ways without detriment to his faith, and might thus attain to the everlasting rewards. What does matter is the answers to those questions: What does a man possess as a result of his love of truth? And what does he pay out in response to the obligations of Christian love? For no one ought to be so leisured as to take no thought in that leisure for the interest of his neighbor, nor so active as to feel no need for the contemplation of God. The attraction of a life of leisure ought not be the prospect of lazy inactivity, but the chance for the investigation and discovery of truth, on the understanding that each person makes some progress in this, and does not grudgingly withhold his discoveries from another."]

50. *Confessions* X, 32, 48: "In this life, the whole of which is called a trial, no one should be sure whether one who can pass from worse to better might not also pass from better to worse. One hope, one trust, one firm promise—your mercy."

thought of his own danger. . . . Peace and love are preserved, therefore, by reflecting in our hearts on the common danger."[51] Thus love rests on the common knowledge of a common danger. For Christians "to be in the world" simultaneously expresses their link with their [A:033363] own past and also means "to be in danger." Even the unified community of the faithful is an expression of this danger. And thus the companionship of fate, the ground on which all live together in the earthly city, is also made newly explicit. This new companionship of fate, rooted in the common danger, is again occasioned by death. Only in Christianity is death viewed as "the wages of sin" (Saint Paul) rather than an event of nature and as the peril common to all. However, it is not the death that puts an end to life on earth, but the eternal death which is the punishment of sin. This eternal death is what Augustine calls the "second death."[52] The fact that there is also the first death, the end of life, expresses the continued existence of our old sinful past, for whose sake alone it existed. By means of Christ's redemption this death can be overcome. It can be our bridge to eternity. However,by the same token, it can turn into eternal death. The same death is good for the good and bad for the wicked. Thus our danger is to relapse into our sinful past—a relapse that amounts to eternal death. Human mortality, which formerly had been a necessity, here becomes a menace. Thus the necessary coexistence in the *civitas terrena* becomes a free inclining *(inclinare)* toward the other who is equally menaced. The mere reflection on the danger has detached the individual from the old companionship of fate. What was once necessary by generation has now become a danger involving a decision, one way or the other, about him—the individual. The pure fact of belonging to the human race is no longer decisive. Death can now mean salvation for the good. Before Christ this very same death had been the inevitable curse and steady [A:033364] misery of all life.

Thus the fact that people belong to each other is no longer determined by generation but by imitation.[53] Through imitation, everyone may initiate the impulse of saving one's neighbor. Imitation rests on mutual love *(diligere invicem)*. But this is never love in our sense which has become impossible in detachment from the world. Mutual love lacks the element of choice; we cannot choose our "beloved." Since the neighbor is in our same situation, he

51. *Commentary on Paul's Epistle to the Galatians* 56.

52. *The City of God* XIII, 2; XIV, 1: "Now the reign of death has held mankind in such utter subjection that they would all be driven headlong into that second death, which has no ending, as their well-deserved punishment, if some were not rescued from it by the undeserved grace of God."

53. *Homilies on the First Epistle of John* VIII, 2 and 9.

is already there before any choices can be made. Love extends to all people in the *civitas Dei*, just as interdependence extended equally to all in the *civitas terrena*. This love makes human relations definite and explicit. Coming from the thought of one's own danger that is experienced in conscience in God's presence, that is, in absolute isolation, this love *(diligere invicem)* also thrusts the other person into absolute isolation. Thus, love does not turn to humankind but to the individual, albeit every individual. In the community of the new society the human race dissolves into its many individuals. Hence, the human race as such is not in danger, but every individual is.

Yet the believer relates in love to this individual, who has been picked out and separated from the human race, only insofar as divine grace can be at work in him. I never love my neighbor for his own sake, only for the sake of divine grace. This indirectness, which is unique to love of neighbor, puts an even more radical stop to the self-evident living together in the earthly city. This indirectness turns my relation to my neighbor into a mere passage for the direct relation to God himself. The other as such cannot save me. He can only save me because the grace of God is at work in him. We are commanded to love our neighbor, to practice mutual love, only because [A:033365] in so doing we love Christ. This indirectness breaks up social relations by turning them into provisional ones. In the earthly city implicit mutual dependence was also provisional since death put an end to it. Yet the provisional nature of these relations was final just the same. There was no eternity to make finality relative. In the city of God these relations are made radically relative by eternity. However necessary *caritas* may be, it is only necessary in this world *(in hoc saeculo)* upon which eternity follows as the last and final salvation. When Augustine frequently quotes Paul's words that love never fails, he means solely the love of God, or Christ, for which all human neighborly love can only provide the impetus and which we are commanded to have only to provide this impetus. The indirectness of the mutual relations of believers is just what allows each to grasp the other's whole being which lies in God's presence. In contrast, any worldly community envisions the being of the human race, but not that of the individual. The individual as such can only be grasped in the isolation in which the believer stands before God.

In raising the question about the neighbor's relevance, we find that the question about humanity's origin is doubly posed and doubly answered by Augustine. First, Augustine inquires about the being of man as an individual. In this inquiry the question about being is identical with the question of whence this being comes—what is its source. The answer is that God is the source of each and every individual. It is at this point that the individual

[A:033366] is discovered. The individual then becomes decisive for neighborly love as the focus of concern for the other's salvation. However, the other person, in his capacity as our neighbor who does not merely happen to be in the same world with us and to believe in the same God, does not come into this field of vision at all. Second, when Augustine asks about the origin of the human race, the answer, as distinct from the self-sameness of God, is that the origin lies in the common ancestor of us all. Analogous to this, man is seen in the first sense as isolated and coming by contingency into the world viewed as a desert. In this second sense, man is seen as belonging to mankind and to this world by generation.

These diverse ways of putting the question suggest that the contradiction in this theory of the twofold origin is merely apparent. Man is the other, whether he understands himself as an isolated individual or as conditioned and essentially constituted by the fact of belonging to the human race. The fact that the two questions are connected is made even clearer by the insight into their specific conjunction, which is derived from the doctrine of neighborly love. It is a twofold conjunction. Although we can meet the other only because both of us belong to the human race, it is only in the individual's isolation in God's presence that he becomes our neighbor. By virtue of this isolation in God's presence, the other is lifted out of the self-evident dependence in which all people live with each other, and then our connection with him is subject to the explicit obligation of kinship. Second, however, the possibility of isolation enters as a fact into the history of the human race and thus comes to be historical itself. According to Augustine's philosophy of history, before salvation through Christ, there was only the human [A:033367] race determined by Adam. Moreover, it is the very possibility of isolation that enables us to detach ourselves from human history and from its irrevocable enchainment by generation.

It is only through this conjunction derived from the two fold origin that we can understand the neighbor's relevance. The other person is our neighbor as a member of the human race and in this capacity, too, is singled out with the explicitness that results from the realized isolation of the individual. The mere common existence of believers grounded in the selfsame God becomes the common faith and the community of believers. With this, the being of man is understood as derived from a twofold source.

REDISCOVERING HANNAH ARENDT

Through remembrance man discovers this twofold "before" of
human existence. . . . This is the reason why the return to
one's origin (*redire ad creatorem*) can at the same time be
understood as an anticipating reference to one's end.

(B:033191)

It is memory and not expectation (for instance, the expectation
of death as in Heidegger's approach) that gives unity and
wholeness to human existence.

(B:033192)

1 / Introduction: "New Beginnings"

The "New" Dissertation

In this work, we return to the Augustinian root of Arendt's critique of modernity to present the first English translation and interpretation of her 1929 Heidelberg dissertation, *Der Liebesbegriff bei Augustin*. This edition of the dissertation is particularly significant as a marker in Arendt's intellectual odyssey because it not only reproduces the translation by E. B. Ashton, which she commissioned, but also includes her subsequent revisions made in anticipation of a 1964–65 publication date.

The Library of Congress revised text is therefore triply significant. First, the dissertation is a crucial missing link in Arendt scholarship that has never before been available to English-reading audiences. Second, by incorporating Arendt's revisions, this new version captures the simultaneity of Arendt's return to Augustine and her "new beginnings" in political theory in America. Third, the dissertation is the only complete book manuscript completed by Hannah Arendt and intended for publication that has remained, until now, unpublished.

Augustine was Arendt's "old friend."[1] She kept the battered text of the dissertation with her in flight from Germany in 1933, and through France to America in 1941. This study presents the dissertation as a bridge from 1929 to Arendt's American classics—*Origins of Totalitarianism* (1951, 1958, 1963); *The Human Condition* (1958); *On Revolution* (1963, 1965); *Eichmann in Jerusalem* (1963, 1965); *Between Past and Future: Eight Exercises in Political Thought* (1968; with expanded essays first published 1954–68); *Men in Dark Times* (1968; essays originally written 1955–68)—which were in progress or being revised while her rediscovery of Augustine was underway. Arendt's characteristic mode of discourse makes its first appearance in the original

---

1. Arendt's depiction of Augustine comes from the remembrance of Jerry Kohn, New School for Social Research.

translation and is reinforced in her revisions. Key terms include *caritas*, memory, natality, foundations, free will, narrative, society, and the world.

Across this bridge and back again, from early Christian philosophy to the twentieth-century *Existenz*, and from Arendt's Heidelberg perspectives to her more overtly political concerns passes her constant inquiry into "the relevance of the neighbor." *Love and Saint Augustine* provides a particularly provocative glimpse into the implied, but rarely articulated, context for Arendt's phenomenology—the social source and moral ground for action in the public realm.

How many Hannah Arendts are there? Is she the German proponent of the *Existenz* who in attacking the "tradition" became its disseminator? The immigrant American champion of political revolutions and the "virtuosity" of public action? The Jewish phenomenologist of statelessness and world-lessness who loved the world? The antifeminist theorist who coined the term "natality"? The Heideggerian "mole" sent to undermine American liberalism, academic political theory, and moral action who wrote her dissertation on the founding of moral communities? The dissertation demonstrates that there is only one Arendt, but one whose nuanced *Existenz* supports a number of diverse readings. All of these "Arendts" can be enriched by a return to her original inquiry into the paradox of a world that humans have "constituted" but that destroys their capacity for authentic community and individual moral judgment.

This interpretative commentary is intended to stimulate new conversations about Arendt's relationship to the "tradition" of philosophy and to theorizing about political experience, not to terminate existing ones. Whether and to what extent she may have been touched religiously by Christianity or Judaism, the religion of her birth, is not at issue here. Others have already plowed these furrows (see, for example, Canovan 1992, 9, 106–7, 180–81; Isaac 1992, 76–78; Barnouw 1988, 30–134). Rather, since Arendt's own fences between her private life and public persona were notoriously rigid, this study approaches the dissertation as she approached Augustine—as a philosophic exercise in "thinking what we are doing" instead of as a study in religiosity.

The foundation of Arendt's interest in Christian theology was laid during her years of independent study at the University of Berlin, where she passed examinations for the *Arbitur* in 1924. There she studied Greek and Latin and also took classes from Romano Guardini, a prominent purveyor of Christian existentialism. Guardini led her to the works of Kierkegaard and to a decision to major in theology when she entered university. She had already read Kant's *Critique of Pure Reason* and *Religion within the Limits of Reason Alone* at the age of sixteen and by 1922 had also consumed Karl Jaspers's *Psychology of World Views* (Young-Bruehl 1982, 33–36).

But for Arendt it was Heidegger's influence, later reinforced by that of Jaspers that catalyzed her lifelong fascination with Augustine. In a retrospective on Heidegger, "Martin Heidegger at Eighty," Arendt discloses her own enchantment with both the aura and the reality of Heidegger's presence in German intellectual life (Arendt 1978a). She dates Heidegger's "fame" to his first lectures in Freiburg in 1919. His reputation spread in a "strange" way, not as a result of publications but solely because of his impact as a teacher, captured in widely circulated lecture notes. Arendt recalls German students' receptivity to the "rebellious element" in Heidegger's teachings, and in those of Jaspers as well. She describes, with distant hindsight, a rebellion against the "schools," "circles," "world views," and their "partisans" dominating German university life in the 1920s. Philosophy was not "rigorous science," despite all the "academic *talk* about philosophy," because it failed to respond to Heidegger's challenge to distinguish "between an object of scholarship and a matter of thought." Within the discipline both the new "schools"—neo-Kantians, neo-Hegelians, Neoplatonists—and the old specialties—epistemology, aesthetics, ethics, logic—seemed to have "drowned in an ocean of boredom."

Into the inertia of ennui and irrelevance came Husserl, Jaspers, and Heidegger. With Heidegger's spreading fame it became clear to Arendt that he alone was the "hidden king [who] reigned in the realm of thinking." Indeed, for her the "rumor" of Heidegger's rebellion came at precisely the right moment. Those drowning in boredom were also seized by an anxiety about "the breakdown of tradition and the 'dark times' which had set in." Heidegger seemed to promise a way out. His secret insight was that because "the thread of the tradition was broken" it was possible to "discover . . . the past anew" (ibid., 295). Arendt's rediscovery of Augustine was part of this journey of antitraditional thought. Her path, however, led beyond "the things themselves" to the question of the relationship between thought and social life, and "the relevance of the neighbor."

Arendt eventually attended Heidegger's lectures, which became the published text of *Sein und Zeit*. She would also study with Jaspers, who turned her attention to the "boundary conditions" of the *Existenz*. Setting out on her own, however, Arendt transformed the "Being" of her mentors' lectures on Greek philosophy into a "Creator," using Augustine as her guide. In a similar move, by the 1960s the "space" between past and future, which in the dissertation she had defined as memory or the *nunc stans*, appears again in a variety of negative and positive guises: the positioning of the

Kafkaesque thinker, the public space "in between" citizens, and the "empty space" in Western traditions resulting from the "catastrophe" of Europe from 1914 to the end of World War II.

As early as 1946, in one of her first pieces published in a non-Jewish journal, Arendt would borrow language and concepts directly from her dissertation to review Hermann Broch's *Death of Virgil*. The title of the review, "No Longer and Not Yet," is one of her many metaphors for the "space" borrowed from the dissertation:

> The chain is broken and an empty space, a kind of historical no man's land, comes to the surface which can only be described in terms of the "no longer and the not yet." In Europe such an absolute interruption occurred during and after the first World War. (Arendt 1946a, 300)

In the same year, Arendt transferred the themes of her dissertation to another article for a prestigious New York journal, *Partisan Review*. The occasion was the answer to her own Augustine-like *quaestio*, "What Is Existenz Philosophy?" It afforded Arendt the opportunity both to declare her independence from Heidegger and to express her admiration for Jaspers on the question of the location and potential for human freedom.

> *Existenz* is never essentially isolated. . . . One's fellow men are not (as in Heidegger) an element which, though structurally necessary, nevertheless destroy *Existenz*; but, on the contrary, *Existenz* can develop only in the togetherness of men in the common given world . . . a new concept of humanity as the condition for man's *Existenz*. In any case, men move together within this "surrounding" Being; and they hunt neither the phantom of the Self nor do they live in the arrogant illusion that they can be Being generally. (Arendt 1946b, 55–56)

This study does not argue that the whole of Arendt's thinking can be reduced to footnotes on Augustine's work or that her subsequent flight from Germany and adoption of a new political homeland had no influence on the development of her *Existenz*. Ideas about the public world do not emerge in a vacuum—either a vacuum of political experience or of prior reflection on the "traditions" of academic discourse. It does maintain, however, that without the historical and conceptual context of the dissertation, Arendt's thought cannot be completely or authentically appropriated. The dissertation is important not simply as a historical artifact from her prepolitical

German past but especially as a concurrent, if not directly explanatory, aspect of her political thought in America.

The evidence for Arendt's intention to publish the dissertation is clear. Documents in the Library of Congress track the progress of the translation, her contract with Crowell-Collier, and her requests for timely payment of royalties (Mss. 33228–022234). Another marker of intent is contained in her 13 January 1964 letter to George McKenna. Asked about the availability of the dissertation, she responds, "An English translation of my doctoral dissertation is now available; it will soon come out either this year or in 1965. I hadn't yet the time to go over it, but I think it is very good" (Arendt 1964). Arendt did, in fact, find the time to begin revising the Ashton translation, but she appears to have left no written trail among her papers in the Library of Congress indicating her strategic plan for the manuscript. Correspondence between Arendt and Mary McCarthy contains a brief, tantalizing reference to the dissertation project. In a 20 October 1965 letter sent from Ithaca, New York, Arendt recounts her recent trips to Italy, Switzerland, and Holland, and meetings with friends and family at each stop (Arendt and McCarthy 1995, 189–91). However, her concern about the failing health of her thesis supervisor and friend Karl Jaspers, whom she visited in Basel, is the dominant leitmotif of the latter. On a positive note, she reports meeting with one of Jaspers's students, who she is sure will complete an "entirely original" thesis on Kant's political philosophy.

It is in the midst of her discussion of the European trip that Arendt references her plans to go ahead with the dissertation project. Even though she is commuting from New York City to Ithaca to teach at Cornell, and as she says, has very little "time for myself," she has become immersed in Augustine once again. Arendt's comments are typical of her prose style, combining a sardonic, detached authorial vantage point with a hint of passionate intellectual engagement.

> I got myself into something absurd—Macmillan asked me years ago for my dissertation on Augustine. I needed the money (not really, but could use it) and said yes. The translation arrived two years ago and now I ran out of excuses and have to go over it. It is kind of a traumatic experience. I am re-writing the whole darned business, tying not to do anything new, but only to explain in English (and not in Latin) what I thought when I was twenty. It is probably not worth it and I should simply return the money—but now I am strangely fascinated in this rencontre. I had not read the thing for nearly twenty years. (Ibid., 190)

Arendt ends the letter with a sad footnote to say that Paul Tillich, her fellow émigré to the United States, has died. "All I can feel is the fear, the certainty that others will die too. All the obituaries mention Jaspers and Heidegger—as though to rub it in." Given both her fear that mentors and friends from her German years would soon be gone and her dismay at the extraordinarily negative worldwide response to her 1963 Eichmann report-age, Arendt may have been particularly drawn to her early work on Au-gustine's concept of *caritas*. Augustine's understanding of evil as habituated *cupiditas* may thus have passed over the bridge of her 1929 dissertation to her own notorious analysis of Eichmann's evil as "banal." Ironically, it may have been the Eichmann affair itself that both reinforced her *rencontre* and denied her the time and attention to carry it through to publication.

There is no record of McCarthy's thoughts on the dissertation, at least in the edited correspondence. Her next letter to Arendt, dated 8 September 1966, notes an earlier visit with Arendt in Basel. Her letter of 11 October discusses the Eichmann controversy. It had been referenced in most of their letters from September 1963 onward. While McCarthy's acerbic critic's eye had already been focused on *Origins of Totalitarianism* (26 April 1951) and *On Revolution* (11 January 1962), she is silent on the dissertation text. If she had seen it, one suspects, her reactions would have been recorded. Their mutual admiration and respect was founded on a division of labor. McCarthy eagerly acknowledged Arendt's philosophic prowess while Arendt deferred to McCarthy's dexterity in English language and letters. McCarthy even felt free to criticize Arendt's Latin and French translations from time to time. "Is your translation of Livy right? . . . As for your translation of 'les malheureux sont la puissance de la terre', words fail me, but I think you could do better" (11 January 1962; ibid., 122).

The considerable volume of correspondence in the Library of Con-gress relating to the Eichmann controversy, much of it personally offensive and threatening, suggests that Arendt was almost wholly absorbed in its repercussions. Case files on the Arendt Papers show that the Eichmann documents were her first gift to the Library. Between December 1964 and December 1965 Arendt shipped eighty-nine folders on the Eichmann affair, including Israeli trial documents and evidence, her own trial notes, research notes, correspondence, newspaper clippings, and five separate versions of *Eichmann in Jerusalem*.

It may be the case that her renewed encounter with Augustine caused her to transfer the *caritas-cupiditas* model to the Eichmann study in order to enrich her examination of the paradox of evil which is not "radical" but pedestrian, bourgeois, and seemingly rooted in everdayness. Augustine's paradigm of immobilized will entrapped in habituated worldliness could perhaps be applied to Eichmann, the routinely civilized bureaucrat incapable of the critical distance necessary for moral judgment. By the late 1920's, Arendt no longer regarded *caritas* as a simple "resoluteness" or "letting be," as in Heidegger and Kierkegaard, but an an active engagement with the "neighbor" made possible by prior self-reflection. The passport on this journey was provided by Augustine's methodological imperative, *quaestio mihi factus sum* " ("I have become a question to myself ").

If a pattern can be discerned in Arendt's editorial activities, it is that segments of the dissertation pertaining to the "tradition" were more heavily reworked than those laying out her basic dichotomy between desire/anxiety and Creator/memory as the cause of the tension inherent in Augustine's understanding of *caritas*. Part III ("Social Life"), for example, may have required little alteration because it is not as dependent upon textual explication and demonstration of Augustine's debt to, or divergence from, Plotinus as the other parts of the dissertation. While Arendt's later research and teaching experience would enrich her revisions of the first two parts, the last part completes her case for understanding Augustine's *civitas terrena* and *civitas Dei* as archetypes for the givenness of the world, on the one hand, and as the "new beginnings" of moral communities, on the other. In revising, Arendt characteristically reconstructed her "traditional" subject around a *quaestio* about the believer's relationship to the human community. In her rendering of Augustine:

> The possibility of imitation, and thereby of freely choosing the grace of God . . . , did not exist until Christ revealed this grace to all people through his historic sojourn on earth. Though freedom of choice recalls the individual from the world and servers his essential social ties with humankind, the equality of all people, once posited, cannot be canceled out. In this process, equality receives a new meaning—love of neighbor. Yet the new meaning denotes a change in the coexistence of people in their community, from being inevitable and matter of course to being freely chosen and replete with obligations. (A:033353)

In Parts I and II, Arendt critiqued Neoplatonic and Greek traditions through the prism of Augustine's "original" definition of Christian *caritas*. By the end of the dissertation in Part III, Arendt clearly shows her preference for Augustine's "Creator" God over the Neoplatonic, and Heideggerian, God of death and desire. The Creator-creature connection roots *caritas* in a search for "the twofold before" of Being, but it also mandates a "return" to the world. Augustine's *caritas* is the basis for founding new communities on common moral judgment as well as the existential, determining "fact" of shared history. In other words, the culminating section of Arendt's 1929 dissertation is the first appearance, in a prepolitical conceptual context, of a major theme in her later political writings. She would keep this argument unmodified in the early 1960s revisions. At the same time, in her political theory texts of the same period, she would insist that it is precisely this common ground of "plurality" in the human social experience and "natality" in public life that have been lost to the tradition of Western philosophy—but not to its "unsystematic" new beginners, such as Augustine and herself.

Arendt makes her intentions clear in the introduction to the dissertation (Copy A), which also remains unaltered. She is interested in Augustine's struggle with the contradictions between the "tradition" of philosophy he inherited and the Pauline Christian worldview. The question that intrigues her in 1929 and continues to dominate her thought when it turns explicitly political is the "relevance of the neighbor" to a solipsistic phenomenology of self-reflection such as Christianity. Contradictions, mostly unacknowledged, seem to her to be the essence of Augustine's project and will be the focus of her reading of him. It is her own "single question" about *caritas* as neighborly love that serves as a "connecting link" amidst the "disjointedness of Augustine's own work" and "mak[es] explicit what Augustine himself has merely implied." The linkage, in other words, is Arendt's and not Augustine's.

> The parallel trains of thought to be shown here defy systematic conjunction. They cannot even be joined in antithetical form, unless we wish to impose on Augustine a systematic and logical exactitude he never had. The several parts of this essay are linked by the question concerning the other human being's relevance. And for Augustine this relevance was simply a matter of course (A:033242).

In fact, it is precisely the conflict within Augustine's Christianized Greco-Roman philosophy that "makes for its particular abundance and fascination."

Arendt's interest in the saint, however, is determinedly nontheological. Following a pattern she repeats in her encounters with Nietzsche, Kierkegaard, Kant, and Marx, Arendt abstracts and transfers only those aspects of Augustine's thought that are useful in formulating her own and leaves the rest offstage. Augustine as bishop and scourge to heretics does not interest her, but Augustine as author of the *Confessions, The City of God,* and commentaries on the letters of John and Paul, Genesis, and the Psalms does compel her attention.

Arendt speaks more directly about her interpretative paradigm in a brief essay on Augustine and Protestantism published in the 4 December 1930 issue of the *Frankfurter Zeitung*. The "breadth and richness of the Christian Augustine," she writes, can be grasped only "if we take into account the ambiguity of his existence as both a Roman and a Christian." Augustine is a "forbear" in that he assisted in the birth of two empires, the Roman Empire reborn in the Catholic Church and the "other, Christian empire that Augustine . . . opened up for centuries to come: the empire of the inner life" (Arendt 1994, 23). In what must have been a surprise to her readers, Arendt valorizes a "heretic" reading of Augustine as well as an "orthodox" one, arguing against the efforts of official Catholic dogma to "exclusively confiscat[e] him." Citing Luther as her proof, Arendt claims that Augustine "carried the same weight" for "the heretic and the orthodox," "the reformers and counter-reformers."

This duality of audience has its parallel in a duality of foundational roles, though Arendt does not make the connection explicit. Like heretic and orthodox readings, confessional and universalistic modes of discourse exist side by side.

> He [Augustine] never stopped trying to understand and interpret the world in philosophical-cosmological terms, and he introduced into the incipient Catholic Church all those elements—the hierarchical order, the rhetorical eloquence and the claim to universality—in whose light we can still today regard the Church as the heir of the Roman Empire. In his *De Civitate Dei*, Augustine gave legitimacy to this legacy by providing the Church with its own history as a secular institution. (Ibid.)

Augustine's pietistic, confessional stream of discourse also broke with the tradition of Western thought by reconfiguring the idea of the soul, not only as rational "essence" but also as "the mysterious and unknown realms of [the] inner world that were no less hidden . . . than the distant realms of the outer world" (ibid.).

In one sense, Arendt's overview of Augustine's significance in her *Frankfurter Zeitung* article reinforces the focus on "hetereogenous" readings in the dissertation. There the pull between a death-based *caritas* and *caritas* focused on natality and memory is the axis of her interpretation. In another sense, however, the irony of her selectivity is striking. Founding

new communities in renewed love of neighbor is the central problematic of
the 1929 dissertation. Arendt wants to show how Augustine can reconcile
the confessional discourse of the individual's journey to the Creator with
obligation to the neighbor in human community. Yet the dissertation is silent on Augustine's role in legitimating the universality of the Catholic
Church. Augustine's public role in defending and extending the parameters
of the Christian community, whether through rhetoric or administrative action, is not the concern of her "philosophical inquiry." By 1930, however,
Arendt would shift ground to claim that Augustine's fusion of late Roman
and Christian philosophic thought was responsible for the emergence of a
public, imperial *metalité* in Western Europe.

The question of the link between thought and action, the vantage point
of the philosophic observer and the grounds for judgment in the public
world, became Arendt's own problematic in her later life and work. Implicit in her handling of Augustine's conflicted thought in 1929 was her own
response to the "break" in the tradition first demonstrated by Heidegger.
Heresy and orthodoxy could coexist in the "space" disclosed by the impotence of institutions and belief systems. From Arendt's perspective, the
radical spirit inherent in Augustine's challenge to inherited Greco-Roman
philosophic traditions was even more important to future public actors on
the cusp of history than his "dogmatic" insistence on order and authority
in the public world. Augustine speaks across centuries to Luther, and also to
the emerging movement of German phenomenology in the void created
by the crises of modernity.

In the introduction to the dissertation, Arendt elaborates on her principles of selectivity. Augustine is not the standard "religious author."

> Augustine's dogmatic subservience to scriptural and ecclesiastical
> authority will be largely alien to our analyses, which are, on prin-
> ciple, in keeping with their essence and significance, not
> dogmatically bound. Such intentional detachment . . . may doom
> the interpretation of a religious author but is relatively easy to jus-
> tify in Augustine's case. . . . None of the philosophical ideas . . .
> that Augustine absorbed in various periods of his life . . . were
> ever radically excised from his thinking. The radical choice be-
> tween philosophical self-reflection and the obedience of religious
> faith . . . remained alien to Augustine. (A:033243–47).

Beginning as she meant to continue, Arendt immediately abandons
Heidegger's death-driven phenomenology with Augustine as her guide. In
one of the few direct criticisms of her mentor in her published works,

Arendt uses Augustine as a weapon against her professor who was raised in a Catholic family, educated in Catholic schools, and gave a course on Augustine at Husserl's request (Krell 1956, 20–21; Caputo 1993, 272–73). Juxtaposing the saint and Heidegger, Arendt assets that "it is memory and not the expectation (for instance, the expectation of death as in Heidegger's approach) gives unity and wholeness to human existence" (B:033192).

Arendt was fond of recounting her life amid other lives as a remembered story created in its telling and imparting a sense of wholeness and continuity to the contingency of experience. *Love and Saint Augustine* is the beginning of Arendt's own story and by incorporating her later revisions, text and story merge. In Arendt's story *Dasein* becomes Augustine's pilgrim soul, whose journey of self-discovery first "takes man out of the world, that is, out of a certain community with men, the *civitas terrena*" (A:033350). The importance of the "neighbor" is a "fact" of history and inheritance in the world of the *civitas terrena*, but is also freely willed in the pilgrim's return to the world and the social life of those made equal by their common origin in the Creator God.

In the dissertation, the term *societas* retains its Latin implications. It is not the "social realm" of modernity, which Arendt later so thoroughly rejected. The *societas, gemeinschaft,* or *civitas,* in Arendt's particular Augustinian renderings, is not the locus of capitalist transactions, parvenu culture, or the regularity state, nor is it a primordial organic community derived from German romanticism. Later, in *The Human Condition,* Arendt would elaborate on the linguistic origins of *societas.* Both there and in her dissertation, the given world provides the challenge to which individuals respond either in the religious mode of withdrawal and reentry for the evangelistic purpose of moral suasion or in the secular mode of constituting public spaces "in-between." Neither form of society/ community is "worldly" in the negative sense of being driven by materialism and fear of death. But both are determinedly engaged in a prepolitical realm (Arendt 1958a, 34–35, 53–56).

The Dissertation and the Arendt Canon

Ironically, Arendt's political thought has been accorded canonical status in the very "tradition" she seemed bent on demolishing. An academic cottage industry in Arendt studies flourishes in departments of political science in America, Western Europe, the Eastern European successor states, and in Japan. At the same time, however, her ambiguous silences on the scope and nature of the existential context of public life are widely interpreted by admirers and detractors alike as evidence of a contentless *Existenz* lending itself to either conservative or radical left infusions of political agenda (see Kateb 1983).

A rather ascerbic, eminent acquaintance, Isaiah Berlin, reacts with scorn to Arendt's observation that in today's world Vico would have studied technology in the same way that he had earlier looked to action as the primary agent in history. To Berlin she will always be the "egregious Hannah Arendt," whose ideas he does "not greatly respect" though "many distinguished persons used to admire her work." She "produces no arguments, no evidence of serious philosophical or historical thought." Instead her work is "a stream of metaphysical free association," which moves "from one sentence to another, without logical connection, without either rational or imaginative links between them" (Berlin and Jahanbegloo 1991, 82; see also 81–85). It is ironic that Berlin accuses Arendt of the same trait of unsystematized thinking for which she praised Augustine, and which marked him in her mind as a philosopher rather than a theologian.

Berlin's response, based as much on quarrels over Zionism as on issues of philosophic merit, is more *ad feminem* than a reasoned assessment. The academic cottage industry, however, has its own problems of orthodoxy. This study is committed to advancing Arendt scholarship beyond its present circumscribed circle of admissible texts and arguments. The question to be addressed is whether Arendt's use of Augustine, whom she called "the only philosopher the Romans ever had," can be accommodated within the existing framework of Arendt scholarship. The fact that the dissertation is pre-Holocaust in origin but already contains the seeds of many of her later ideas and modes of discourse is disconcerting to those adhering to the orthodox reading in which Arendt is primarily either a theorist of totalitarianism writing in response to the Holocaust, a relentless classicist bent on reinventing a postmodern Greek *polis*, or a phenomenologist of the public realm who ignores class, race, and gender.

Comparable "canon" problems are well documented in the study of other major theorists from Plato to Walter Benjamin, but have yet to be clearly confronted in the literature on Arendt. Taking Augustine as seriously as Arendt did has not before now been an acceptable approach among mainstream Arendt scholars. Most demarcate an "early" Arendt, who was influenced by Augustine only through the medium of her mentors' German phenomenology, from a "mature" Arendt, who set aside the idylls of her youth for a public philosophy of word and deed influenced more by Aristotle, Kant, and Tocqueville than by the Christian *Existenz*. The gap, as measured by the canon, is historical and cultural, with not a little American academic hubris thrown in for good measure.

Arendt needs to be rescued from her earlier dalliances. Otherwise, in guilt by association, she will be tarred with the brush of Heidegger's German "political existentialism," and her valiant effort to rescue the public world from oblivion will itself be doomed. Critics such as Martin Jay, Luc Ferry, and Thomas Pangle have, from widely varying perspectives, all pointed to the Nietzschean/Jacobin temptation they discern lurking behind Arendt's seemingly noble Greco-Roman political theory of action and natality (Jay 1985, 237–56; Ferry 1992, 5–30, 59–62, 76–68, 83–93; Pangle 1988, 48–52). Pangle even suggests that Heideggerian phenomenology, which he claims Arendt insinuated into American departments of political science, is dangerously un-American.

For those interested in maintaining the orthodox Arendt cannon, defending Arendt's virtue is the primary agenda. For them a clear break between Arendt's pre- and post-Holocaust writings is fundamental and necessary. Central to this plan, however, is the marginalization of Arendt's dissertation and a renewed interest in her study of Rahel Varnhagen. Arendt's 1930 Varnhagen book, another of her "rencontre" projects, appeared in English in 1958. Because it concerns the pariah-parvenu theme in a German Jewish-gentile context, it can be easily included in the Arendt canon as a prefigurement of both her Holocaust studies and her critique of liberal bourgeois culture. The dissertation is also centrally concerned with the tension between worldliness and disengagement, but because it pursues the theme by means of an engagement with Christian philosophy heavily indebted to Heidegger's "project," it is set aside as uncharacteristically idealistic.

The effect of selective emphasis shows clearly in Dagmar Barnouw's important intellectual history of Arendt as a German-Jewish thinker, *Visible Spaces: Hannah Arendt and the German-Jewish Experience*. Barnouw takes specific issue with Martin Jay's unflattering picture of Arendt's connection to Heidegger, Carl Schmitt, Ernst Jünger and Alfred Baeumler. To show that Arendt was no political naïf, Barnouw argues that she "has proved herself in all her writing since the Rahel biography a writer with deep political concerns" (Barnouw 1990, 254 n. 28).

These political concerns do not include right-wing German nihilism, voluntarism, and a disregard for the constraints of history and social convention. Barnouw rejects Jay's claim that Arendt "view[ed] . . . history as an illegitimate source of constraints on freedom" (Jay 1985, 243). Barnouw's reading of Arendt's political thought, however, does attribute to her "a general tendency beginning with works like 'Tradition and the Modern Age' (1954) . . . to locate her political philosophical models in a tradition informed by (meta)political norms formulated in antiquity" (Barnouw 1990, 254 n. 17). Barnouw also acknowledges that Arendt "shared with the majority of Weimar intellectuals a preoccupation with the dichotomy between positive paradigms of community and negative models of masses and 'collectivity'" (ibid., 255 n. 32).

Yet the dissertation in which Arendt's basic metapolitical paradigm is first formulated, including both pariah-parvenu and *civitate Dei/terrena* themes, is given the briefest of references. In the introductory paragraphs to the chapter analyzing the Varhnagen study, Barnouw dismisses the dissertation in two sentences. One sentence remarks that Arendt completed her dissertation under Jaspers the year before she wrote the biography. Another sentence reports Jaspers's concern that Arendt spend more time proofreading the dissertation prior to its publication in the series *Philosophische Forschungen*. A note briefly references Augustine on the willing faculty, but locates the source only as *The Life of The Mind* (ibid., 256 n. 13).

The discursive strategy of marginalizing the dissertation, so evident in Barnouw's otherwise balanced contextual approach, was pioneered in 1982 by Elisabeth Young-Bruehl in an exhaustive biography of Arendt. Her *Hannah Arendt: For Love of the World* has become the benchmark in Arendt studies. Young-Bruehl confines the dissertation to an appendix and Arendt's interest in Augustine to an early, romantic enthusiasm long since put aside for a focus on the public world. She credits Augustine with the genesis of Arendt's themes of natality and mortality but argues that in her later works Arendt "shifted the emphasis from the theological side of these existential determinants," predominant in the dissertation, to the "political side." She adds that "Arendt was no theologian, not even an Augustinian one" (Young-Bruehl 1982, 494, 366–70, 499).

Of course, as Arendt made clear in the dissertation, theology was not the point of the exercise. She did not think Augustine was a very consistent or dogmatic theologian, and for that reason felt justified in pursuing a "philosophic" study of his idea of *cartias*. To prove that Arendt drew a line between her early concerns and later political interests, Young-Bruehl produces one partial quotation from *The Human Condition*:

To find a bond between people strong enough to replace the world was the main political task of early Christian philosophy and it was Augustine who proposed to found not only Christian brotherhood but all human relationships on charity. . . . The bond of charity between people, while it is incapable of founding a public realm of its own, is quite adequate to the main Christian principle of worldlessness and admirably fit to carry a group of essentially worldless people through the world.

However, what is omitted in the ellipsis considerably qualifies what would otherwise appear to be a negative assessment of the relevance of *caritas* to the modern world of public politics. In fact, Arendt amplifies her comments with a statement that, taken together with the other two, seems to be a direct paraphrase of the dissertation's central argument:

But this charity, though its worldlessness clearly corresponds to the general human experience of love, is at the same time clearly distinguished from it being something which, like the world, is between men. "Even robbers have between them (*inner se*) what they call charity." (Arendt 1958a, 53)

Arendt follows up by observing that the robber analogy is Augustine's surprising but very well chosen example of what she calls the "Christian political principle." Arendt's citation for the robber analogy is Augustine's *Contra Faustum Manichaeum*, and its context is alienation from a doomed or hostile world.

Worldlessness as a political principle is possible only on the assumption that the world will not last; on this assumption, however, it is almost inevitable that worldlessness, in one form or another, will begin to dominate the political scene. This happened after the downfall of the Roman Empire and, albeit for quite other reasons and in very different, perhaps even more disconsolate forms, it seems to happen again in our own days. . . . There is perhaps no clearer testimony to the loss of the public realm in the modern age than the almost complete loss of authentic concern with immorality, a loss somewhat overshadowed by the simultaneous loss of the metaphysical concern with eternity. (Ibid., 54–55)

The dissertation is present throughout *The Human Condition* as a subtext for Arendt's phenomenology of public, private, and social life. It generates the paradox of a Christian political principle producing an "unpolitical, non-public" social grouping or "corpus" as in "monastic orders. . . the only communities in which the principle of charity as a political device was ever tried" (ibid., 54). On the assumption that immortality can be achieved only in the relationship of the soul to God or in the common practice of faith, the public realm is emptied of its significance. *Caritas* functions under these circumstances as the moral equivalent in civil society of natality in politics.

Another example of Young-Bruehl's dismissive approach to the Augustine-Arendt connection occurs in her discussion of Arendt's shift from the concept of "radical evil" in *Origins of Totalitarianism* to a definition of evil as "banality" in her study of Eichmann. Students of Augustine will immediately recognize a similar movement in his thought as he evolved from a belief in the material reality of evil during his Manichean period *(De Libero Arbitrio)* toward his "mature" position in which evil is described as a bondage to habitual sin, a worldliness that free will is powerless to break *(De Natura et Gratia)*. Although Young-Bruehl devotes considerable time to the controversy surrounding the shift in Arendt's approach, she dismisses the possible Augustinian parallels out of hand.

> The idea of radical evil evokes the Manichean or Gnostic doctrine that both the good and evil are primordial. . . . When Hannah Arendt rejected this idea, she moved in the direction of the doctrine that has been the chief alternative in the Western tradition; evil is merely a privation of the good. . . . But despite her admiration for the greatest of the ex-Manichees, Arendt was no theologian, not even an Augustinian one, and she explained the privative nature of evil in secular terms. (Young-Bruehl 1982, 369; see also 505 n.43)

Reading the dissertation out of Arendt's work distorts as well as contracts the scope and nature of scholarly discourse on her contribution to political thought. The "politics-only" Arendt, excluding issues of moral judgment, the formation of prepolitical communities, and the conjunction of religious and political discourses, is not an authentic Arendt. Barnouw, too, observes the missing linkages and cultural context that mar Young-Bruehl's portrait of Arendt.

> Young-Bruehl's biography is richly documented and usefully answers many questions, but it does contain many serious errors, and it does not deal well with the European-German part of Arendt, especially not in its relation to her American experience.

The result is that Arendt does not really become present intellectually. (Barnouw 1990, 258 n.46)

If there is a dawning sense among Arendt scholars that the portrait of Arendt lacks depth, the "party line" still hesitates to expand the scope of inquiry beyond safe boundaries. Recent feminist readings of Arendt, conducted explicitly against the grain of her texts themselves, have been willing to take significant risks—with mixed success. Here the expansion of discourse is not contextual but postmodern, not conducted according to Arendt's rules but with those devised by a new generation of scholars. They are doing to Arendt what she did with impunity to the "tradition" preceding her, including Augustine (Honig 1992).

The orthodox mainstream within political science has recently produced another admirable, Barnouw-like attempt to reconnect the fragments of Arendt's life and works. It still, however, makes a point of marginalizing her dissertation and Christian philosophy generally. Margaret Canovan's *Hannah Arendt: A Reinterpretation of Her Political Thought* (1992) argues for the importance of political history. What Canovan reinterprets is her own 1974 study of Arendt in light of what she judges to be a counterproductive bipolarity in Arendt studies. But even Canovan adheres to the canonical interpretation of Arendt's apolitical interest in Augustine and the resulting irrelevance of the dissertation to Arendt's later public philosophy.

Ironically, Canovan insists that the Arendt scholarly community needs to recontextualize her work by linking political to phenomenological texts. What Canovan proposes is only that Arendt's political *Existenz* in *The Human Condition* be reintegrated with her historical phenomenology in *Origins of Totalitarianism*, not that her American works be reintegrated with the dissertation. Indeed, Canovan argues that Arendt's study of totalitarianism provides the real-world animus for the abstract *Existenz* of *The Human Condition*, and that both texts should be read together with her other "political" discourses (Canovan 1992, 7–12, 63, 154, 279).

Canovan also seems to accept the premise that all of Arendt's originality in argument and language emerged in direct response to her personal experience of the Holocaust. Though she "thought about him [Augustine] for the rest of her life," Canovan acknowledges, Arendt's response to the crises of her century was a "thoroughgoing rejection of anything resembling his approach" (ibid., 8). She provides no references or footnotes to substantiate this claim. Though Canovan implicitly introduces the dissertation's research question about the relevance of the neighbor in Augustine's thought, she provides only a negative reading that dramatizes the apparent gap between Arendt's thesis and her later political thought.

> In light of her subsequent political commitments it is piquant that her doctoral thesis, on "The Concept of Love in Saint Augustine," should have been concerned with a form of Christianity for which rejection of this world and its concern was an essential prerequisite for the love of God. (Ibid.)

Nevertheless, Canovan is one of the few Arendt scholars to have worked with Library of Congress sources and even read the dissertation. Yet, when citing it (ibid., 8 n.3) she makes a partial error that supports her position but leads the reader to ponder other possible readings. After acknowledging Arendt's frequent quotations of Augustine's natality statement, translated as "that a beginning be made man was created," she says that Arendt meant to reference only hopeless situations and even then had to add "natality" as a term "to her original dissertation when she later thought of revising it for publication in English" (ibid., 8).

The effect of Canovan's reading is, first, to discount the transferability of Augustine's "natality" to other than theological contexts and, second, to suggest that Arendt was unhappy with the original dissertation and only "thought of" but did not actually set in motion a revision for publication. However, the dissertation text clearly shows that Part II, chapter 1 of the first translation (Copy A) does in fact contain a direct discussion of "beginning," though Arendt added the exact term "natality" and its associated idea of narrative as she reworked the text for Crowell-Collier in the early 1960s.

> Because the world, and thus any created thing, must originate, its being is determined by its origin (*fieri*)—it becomes, it has a beginning. Yet thereby it is subject to mutability. . . . The creature is governed in time by the fact of having become. Along with its mutability, time has been created. Only by memory and expectation can it make a whole out of the temporal extension of its being presented in past and future, and thus approach the eternal today, the absolute present of eternity. (A:033293–94)

Comparing this passage to its revision in Copy B shows that what has changed is primarily terminology and clarity of focus. Arendt now speaks of "natality" rather than simply "beginning."

> To put it differently, the decisive fact determining man as a conscious, remembering being is birth or "natality," that is, the fact

that we have entered the world through birth. The decisive fact
determining man as a desiring being was death or mortality. . . .
What ultimately stills the fear of death is not hope or desire, but
remembrance and gratitude. (B:033187)

Three pages later in Copy B, Arendt is still adjusting text by adding terminology and elaborating upon her basic insight into Augustine's fundamental
"originality." Augustine is interesting to her not only because he clearly
chafes at the restraints of the Neoplatonic and Stoic God, static in his
abstract eternity, but because he is bold enough to attempt a completely contradictory line of argument within the shell of the tradition he inherited.
Dissatisfied with the dichotomy of death-driven appetite versus contemplative disengagement, Augustine searches for a Creator God to legitimate
freely willed new beginnings. The theme of life experience as a "story" linked
to natality as *initium* was also inserted in the 1960s revisions.

"In the Beginning God created the heavens and the earth" (Gen.
1:1). However, *initium* refers to the beginning of "souls," that is,
not just of living creatures but of men. Augustine writes that "this
beginning did in no way ever exist before. In order that there be
such a beginning man was created before whom nobody was." . . .
Hence, it was for the sake of *novitas* . . . that man was created.
Since man can know, be conscious of, and remember his "beginning" or his origin, he is able to act as a beginner and enact the
story of mankind.
     Everything that has a beginning, in the sense that a new story
begins with it *(initium* and not *principium)*, must also have an end.
(B:033190)

Canovan does not explore the important thematic continuity between the
original translation and Arendt's revisions. Nor does she suggest linkages
between the revisions and Arendt's contemporary works, which might clarify Arendt's approach to the origins and limitations of the "tradition" of
Western philosophy. However, even if Canovan's interpretation were definitive, why should significant revisions indicate a lesser status for the entire
concept of "new beginnings" in Arendt's work? A theme reiterated is a
bridge strengthened.
     Canovan's project is an integrative one. She notes that scholars like
George Kateb criticize Arendt for her abstract "male Greeks in togas" paradigm, which seems to ignore the substantive issues and moral concerns ani-
mating public life. If Arendt's work on totalitarianism were merged with her

phenomenology of action, Canovan suggests, her political thought would be "more generally relevant" (Canovan 1992, 197, 279). In other words, Canovan is arguing against one of the strategic moves characteristic of Arendt "orthodoxy." In the latter, the Archimedean point of Arendt's political thought is either *The Human Condition* or *Origins of Totalitarianism*, not both. The earlier text can be critiqued for its inattention to historical detail while its core insights into the threats to public life inherent in totalitarianism are preserved and transferred to the former's "mature" discussion of the *vitae activa* and *contempliva*. This study takes up Canovan's challenge but casts a wider net. Canovan states her case against the orthodox approach to Arendt by saying:

> This traditional strategy is counterproductive. If (in quest of ideas of general interest) we start from *The Human Condition* what we find seems exotic but marginal. It is only when we go back to the roots of her thought to be found in her reflections on the specific events of her time that we get at the important things she had to say. . . . If we trace her thought trains to their source, it must be admitted that the first thing we find when we go back . . . may be something of an embarrassment. (Canovan 1992, 279)

Whether or not the dissertation is an embarrassment depends, however, on predetermined principles of inclusion and exclusion. Unfortunately, Canovan's principles, like Young-Bruehl's, are too restrictive in retrieving the context of Arendt's political thought. What is missing is not just the link to totalitarianism but to the dissertation as an important, missing context for her explicitly political thought.

The dissertation seems to have had a significant impact on Canovan herself. Comparisons of terminology and phrasing demonstrate its influence. Canovan argues that her interpretation of Arendt's ideas "will not attempt to supply . . . the system that she herself did not build, but will try instead to follow the windings and trace the interconnections of her thinking" (ibido., 12). In the dissertation, Arendt, describing her approach to Augustine, says that her "systematic approach" will not seek "to yoke Augustine to a consistency unknown to him" but instead "attempts to interpret even seemingly heterogenous statements and trains of thought in the direction of a . . . common base" (A:033243).

First and Last Things: *Love and Saint Augustine* and *The Life of The Mind*

From the vantage point of the dissertation, the Gifford lectures, which Arendt gave in Aberdeen, Scotland in 1973 and which were published post-humously as *The Life of the Mind*, are a return to first causes—a Heideg-gerian and/or Nietzschean "throwback" within her own work to its "new beginnings." By 1974, after decades of fertile juxtaposition between the mind-death of totalitarianism and the revelatory virtuosity of action in the *polis* space, Arendt shocked her audiences with the drama of the return. The shock was particularly acute because her first concerns were virtually un-known. For Arendt's overlapping audiences of academics and literati, *The Life of The Mind* was a puzzle, a mysterious journey inward yielding the alarming conclusion that, for Arendt, the life of the mind was itself a dis-puted terrain of thought silenced and will divided.

Though the *"quaestio"* that stimulated the lectures is the puzzling phe-nomenology of evil, Arendt's mode of presentation is a fairly narrow "cri-tique" of the tradition, not only confined to the classics but also walled off from the world in an internal dialogue of the mind with itself. Technical discussions of the divided will and mind are drawn from the dissertation. But the rich context of *caritas* in community, "natality," and "the constituted world" that dominated the dissertation is missing in the lectures. The *Will-ing* volume of *The Life of the Mind* focuses only on the weakness of the tradi-tion's understanding of the will. Even within that context, however, Arendt limits her use of Augustine to an exploration of the "monstrosity" that "to will and to be able are not the same." Leaving the *Existenz* almost entirely behind, Arendt returns to the *bios theoretikos*. Augustine is cited as "the first Christian philosopher and . . . the only philosopher the Romans ever had" (Arendt 1978b, 2:84), but not as a source of insight into the paradox of being "in" but not "of" the world.

In *Willing*, Augustine is invoked mainly as the sorcerer of immobilized will healed, suddenly and contingently, by *caritas*. Augustine is also implic-itly present in her discussions of memory and the *nunc stans* where past and future meet (ibid., 2: 75–78, 85–87) and in the Kafka metaphor (2:202–11), both of which are drawn primarily from the dissertation. These particular returns to Augustine occur, however, only in the *Thinking* volume. In *Will-ing*, his role is to establish a defense of free will against the determinis-tic implications of both the official providential order and earlier Greco-Roman determinism. In the introduction to the *Willing* volume, Arendt announces that by the end of her discussion she will address Heidegger's "conversion" to ancient philosophy and "repudiation" of the willing faculty. Strikingly, the entire framework for her exploration is Augustinian.

> What will be at stake here is the Will as the spring of action, that is, as the power of spontaneously beginning. . . . No doubt every man, by virtue of his birth, is a new beginning, and his power of beginning may well correspond to this fact of the human condition. It is in line with these Augustinian reflections that the will has sometimes, and not only with Augustine, been considered to be the actualization of the *principium individuationis*. (ibid., 2:6)

Equally at stake, she continues, is "how this faculty of being able to bring about something new . . . can function in . . . an environment of factuality which is old by definition." But the promise is not fulfilled. This question, taken almost directly from the dissertation, remains unanswered in *The Life of The Mind* in the absence of a satisfactorily completed section on judgment.

Arendt repeats her praise for Augustine's willingness to abstract his arguments from their polemical context and "to draw the philosophical inferences and articulate the consequences of the strange phenomenon which Paul had described"—that is, "to will and to be able are not the same" (ibid., 2:87; see also 2:86–93). But the locus of Arendt's drama of freedom in *The Life of the Mind* is "the inner empire." Only part of the problem of the "I will" versus the "I can" is solved by eliminating the dimension of habituated cupidity in favor of conscience-inspired free choice in the social realm. Breaking the bonds to outside desires, laws, and human dependence still leaves the internal dilemma of a will beset by contrary impulses and thus rendered powerless to act (see, in general, B:033191–98). Throughout, Augustine thus provides the substance and form for Arendt's extended disquisition on the problem of critical distance, judgment, and freedom.

She cites the famous passages from the *Confessions* and *De Libero Arbitrio* in which Augustine grapples with the "monstrosity" of will enchained by habit, passages that are also referenced in the dissertation.

> As the will commands, there must be a will . . . [but] it does not command entirely, therefore its command is not fulfilled. . . .
> Hence, it is not a monstrous thing to will a thing and partly to oppose it; it is rather an illness of the mind which cannot wholly rise, being uplifted by truth, weighed down by habit. (Arendt 1978b, 2:93)

Free will, judgment, and human community are in constant danger. In *Willing*, Arendt's Augustinian remedy for the divided will is still *caritas*.

But while in the dissertation *caritas* was directly linked to divine grace bestowed on the creature who stands *coram Deo* (in the presence of God) and to the resulting love of neighbor, in *Willing* love functions as an internal binding force with no apparent external mediation. *Caritas* is the internal evidence of the efficacious will, but its origin and external manifestation remain unspecified. Arendt remarks only, citing Augustine, that "compared to the will which nature has implanted in us, love is the stronger will." Her exposition of Augustine in *Willing* is so narrowly focused on rescuing free will from external entanglements that the effect is not only to jettison grace and the providential order but the link to public life and judgment as well. In a statement that no doubt would surprise scholars of Augustine, Arendt insists that for the saint, "the healing of the Will, and this is decisive, does not come about through divine grace. . . . He diagnoses the ultimate unifying Will that eventually decides a man's conduct as Love" (ibid., 2:95).

The concept of love as "the weight of the soul," she hastens to add, might "look like a *deus ex machina* in the *Confessions* [but] is derived from an altogether different theory of the will" (ibid., 2:96). That is, Augustine proposes a concept of love that is not only sui generis because of its originality, but also because it possesses a binding force that is spontaneous and inwardly generated. *Caritas* constitutes a decisive burst of purposive activity that ends the "hot contention" of the will. The unaided will cannot achieve the power of external action because it is itself lacking in the inner power of unified choice. Arendt sets aside the issue of power in the sense of "being able" to act in the world as a questionable phenomenon, fraught with problems of violence and "sovereignty." Instead, power is given its internal meaning as *caritas* generated within the mind-will-memory trinity.

The change from the enthusiastic embrace of Augustine's panorama of the pilgrim self in the dissertation to the broken will entombed in a solipsistic world is a striking one indeed. The drama of confrontation with death, the search for the Creator, and the "return" to the "vast camps" of memory and communal life are not replayed in the Gifford Lectures, even though they were occasioned by Arendt's unanswered question concerning the origin and effects of evil. Of course, the lecture format requires selectivity, and the texts were not completed before her death. Thus, without the dissertation not only is Arendt's last work a puzzling, constrained inquiry, but the possible connection to judgment remains elusive. Arendt's lectures on judgment, also published posthumously (Arendt, 1982), do not provide a direct enough link to the Gifford Lectures to fill in all the gaps, though they do provide important clues.

The dissertation provides even more clues—not only about Arendt's views on the context for judgment and its phenomenological dynamics, but also about the will's links to the human world. As Arendt noted in her essay "What Is Freedom?" Augustine's Roman *mentalité* worked to counteract "the strong anti-political tendencies of early Christianity." He was "the first to formulate the philosophical implications of the ancient political idea of freedom" (Arendt 1977, 167). The paradox of religiously inspired thought generating philosophic insights into public life would seem less puzzling, Arendt observed, "if the sayings of Jesus of Nazareth were taken more seriously in their philosophic implications. We find in . . . the New Testament an extraordinary understanding of freedom, and particularly the power inherent in human freedom" (ibid., 167–68).

Arendt's idea of freedom flows from Augustine's notion of *caritas*. Arendt's dissertation explains her silences and her selective emphases by providing the missing contexts for her subsequent explorations of the various internal and external, individual and communal manifestations of freedom. Indeed, without the dissertation, Arendt's linkage between *caritas* and the Godlike manifestation of natality, and her frequent oblique references to "an entirely differently conceived notion" of freedom, remain elusive. The following observation comes from her essay, "What Is Freedom?" in *Between Past and Future*:

> We find in Augustine . . . the great Christian thinker who in fact introduced Paul's free will along with its perplexities into the history of philosophy . . . not only the discussion of freedom as *liberium abritrium*, though this definition became decisive for the tradition, but also an entirely differently conceived notion which characteristically appears in his only political treatise, *De Civitate Dei*. (Ibid., 167).

For Arendt, Augustine's idea of freedom in *De Civitate Dei* grew out of the existential ground of his own Roman experience, in which "to be free and to begin [were] interconnected." She repeats her favorite quotation from Augustine, *"[initium] ut esset, creatus est homo, ante quem nemo fuit,"* including the important observation drawn from her dissertation that man comes into a given world that possesses an independent origin and history (ibid., 166, 167).

In the essay on freedom Arendt imports the Augustine of her dissertation and adapts him to a discussion of the exemplary power of natality and foundation in the world. That there is a "valid political idea of freedom in Augustine" is surprising, she argues, only if the standard reading of the history of ideas is accepted without question. In reality, Arendt maintains,

Augustine formulated a Christianized language for the Roman experience of freedom. *Caritas*-infused free will is not only portrayed by Augustine "as an inner human disposition" but also, and most importantly, "as a character of human existence in the world." As Arendt understood him, from 1929 until her death, Augustine was the product of dual citizenship—Roman and Christian. His life "in between" ideally prepared him to "formulate . . . the central political experience of Roman antiquity" for a Christian world, which was that freedom as new beginnings can be institutionalized in the "act of foundation" (ibid., 167).

Conclusion

How could Arendt bridge the gap between the battlefields of the mind and will, the canonic "tradition" of philosophy, and her categorical imperative of public works and deeds? The dissertation is an important pathway to the enigma of Arendt's *nunc stans*, her authorial vantage point. As a bridge between decades and texts, the revised dissertation provides a missing foundation for Arendt's work. The Augustinian faculty of memory is substituted for Heidegger's "woodsman's path" or "clearing." Significantly, it is a much broader and more temporal terrain than the epistemology of thinking and willing presented in the 1973 Gifford Lectures *(The Life of the Mind)*. In the dissertation, memory provides the vantage point "out of the world" required for self-definition, which Arendt would explore in other contexts through the metaphors of Kafka. Memory also binds past and future in a timeless present. When the self can no longer act authentically in public, the "vast camps" of memory beckon, spaces that would be condensed, by 1974, into the narrower fields of thought and will.

In 1929 Arendt's world was Augustine's. She would return to his metaphors of imperial decline in *Origins of Totalitarianism* and in her last looks at America in the age of Watergate and Vietnam. More dramatically than ever before, for Arendt's generation the "world" was indeed man-made. Heidegger's dichotomy between *das Man* (the "they" of public opinion) and *Dasein* (the existential self) was a metaphor for the sensibility of intellectuals on the left and right in what came to be called the "Gray Republic" of the 1920s. This world was clearly not the powerful "public realm" of Arendt's later American works. In the dissertation, she explores instead a phenomenological "world" constituted by the web of relationships between Creature and Creator and "between men."

Arendt intentionally merged Augustinian and Heideggerian discourses to consider the tension between context and transcendence. The complexity and variety of human lives ("plurality") have a point of congruence in an existential dilemma—the nature of Being. Before politics, both historically and phenomenologically, the personal voice of Augustine's *quaestio* ("I have become a question to myself") summons the individual to an inward journey. Arendt's "creature," recognizes a source beyond itself, and is "thrown back" to the *nunc stans* of memory, where future and past meet in the "sempiternal present." The questing, anxiety-driven appetite for elusive permanence in the world is replaced by *caritas* in the presence God. Love of self as a creature of God entails love of the Creator and of all other creatures.

The "neighbor" is relevant and morally necessary, first through common inheritance and a shared "constituted" world and second as the object of moral action after returning to the world. The specifically Christian commandment to love one's neighbor as oneself strengthens the pre-existing natural law "written in the hearts of men." Translating Heidegger and Jaspers into Augustinian discourse, Arendt reiterates the constancy of social context. Human collectivity is a pre-Christian, historical "given," one that Augustine never questioned even as the Roman public world disintegrated around him. Arendt was struck by the fact that among the late imperial Christian fathers of the Church, only Augustine fully accepted the necessary link between *libertas* of the spirit and the complexity of customs, languages, and methods of governance within and beyond the reach of Roman law.

At the same time, the givenness of social context did not obviate the obligation to make moral distinctions and act upon them. Arendt's oblique references to moral judgment in her American works are direct encounters in the dissertation. In 1929 and in her 1960s revisions, Arendt was ready to press the Husserl-Heidegger-Jaspers methodology farther than they had yet done to an understanding of the human condition in situ. Instead of writing about Being abstracted from life, she focused on paradigmatic individuals moving in and out of engagement with the "world"—Aurelius Augustinus and, shortly thereafter, Rahel Varnhagen. Arendt writes in the dissertation that "in estrangement from the world, divine grace gives a new meaning to human togetherness—defense against the world" (A:033361). In *caritas*,

> the *civitas terrena* as such is abolished, but at the same time the believer is called upon to fight it. The past remains at work in the impossibility of complete isolation for the believer, who cannot act by himself *(separatus)*, only with others or against them. Even though the believer is estranged from the world he continues to

live in the world. . . . Salvation is itself made to depend on the conduct of the world, or rather, on its conquest. (A:033359)

In a symposium on "Religion and the Intellectuals" published in *Partisan Review* in 1950, Arendt remarked that philosophers such as Heidegger, Spinoza, Descartes, and herself never "explicitly rejected . . . traditional religious beliefs" or, for that matter, "accepted" them. If belief were as necessary precondition for understanding, "then we would be forced to throw out more than one thousand years of philosophic thought." Arendt declares herself to be in "fullest sympathy with a *Zeitgeist* that would bring the intellectuals to the point of no longer considering the tremendous body of past philosophy as errors of the past" (Arendt 1950, 113–16). Here Arendt appears as she was in 1929, in 1964, and in all her "futures" until her death in 1975. Her description of Augustine's "thought trains" can as easily apply to her own: "The return to one's origin (*redire ad creatorem*) can at the same time be understood as an anticipating reference to one's end" (B:033191).

2 / "Thought Trains"

Major Themes and Terminology

The themes and modes of discourse Arendt introduces in her dissertation are major "thought trains" in her subsequent work. All of them carry her through and beyond the thicket of Heideggerian phenomenology with Augustine's *caritas* as her primary conceptual vehicle. "Love" is the source of both individuation and collectivity, an existential link between past and future as well as the means of banishing the fear of death. Augustine's *caritas* allows Arendt to redefine Being as transcendent Creator and at the same time to engage Being directly in the human condition, thereby overcoming a fundamental tension in Heidegger's work. The effect of Arendt's appropriation of Augustine's *caritas* is to merge, and thereby transcend, both Jaspers's "factual-life-in-process" and Heidegger's "question of Being."

In Arendt's hands, mortality, the quintessential "limit condition," is the occasion for a personal search for the Creator. The focus of her inquiry is the ontological source rather than its negation in the oblivion of death. Via Heidegger, Arendt uses the concept of time, within which to situate the "throwback" of the search. But Arendt's understanding of time, mediated most directly by Augustine, is *memoria*. Both Being and Time are returned to the level of personal experience. As a mental faculty explored in depth in the dissertation, memory provides the means by which future and past meet in the mental *nunc stans*, or "space" of memory. Projected outward in her later works, the locus of encounter is transformed into the "public space," where immortal acts of word and deed take place. *Caritas* bridges reason and judgment in the space provided by memory. It is *caritas* and its targeted mental faculty, free will, that transform Heidegger's anxiety-ridden "they" into the community of "neighbors" in the world, who are loved both for themselves and for the sake of their common Source.

When Arendt came to America and shifted her conceptual venue to an explicitly public space, her Augustinian neighbors in the "world constituted by men" would become citizens of similarly constituted republics, bound by social and political contracts at their "founding." Then, too, the *nunc stans* as mental space in which past and future meet in a "sempiternal" present would appear in her American works as the vantage point for an observer/ actor—the foundation for judgment as well as for thought and free will.

"Quaestio Mihi Factus Sum" ("I am become a question to myself")

Arendt uses this text from Augustine's *Confessions* as the opening theme for her philosophical analysis. In the introduction to the dissertation she characterizes this *quaestio* as "human existence reflecting on itself" and identifies it as the pivotal existential dilemma. According to Arendt, formulating the *quaestio* begins the lifelong task of thinking through the human being's fundamental relationships to the world, to God, and to other human beings. The *quaestio* is Heidegger's "call" translated into a theological context. Once asked, the *quaestio* initiates what Arendt terms the "transit" out of this world. Through this spiritual journey, the questioner discovers his true source in the eternal Creator and then returns to constitute the world as the human community. Raising the *quaestio* itself is a fundamental act of freedom because it is a "new beginning." At the same time, the choice "out of the world" is made efficacious through contingent grace. However, although Arendt acknowledges the dogmatic rigidity of Augustine's later works in her introduction, in the rest of her analysis she is silent about his evolving views on predestination and the coercion of grace. Convinced that she can proceed with a "philosophical" analysis, Arendt neatly bypasses this theological minefield.

Just as Arendt sees the *quaestio* as the key to understanding Augustine, her use of the Augustinian *quaestio* is central to understanding her own works. The *quaestio* figures prominently in *The Human Condition* (Arendt 1958a, 10–11) and in her last work, *The Life of the Mind;* where she titles the second section of the *Willing* volume *"Quaestio Mihi Factus Sum:* The Discovery of the Inner Man" (see also Arendt 1978b, 2:85–86 for greater elaboration on the *quaestio*). In her essay "Karl Jaspers: Citizen of the World?" Arendt writes of the "axial age" as the time "when, for the first time, man becomes (in the words of Augustine) a question for himself" (Arendt 1968, 88–89).

Caritas and *Cupiditas (Habitus)* as *Appetitus*

In Arendt's reading of Augustine, *appetitus* is the existential link between the fundamentally isolated individual and the rest of reality. Without *appetitus*, the human being who raises the *quaestio* and embarks on the transit out of the world would devolve into the Cartesian *cogito*, the nonmaterial "thinking thing" gazing on its own thoughts and disconnected from the world. Expressed as *caritas*, *appetitus* leads to the reconstitution of the world on the basis of shared values; expressed as *cupiditas*, it reinforces the existing world of materialism and force.

Cupiditas is routinized as habit, which "puts sin in control of life." In habit man tries to avoid "recollect[ing] his real source" and insists that he is "of the world" (A:033320). This avoidance of thinking and responsibility for behavior may be the paradigm for her notorious exploration of the "banality of evil" in *Eichmann in Jerusalem*.

Memory/Time/*Nunc Stans*

Memoria, one of the richest and most complex concepts in Augustine's philosophy, is the centerpiece of Arendt's dissertation. Taking up the Augustinian notion of memory as the vast "spaces" and fields of the inner life within which the infinity of past and future are perceived and preserved, Arendt reconfigures Heideggerian "space," moving it from the terrain of "Being" to the soul's inner realm. Unlike Augustine's understanding of grace and free will, which underwent significant modification of emphasis over time, his *memoria* remained relatively unchanged from his earliest to his latest works, from *Confessions* to *The Trinity*. For Augustine, without *memoria* there can be no *confessio*, and thus no journey to the Creator. Arendt's literal application of Augustine's *memoria* allowed her to locate the drama of alienation and reconciliation in the "timeless present," removed from "they" but not unconnected to the "world" of remembered existence. By means of memory, Arendt's pilgrim soul reflects on its origins in the image of the creator *(imago Dei)* and prepares to "return" and to "constitute" community. Memory is the precondition for the human being's search for his true origin and source, what Arendt in another vein calls the "twofold 'before' of absolute past and absolute future" (B:033193).

Arendt uses Augustine as an exemplar of the Western metaphysical struggle between necessity and freedom. In Augustine, this struggle is expressed as a dialectic between the Greek notion of Being as permanence and the Christian view of creation ex nihilo. As a product of creation, time is transitory and is perceived as such by human beings who are exemplars of "natality." Time's eternal anchor is *memoria*, through which the journey to the self leads both backward and forward to the Creator as the source, and final goal, of existence.

As the student of eminent phenomenologists in the 1920s, Arendt learned that modernity was characterized by a "crisis" of cultural continuity, the most important aspect of which was the severance of thought from existence. Later, in America, she would speak directly to the "break" in the history of philosophy, particularly to its denigration of political action (see especially the preface to *Between Past and Future, The Human Condition, The Life of the Mind*, and the Christian Gaus Lectures). But in her 1929 dissertation, the selection of memory as the mental context for thought and action more directly evokes the German phenomenological project and does not suggest the role memory would play in her later political thought. Later she would write that modernity has put *memoria* in jeopardy; in Augustine's lifetime, the end of the Roman Empire had threatened to do the same thing. Arendt follows a "woodsman's path" comparable to Heidegger's, but she reaches a different "space"—*memoria*—with the help of Augustine's rich and evocative concept.

But hers is no exercise in nostalgia or antiquarianism, her appeal to Augustine no attempt at a neo-Augustinian or specifically Christian solution to the crises of modernity. Arendt gazes without flinching on the modern loss of ontological bearings. Her own intellectual inquiry was both a critique and recapitulation of the tradition that had been lost. No wonder, then, that *memoria* is so central: complete cultural amnesia opens up the abyss of nothingness. Having no past would be too much to bear in addition to facing the "abyss of nothingness" that, as Arendt says, "opens up before any deed that cannot be accounted for by a reliable chain of cause and effect" (Arendt 1978b, 2:207). Every act of freedom entails a glimpse into the abyss, even more so the grand performance of political foundation. Capricious, uncharted newness is, perhaps, more than enough to bear without the loss of the guiding paradigms from the past. Here, in the last section of her last work, the *Willing* volume of *The Life of the Mind* (which she entitled "The abyss of freedom and the *novus ordo seclorum*"), Arendt stands poised precariously between the unpredictable newness of the free act and the fading contours of the ever-vanishing tradition (see especially ibid., 2:207–14). In such a setting, *memoria*, frail and fragile though it may be, is called upon to perform heroic deeds.

In her later works, Arendt continued to conjure up the power of memory and remembrance (see especially the preface and "What Is Authority?" in *Between Past and Future* and *The Life of the Mind, Willing*). Whenever she discussed the "gap" between past and future, and the freedom of the individual "inserted" between them, Arendt evoked Augustine—together with an assortment of similarily pivotal thinkers, such as Kafka, Heidegger, Hegel, and Nietzsche. "Only insofar as he thinks, and that is insofar as he is 'ageless'—a 'he,' as Kafka so rightly calls him, and not a 'somebody'—

does man in the full actuality of his concrete being live in the gap of time between past and future. The gap I suspect, is not a modern phenomenon; it is perhaps not even a historical datum but is coeval with the existence of man of earth. It may well be the region of the spirit or, rather, the path paved by thinking, this small track of non-time that the activity of thought beats within the time-space of mortal men and into which the trains of thought, of remembrance and anticipation, save whatever they touch from the ruin of historical and biographical time. This small non-time-space in the very heart of time, unlike the world and the culture into which we are born, can only be indicated; it cannot be inherited and handed down from the past. Each new generation—indeed every new human being as he inserts himself between an infinite past and an infinite future—must discover and ploddingly pave it anew" (Arendt 1977, 13). Arendt found their confrontation with modernity compelling both for its metatheoretical force and its epic dimensions. These men were storytellers, invoking the realm of memory with poetry as well as rational discourse. Arendt often remarked that the storyteller creates the mythology of the modern world by recalling and reconstructing events in the timeless realm of *memoria*. Later, whether citing Kafka, Rahel Varnhagen, or Isak Dinesen, Arendt put into play the insights of the dissertation. In *The Human Condition* she quotes Dinesen: "All sorrows can be borne if you put them into a story or tell a story about them" (Arendt 1958a, 175).

Natality

Not only is natality central to Arendt's appropriation of Augustine; it is also central to her own thinking and has particular significance for her later understanding of the public realm. The context for natality is established in the original dissertation (A:033290–92). In her subsequent editing of the text Arendt coins the term "natality," adding substantial new material and further working out its meaning and implications (B:033187–88; 033190). Augustine's emphasis on "entering the world through birth" as the model of human creativity and the precondition for freedom enables Arendt to challenge Heidegger's notion of "death or mortality" as the spring of action.

In close proximity to the inserted term "natality" in the Copy B section of Part II, chapter 1 are new references to "gratitude for life having been given at all" as the "spring of remembrance" and, in turn, to remembrance as the cause of being "able to act as a beginner and enact the story of mankind" (B:033187, 90). These are only hints of the linkages between narrative and new beginnings that Arendt develops more fully in her political thought, suggesting that she traveled back across the bridge from the 1960s to 1929 to enhance her original theme of "the fact of having become."

In her chapter on "Action" in *The Human Condition*, Arendt opens her analysis by striking the Augustinian chord of natality, which then sounds throughout this central section of her book. Without freedom and its ground in natality, there is no human action in the world, and the political realm ("the public space") disappears entirely. As with many of her favorite "thought trains," Arendt returned repeatedly to the key concept of natality, often citing the Latin text from *The City of God* (XII, 20) that inspired her interpretation: *"Initium ut esset, creatus est homo, ante quem nemo fuit"* (Arendt 1977, 167; see also Arendt 1973, 212–13, 215, 1958b, 177; 1978b, 2:108–10). Her essay "What Is Freedom?"—a version of which first appeared in 1960 at the time Arendt was in the process of revising the dissertation—is typical of her use of the term. "Because he is a beginning, man can begin; to be human and to be free are one and the same. God created man in order to introduce into the world the faculty of beginning: freedom" (Arendt 1977, 167). In *Origins of Totalitarianism*, at the close of the pivotal chapter on "Ideology and Terror" which Arendt added to the second edition in 1958, the natality quotation from Augustine appears again, this time to emphasize that "new beginnings" in freedom, which she elsewhere termed "miracles," are always possible even under a new and unprecedented form of government: totalitarianism. "But there also remains the truth that every end in history necessarily contains a new beginning; this beginning is the promise, the only 'message' that the end can ever produce. Beginning, before it becomes a historical event, is the supreme capacity of man; politically, it is identical with man's freedom. *Initium ut esset homo creatus est*, 'that a beginning be made, man was created,' said Augustine. This beginning is guaranteed by each new birth; it is indeed every man" (*OT*, p. 479).

Without Arendt's reading of Augustine, whom she celebrated as the first philosopher of the will and the Romans' "only" philosophical mind (Arendt 1978b, 2:84), it is difficult to imagine the context out of which her analysis of freedom and its relationship to politics might have emerged. Her dissertation on Augustine sounded the first notes, which continued to ring thoughout her work virtually to the very last thing that she wrote for publication, *The Life of the Mind*, volume 2: *Willing*. There she cites once more and, as it turns out, for the last time, the same text from Augustine on God's creation of man as the introduction of new beginnings in the world: "This very capacity for beginning is rooted in *natality*, and by no means in creativity, not in a gift but in a fact that human beings, new men, again and again appear in the world by virtue of birth." Arendt calls Augustine's argument on this point opaque: "it seems to tell us no more than that we are *doomed* to be free by virtue of being born no matter whether we like freedom or abhor its arbitrariness." Presumably, Arendt hoped that the opacity might have yielded to some enlightenment had she completed the final volume of her trilogy: *Judgment*. The human faculty of judgment Arendt calls "no less mysterious than the faculty of beginning" (ibid., 2:217). Even though the mystery is not solved in her last work, her first work on Augustine provides important and tantalizing clues.

Conscience and Judgment

Arendt's rendering of Augustine's *caritas* entails a move "out of the world" followed by a triple "return": a return to the future of death and reunion with the Creator; a return back to the historical origin of life in creation; and a final return to the constituted world, which is born anew in "natality." Arendt would find this triple return a particularly useful vehicle for exploring "the relevance of the neighbor." It also would prove equally applicable to her later, political writings in America. In those later works, the problem of vantage point for judgment moved to the foreground. At the time of her death, Arendt had just begun the third volume, *Judging*, for *The Life of the Mind*. In most of her earlier works (*The Human Condition, Eichmann in Jerusalem*, and especially the first two volumes of *The Life of the Mind*), various "thought trains" on judgment are introduced or hinted at without being fully developed. In *Between Past and Future* and *The Life of the Mind*, discussions of Kafka's and Heidegger's views on time and critical distance seem to echo the Augustinian paradigm. While Arendt's lectures on Kant's *Critique of Judgment* are suggestive, they lack the full context of vantage point provided by the bridge of the dissertation. The missing link is Arendt's use of *memoria* as the "space" between past and future, which is the existential context for the mental act of judging.

Arendt invokes "conscience" as the inner voice "of God." The journey to the *nunc stans* of *memoria* is begun because "the law calls on conscience" and breaks "the security of habit." The basis of moral judgment, therefore, is not the neutral Heideggerian "call" occasioned by anxiety; instead, conscience is evidence of *caritas*, which links the creature to his Creator and then to his neighbors. Conscience, therefore, speaks in the language of God but is "in ourselves." The world's language is "another's tongue." It is evil only to the extent that it "determines man's being, whether good or evil, from outside and from what man has founded" (A:033321). The vantage point attained by the journey inward to the Creator views the man-made world as a "desert" only in that the world is then seen as enchained by habit and thoughtlessness.

Arendt's analysis of Augustine's model of judgment emphasizes ambiguity. On the one hand, the world is rendered alien and remote because the *appetitus*-driven model of love sees the divine object of desire as eternal, beyond the impermanence of the world and its lesser objects. The behavioral effect of desire for God is achieving a "point of reference" in the "absolute future," which allows the pilgrim soul to "regulate" his life and relationships according to the "highest good." On the other hand, this renders the individual's life itself an object of regulation, an objectified entity in the divine ordination *ad unum*. "He who returns. . . to regulate the world" finds "even his own present existence as a 'thing' . . . to be fitted into the rest of what exists" (B:033 167). Arendt does not eliminate this option. Instead she counterposes it to another idea of love, which is not Greek or Roman in its regulatory impulses but Christian in its emphasis on loving union with a remembered Creator. Both notions of the journey—passion and memory—have their counterparts in Arendt's primary dialectic of death and birth and exist simultaneously in Augustine's *Existenz*. For Arendt, Augustine stands as one of the sources of the Western ambiguity of contingency and determinism, freedom and law.

By implication, judgment is more a function of *caritas* as desire for an eternal, fixed truth than of *caritas* as the union of Creator and creature. In the former, a point of reference is attained whereby judgments can be rendered (by the order of love) in the "world" constituted by men. Judgment based on *caritas* inspired by *appetitus* is the counterpoint to habits formed by *cupiditas* in that it is the expression of the efficacy of free will. Both forms of *caritas*, however, entail a return to the world, either to regulate it or to found new moral communities.

The Will

In Augustine, Arendt discovered not only the philosophy of the will's power but an account of its inner divisions and impotence: "To will and to be able are not the same" (*Confessions* VIII, 2, 20). She never tired of exploring this paradox, both in her analysis of the tradition and in her critiques of postmodern society and culture. Arendt explicitly used Augustine's paradigm of powerlessness healed by *caritas* in "What Is Freedom?" where she writes: "Only where the I-will and the I-can coincide does freedom come to pass" (Arendt 1977, 160; see also 1978b, 2:86–92). The power to perform the choice of the will comes from *caritas*, which is the expression of grace. In the dissertation Arendt follows Augustine and stresses the search "out of the world" for the source of grace. In later works, such as "What Is Freedom?" and the *Willing* volume of *The Life of the Mind*, Arendt returns to the theme of free will but deemphasizes the theological aspects of grace and the divine healing of the divided will. Love *(caritas)* as the binding and healing function of the will appears as a self-generated inner power, externalized as action. In these analysis Arendt relies on Augustine's notion of the inner life, particularly as he developed them in *The Trinity*. Arendt extrapolates from the theological framework within which Augustine developed his Christian philosophy. She specifically declines to discuss his doctrine of predestination, which she called "the most dubious and also most terrible of his teachings" (Arendt 1978b, 2:105–6). In doing so, Arendt engages in her characteristic, selective reworking of Augustine to emphasize the complexity in trains of thought which exist side by side in his work but are not identified as such by Augustine. His later works were constrained by the Pelagian controversy and, for polemical reasons, emphasized unmerited grace and the impotence of free will. For her own discursive purposes, Arendt wants to highlight Augustine's earlier line of reasoning based on natality and free will. Yet, though she resists the "dogmatic" conclusions of the late Augustine, Arendt preserves throughout the essence of his *confessio* mode of discourse.

The World

Arendt analyzes the double meaning Augustine attributed to the "world." First, he speaks of the physical universe ("the fabric of the heavens and the earth") created by God; second, he examines the world "constituted" by men in their search for permanence and meaning (B:033193). The man-created world "is the place where things happen," whereas "outside of the world" there is "whoever makes them happen." All of this analysis is in the original dissertation and suggests Arendt's first exploration of the meaning of action. Typical, too, of her later work is her reminder, through Augustine, that "events in the world" are only "partly constituted by man who inhabits the world" (A:033299). Causality is not negated but its mechanisms remain mysterious to the human agent.

This is an explicit commentary on, and revision of, both Heidegger and Jaspers. Notable, too, is Arendt's repeated use of the latter's term "the encompassing." In the dissertation, the constituted world is both loved and the cause of estrangement. Her treatment of the "world" suggests the tension in balancing critical distance with engagement, which was so pivotal in her later works. Using Augustinian terms, Arendt laments that in the "human world established by man," the voice of conscience can be stilled by "'another's tongue' *(aliena lingua)"* (A:033323). Many years later she would discover this was true of Eichmann's conscience. (Arendt 1965, 114–17).

The individual who has not performed the transit and encountered the "twofold before" lives in habit, "in the view of the world and . . . subject to its judgment." In the return to the Creator man stands *"coram Deo,"* in "the presence of God." By freely willing *caritas*, the individual is bound by conscience not only to know the good but to perform the good by returning to the world constituted by men and acting accordingly in concert with others. The precursor for external "neighborly love" is the journey to the source. Arendt elaborates on Augustine's understanding of being in but not of the world by observing, "There is no togetherness and no being at home in the world that can lessen the burdens of conscience" (A:033323).

Many years later, in *The Human Condition*, Arendt would return to the twofold meaning of the world to distinguish labor, work, and action. Labor belongs to the realm of the physical universe because it shares the repetitions and cycles of the natural order. Work and action are correlated to the second sense of the world as constituted by men, since work brings artifacts, which have a quasi-permanent character, into existence. Action introduces words and deeds into the public space where they can be judged, praised, or blamed by others. Arendt's concept of plurality as being among others *("inter homines esse")* and appearing in the public space also develops from this second sense of the world. All of these are also central ideas in *The Human Condition*.

Foundation

In the dissertation Arendt sees man as having "a hand in founding the world" he lives in (A:033310). This is accomplished either through *cupiditas*, wrongly directed love of the world, or through *caritas* after one has exercised the transit and discovered one's true source in God. Foundation imitates God's creation of the "divine fabric"—the heavens and the earth. Yet since human life cannot be its own raison d'être, its drive for permanence and stability through *cupiditas* reveals the futility of the effort to find one's ultimate home in this world. *Caritas*, which binds man to God and men to each other, is the transmundane principle that both grounds the true human community and radically relativizes it.

Arendt works within the framework of Augustine's fundamental distinction between the two cities that receive their particular character from the nature and quality of their love. In her works written in America, Arendt shifts contexts and explores foundation as the *novus ordo saeculorum* (*On Rev-*

olution, Origins of Totalitarianism, and *Between Past and Future*). It is interesting to note, however, that while she attached a great deal of importance to the American "Founding Fathers" as exemplars of natality because they created public realms and constituted institutional foundations to assure their permanence, she made no similar institutional claims for Augustine. In the dissertation, Augustine as the "Father" of the Roman Church in North Africa makes only brief appearances. Arendt finds his founding role as "first philosopher" of the Christian idea of citizenship much more central.

Making, Creation, and Labor

In the 1929 dissertation, Arendt emphasizes the distinction between the Creator's "product" as an extension of Being and as human artifice which produces an estranged "world." This is an important early version of Arendt's later distinctions in *The Human Condition* between labor, work, and action, on the one hand, and the *vita contemplativa* on the other hand. The original dissertation (Copy A) predates Arendt's reappraisal of Marx's labor theory of value in her Guggenheim year, 1952–53, and approaches labor in terms that are more Hegelian than Marxist. Significantly, when revising the dissertation for publication in the early 1960s, Arendt retained all of this material from the original text.

The Neighbor, Society, and Community

Conscience hears the "call," which leads "out of the world." But *caritas* looks both to the Creator and to the "neighbor," binding the pilgrim soul to both. After the "return to the twofold before" (the Creator as past and future), the final return to *societas* is achieved not in dependence, habit, and *cupiditas*, but in equality, freedom, and *caritas*. In the final chapters of each part of the dissertation, the "relevance of the neighbor" is explored within the paradigms of love as cupidity and love as *caritas*.

In her brief Part III, "Social Life," Arendt presents the final accounting and reconciliation of different approaches to *caritas* in Augustine's often conflicting discourse. She asks, "why does love of neighbor . . . play so large a role" in Augustine's work, even though he is describing a "freedom of choice" that "recalls the individual from the world and severs his social ties with humankind" (A:033348, 53)? The answer is the fact of human social life. "What makes my neighbor appear in the relevance required for the commandment of love is not that 'I have become a question to myself.'" Instead, "it is a historically pre-existing reality . . . the factuality of history" which presents human community, the genealogy of Adam, and the death of Christ as existential "givens" (A:033350).

The theme of the individual's relationship to the human community pervades all of Arendt's works, both in Germany and America. Her 1929 gloss on Augustine provided her with a way of rooting "plurality" in the "multiplicity" of human society while balancing it against collective common purpose. In the dissertation, not unexpectedly, she makes this move within the framework of the Christian commandment to love one's neighbor. In a footnote to Part II chapter 3 of the dissertation Arendt writes, "The fundamental question for an understanding of neighborly love, as commanded by Jesus, reads as follows: As one seized by God and detached from the world, how can I still live in the world?" (A:033345). The answer is only by "founding society anew." As a result the "new social life . . . is defined by mutual love." It replaces "mutual dependence" and therefore "dissolves the bonds that tied men to the world in its original sense of the earthly city" (A:033361). It does not deal with "mankind" but with "the individual, albeit every individual." The collectivity is the sum of the ties that bind "many individuals" rather than an abstract "human race" as such.

Arendt continued to explore this dilemma throughout her works. Her approach may be seen as an implicit counterpoint to the paradigm of "mass society" already being analyzed in the 1920s and 1930s by German sociologists (for example, Lederer and Weber on bureaucracy). She interjected the concept of mass society into *Origins of Totalitarianism*; later, in *On Revolution*, she returned to the problem of mass society overrunning the boundaries of private and public life. Arendt's primary negative model was the French Revolution in which the socioeconomic "Rights of Man" threatened the "public world" of political action. Her positive model was the American Revolution, which maintained plurality by placing "fences" between the community and individuals in society while at the same time constituting the public realm.

The dissertation does not contain any of the distinctions between the *vita contemplativa* and *vita activa* or between the political and social realms that so mark *The Human Condition*. Augustine's conceptual originality is noted repeatedly and thus, by implication, is tied more directly to the "natality" theme, at least with respect to philosophical creativity. Even in Arendt's later repeated citations of, and admiring comments about, Augustine's *civitas*, she does not explicitly compare or contrast him to other institutional founders. His transition from thought to action may have suggested to Arendt a fall from philosophical grace rather than an enrichment. In the context of theology, the shift of venues seemed inevitably to imply the descent into "dogmatic rigidity."

Arendt makes fleeting references to the external manifestations of *caritas* in *societas*. The "world" as the locus of action makes only a brief, tantalizing appearance as the "place where things happen" (A:033299). In effect, had Arendt published the dissertation in 1964–65, it would have become part of a triptych uniting her work on human *Existenz* in the world *(The Human Condition)* and the phenomenology of revolution in history *(On Revolution)*. All three texts were written or revised in the late 1950s and early 60s, and were thus important formative influences on each other and on *Eichmann in Jerusalem*. The published dissertation might have provided a paradigm for the illusive "point of reference . . . out of the world" Arendt had sought as she struggled with the problem of "judgment." From 1929 to 1973, when she presented the Gifford Lectures in Aberdeen, Arendt's "thought trains" had come full circle.

Arendt's Revisions, 1958–65

Arendt did not rework her dissertation in a vacuum. Her own intellectual development and the political and cultural discourse of the 1950s and early 1960s New York inevitably shaped her response to the English translation. Remarkably, however, none of the stylistic and substantive revisions Arendt made to Copy A, whether interlinearly or in appended new text, changed the general thrust of her analysis or its specific components. All of the changes seem intended to clarify, elaborate, emphasize, or document Augustine's exploration of the natality-mortality couplet.

This continuity is remarkable for the evidence it gives of Arendt's commitment to past work in present contexts. It is important, too, because it proves that Arendt's consciously selective, and frequently critical, approach to the work of her mentors, Heidegger and Jaspers, had not substantially changed since 1929. Even the original dissertation (Copy A) broke new ground by testing Heidegger's phenomenology of Being and Jaspers's *Existenz* in the intellectual laboratory of Augustine's encounter with God. Her experiment was a daring one.

Arendt's application of *Existenz* phenomenology to the case study of Augustine's thought creates a dissertation of layered discourses. Augustine's *quaestio* occasions a discussion of *liberum arbitrium* versus *gratia*, *caritas* versus *cupiditas*, and the *civitas terrena* versus the *civitas Dei*. But the *quaestio*, and Jaspers's *Existenz* philosophy, also provide the ammunition for her assault on Heidegger's thesis that the meaning of Being for the individual is irremediably shaped by its negation in death. *Caritas*, therefore, is the foundation for an alternative phenomenological vantage point—"that a beginning be made, man was created."

By the early 1960s, Arendt felt sufficiently at home in the English language to elaborate upon the basic themes and logical structure of her dissertation in translation by incorporating some of her other work in progress without altering her original purposes. For that reason, the arguments of "What Is Freedom?" *The Human Condition, On Revolution,* and *Eichmann in Jerusalem* seem to be just below the surface of her revisions in Copy B.

The question of why she broke off revisions at the end of Part II, chapter 1 and returned to the original text for the last pages of the chapter remains to be answered. One possibility is that she was displeased with the results thus far and gave up the idea of getting the manuscript ready for her contractual deadline. However, the continuity between her past and present concerns suggests that this was not the case. Her essays on freedom and authority, *The Human Condition,* and *On Revolution* are filled with the terms and problems of the dissertation. The moral foundation of communities, the limits of free will, the constraining force of worldly habits, and the prospect of choice are all under continuing examination from 1929 to the 1950s and early 1960s.

Careful review of materials in the Library of Congress, and interviews with her friends and colleagues, have yielded no direct evidence of the plan Arendt pursued with the English translation. There is only the mute yet eloquent evidence of her handwritten interlinear changes and added pages of handwritten text in Copy A, and further marginal notations and revisions in the new text of Copy B, which she herself typed out. The current text, incorporating all revisions and including editorial changes to facilitate the flow of the text, is a third version of the manuscript reflecting Arendt's abiding concerns.

From an examination of the typescript versions of the dissertation in the Library of Congress collection of her papers, it is obvious that Arendt worked intensely and repeatedly on revisions of the translation by E. B. Ashton. Differences in typefaces and style of marginalia attest to this fact. Throughout her rediscovery of Augustine, however, the path she had embarked upon in 1929 was not set aside for another. In tone and mode of discourse, as well as in substantive emphasis and argumentation, the original dissertation is preserved. As a result, the significance of this preservation project lies only partly in the evidence it provides of Arendt's place in the German conversation on existentialism in the 1920s. Arendt's deliberate plan to retrieve and update the thesis for publication in 1964–65 also testifies to its bridging role. The revision process evidently reflected, as well as influenced, her works on politics, society, and moral judgment during the most productive period of her career. Arendt's return to the dissertation sig-

nals her use of Augustine as a radical critic whose challenges to his own philosophical predecessors was a paradigm for her own critique of the tradition.

Arendt broke off the process of revising the English translation in Part
II, chapter 1, but not before she had introduced Augustinian concepts of
foundational importance to her own work at the time: the concepts of
natality, initium, and *novitas.* In the last part of this edited section, Arendt
was working through Augustine's twofold notion of the world as both the
human world constituted by men and as the physical universe. In considering the latter, she analyzed both the Greek philosophical and Christian
theological influences on Augustine's notion of the cosmos, using texts—
Plato, Aristotle, and Plotinus—largely taken from the footnotes in the original dissertation. She also added illuminating commentary to this section by
sharpening the tensions between the Greek understanding of the cosmos as
eternal and uncreated (as in Aristotle) and the Christian notion of a created
and temporally limited cosmos. Her point was to demonstrate that while
"imitation" is a concept that spans both approaches, it is not sufficient to
resolve the underlying contradictions in Augustine's effort to unite Greek
philosophy and Christian theology.

This is a good example of the sort of change Arendt made to her 1929
dissertation. Tensions are pushed further and placed in bolder relief without
any attempt at resolution or compromise. Unfortunately, Arendt did not
continue her revisions to examine Augustine's other sense of the world, that
is, the world as constituted by men. Reference is made to the world as "the
place where things happen" and to community renewed by the bonds of *caritas,* but the discussions of "social life" and the phenomenological "world"
are not linked. The silence of the dissertation on this point is remarkable
since this notion of world is much more akin to her abiding concerns with
foundation, community, and political action than is the idea of the physical
cosmos. Had she proceeded along these lines with her exploration of the
human world, the "shining pearls" noted by Jaspers in Heidelberg might
have been set out very differently.

Below are some illustrative examples of revisions and additions that
Arendt made to the English translation of the dissertation.

Part I, Chapter 1 (B:033131–42)

In Copy B Arendt adds many quotations from Augustine that she originally had placed in footnotes to the 1929 text. She also places directly in
Copy B a great deal of material that had originally appeared in an addendum
to the first chapter. None of these changes will be noted here in any specific way since they do appear in the German original and do not constitute

substantive revisions. The following revisions, however, are more significant and substantive. For example, Arendt introduces a critical and reflective summation of Augustine's notion of craving and his uses of the Greek tradition. She adds this passage in Copy B:

> The reason for this incongruity lies in Augustine's terminology, which he took over from the tradition of Greek philosophy even when he wished to express experiences that were quite alien to it. This is especially true of the *appetitus* reflections, which can be traced back to Aristotle via Plotinus. Aristotle defined death as the "evil most to be feared" without, however, insisting on this fear for his understanding of man. (B:033134)

In the next addition to the text, Arendt takes quotations from Augustine that had originally appeared in the footnotes and inserts them into Copy B while adding more specific details of Augustine's life:

> There can be no doubt that death, and not just fear of death was the most crucial experience in Augustine's life. With exquisite eloquence he describes in the *Confessions* what it meant to him to lose his friend, and how "he became a question to himself" as a consequence of this loss. After "the loss of life of the dying" followed "the death of the living." This was the experience that initially turned the young Augustine toward himself when he had first fallen in love with philosophy at age nineteen after reading Cicero's *Hortensius* (one of his lost works, an exhortation to practice philosophy). (B:033136)

In Copy B, Arendt is especially concerned with underscoring the actual experience of loss as the catalyst for Augustine's phenomenological *quaestio*. Experience produces the "fear of death," for nothing else had so strongly recalled him from "carnal pleasures." The path she demarcates for him leads away from Neoplatonism toward the apostle Paul, who, she emphasizes, finally convinced Augustine: "Nowhere else in the New Testament is the fact of death, life's imminent and final 'no more,' invested with such decisive importance. The more Christian Augustine grew in the course of a long life, the more Pauline he became" (B:033136).

That Arendt chooses to underscore rather than to diminish Augustine's death-driven quest in Copy B is significant. Her chosen mode of discourse immediately evokes Heidegger's premise of death-driven anxiety and Jaspers's "boundary conditions" while at the same time advancing beyond the parameters of the German *Existenz* by means of Augustine's paradigm of *caritas*.

Arendt clearly intends to heighten her audience's sensitivity to Augustine's "originality," and her own, by repeatedly emphasizing his transformation of Greek and Roman philosophical traditions.

For example, she inserts an aside on Augustine's terminological "incongruity" to illustrate his role in transforming the tradition. Death and *appetitus* illustrate the powerlessness of the individual in the world yet are founded on an implied possibility of permanence and possession—"something that can be achieved." This tension, underscored in Copy B, is a function of "Augustine's terminology." Throughout the dissertation, both in its original and revised forms, Arendt reiterates the ambiguities resulting from Augustine's uses of traditional Greek and Neo-Platonic language to express a new Christian sensibility (B:033134). As the 1960s begin, Augustine is framed as the radical philosopher of his own transitional era, straining at the bonds of inherited language and beliefs.

The next addition contains a theme that is decisive for Arendt's political thought: the human being's love of the world, and the continual frustration it entails. Love of the world arises from the fear of death and the urgent need to establish a stable bulwark against it. This effort can never succeed. Yet it does account for constituting the world as a place of human habitation. Arendt introduces Augustine's distinction between *cupiditas* and *caritas* at the close of this chapter where she adds: "Augustine calls this right love *caritas:* the 'root of all evils is *cupiditas*, the root of all goods is *caritas*.' However, both right and wrong love (*caritas* and *cupiditas*) have this in common— craving desire, that is, *appetitus*. Hence, Augustine warns, 'Love, but be careful what you love'" (B:033139).

Finally, Arendt appends several pages of handwritten notes to the end of Copy A, Part I, chapter 1, expanding on the location of the "space" of eternity through which the "not yet" passes on its way to "no more." These notes, which were revised and retyped for Copy B, sound a significant Heideggerian theme, but with Arendt's characteristic Augustinian variations. As in discussions of death and *appetitus* above, Arendt weaves into her analysis of Augustine more examples of his encounter with, and departure from, the Neoplatonists, especially Plotinus. While the present is seemingly "real," mused Augustine via Plotinus, "how can the present (which I cannot measure) be real since it has no 'space'?" (B:033136). Yet experience belies the apparent insubstantiality of both time and life, which are "always either no more or not yet." Men measure time in the "space" of their minds, a space that Augustine called *memoria* and that transcends "both life and time" (B:033137).

In Copy B, Arendt's excursus on time becomes the basis for her repositioning of Heidegger's "woodsman's path" or "clearing" as the Augustinian "space" of *memoria*. Most of these added references are drawn from the *Confessions*. For instance, she merges her own text with Augustine's to conclude:

> Therefore, I do not measure what is no more, but something in my memory that remains fixed in it. It is only by calling past and future into the present of remembrance and expectation that time exists at all. Hence the only valid tense is the present, the Now. (B:033137)

These turns of argument and discourse are significant because they show Arendt's engagement with the problem of *nunc stands*, or vantage point out of the world, precisely at the time when she developed her phenomenology of the *vita activa* and of specific political experiences, such as revolution and Holocaust. Arendt argues that "it is this Now that becomes Augustine's model of eternity for which he uses Neoplatonic metaphors—the nunc stans or stans aeternitatis." To make them useful, however, Augustine has to first "divest . . . them of their specific mystical meaning" (B: 033137).

Part I, Chapter 2 (B:033143–65)

In this chapter Arendt continues to augment the text by inserting quotations from Augustine's works that had originally appeared in the footnotes of her 1929 dissertation. She also inserts the major part of an Addendum that had first appeared at the end of Part I in the German original. The net effect of these changes is to substantially expand the scope and depth of her argument while retaining the same focus and intent as in Copy A.

On the first page Arendt reprises the theme of isolation and lack of self-sufficiency from which the individual moves through *caritas* or *cupiditas* to the eternal or temporal world. Pushing this paradox even further she adds a new *quaestio*:

> Would it not then be better to love the world in *cupiditas* and be at home? Why should we make a desert out of this world? The justification for this extraordinary enterprise can only lie in a deep dissatisfaction with what the world can give its lovers. Love that desires a worldly object, be it a thing or a person, is constantly frustrated in its very quest for happiness. (B:033143)

To reject the natural impulse to love the world is not, she will emphasize, a complete rejection of the world constituted by men.

Instead, the next revision in this chapter shows Arendt reemphasizing the Stoic source of Augustine's apparent "contempt for the world." The tension between Stoic and Neoplatonic influences, on the one hand, and Paul's teachings on the other, is elaborated as an explanation for equivalent "incongruities" in Augustine's understanding of *appetitus*, death, and the nature of Being. Arendt incorporates into the text a long digression from her handwritten notes at the end of Copy A on the ideal of self-sufficiency and alienation from the world. This theme was central to the pre-Augustinian tradition, which had identified freedom with self-sufficiency and with overcoming the fear of loss.

For emphasis, Arendt adds to Copy B a text from Epictetus that did not appear in the original. Here the Stoic philosopher enjoins his readers to despise those things that are not in their power. In Copy A Arendt had written: "This self-sufficiency is expressed in disdain, which need not yet be Christian in kind." In Copy B, that sentence is replaced with: "Hence, we see that contempt for the world and its goods is not Christian in origin. In this context God is neither the Creator nor the supreme judge nor the ultimate goal of human life and love. Rather, as Supreme Being, God is the quintessence of Being" (B:033145). The effect of her revision is to stress that Christianity is not the source of the "radical" alienation that entered the tradition with Stoicism and Neoplatonism. Neither, by implicit extension, is Augustinian Christianity the cause of the even more radical "loneliness" that Arendt discusses in her 1958 chapter on "Ideology and Terror" added to *Origins of Totalitarianism*. In the latter, she again cites Epictetus to establish that contempt for the world or "isolation" is not necessarily the same as the "loneliness" that is "the common ground for terror . . . and ideology" in totalitarian rule. (Arendt 1958b, 174) Loneliness means dependence upon others "with whom one cannot establish contact," or who are hostile. Arendt's Augustine rejects both a static understanding of Being and alienation from human community, though not the fruitful "isolation" in which the *quaestio* is pursued. In this, she observes, he is much more Christian than Greek, just as Arendt's "natality" marks her as much more than a transmitter of German phenomenology.

In the next few pages of this chapter Arendt continues to incorporate new material from her notes and the Addendum to illustrate the enormous influence of Plotinus on Augustine's thinking and the difficulties encountered in fusing the Plotinian and Christian frameworks. The Plotinus citations are derived from the original Addendum, but with the contrasts between Plotinus' language and intent and that of Augustine more sharply delineated. Christianity is premised on the Creator as the highest good, while for Plotinus the inner activation of the spirit or *nous* brings human fulfillment. Although Augustine was inspired by the Stoics and Plotinus, Arendt sees him engaging in an analysis of man's relationship to the world that is far more complex and subtle, deriving from experience and faith as well as from philosophical reflections. In her notes incorporated in Copy B, she adds that in addition to Augustine's dependence on the Stoic and Neoplatonic tradition in his definition of love as desire, he also draws on his own experience of "the deplorable state of the human condition." At least at first, Augustine is enmeshed in his own *Existenz* rather than finding a "starting point [in] God who revealed himself to mankind" (B:033145–46). Arendt also makes the point that Augustine's debt to the tradition is clearly demonstrated in his eagerness to contrast "dispersion" in worldliness not with *caritas* but with free will based on moral self-sufficiency.

In Copy A Arendt had noted Augustine's key concept of *dispersion*, through which human beings lose themselves in the world. In Copy B she adds: "Since dispersion brings about loss of self, it has the great advantage of distracting from fear, except that this loss of fear is identical with less of self" (B:033148). Arendt then proceeds to view "lust of the eyes" as fundamentally different from other sensuous pleasures. It is paradigmatic of a curiosity that seeks knowledge for its own sake, a curiosity that also brings about the loss of self. She cites 1 John 2:16 for Christian support of this interpretation. This kind of desire is so strangely selfless both in origin and in effect that it holds a particular danger and fascination for human beings. It also stands in stark contrast to the self who finds his highest good and true identity in God.

But here, too, Arendt focuses on perplexity—"the question that I have become to myself." The answer to this question is by no means self-evident. At this juncture, Arendt adds entirely new material to dramatize the beginning of Augustine's journey of self-definition.

> Whoever wishes to say "I am," and to summon up his own unity and identity and to pit it against the variety and multiplicity of the world, must withdraw into himself, into some inner region, turning his back on whatever the "outside" can offer. (B:033149)

Augustine's new beginning, however, is also a departure for the tradition of philosophy, says Arendt. He "strikes out on his own." Unlike Epictetus or Plotinus, he does not find either self-sufficiency or serenity in this inner region of the self: "he does not belong to those 'who can act well within themselves so that actual deeds will result from this.' . . . On the contrary, may God see 'where I am . . . and have mercy and heal me (Psalm 6:2)" (B:033149). Arendt retains the "question I have become to myself," which appears in Copy A, and then continues:

> Hence, it is by no means a simple withdrawal into himself that Augustine opposes to the loss of self in dispersion and distraction, but rather a turning about of the question itself and the discovery that this self is even more impenetrable than the "hidden works of nature." What Augustine expects of God is an answer to the question "Who am I," the certainty of which all previous philosophy had taken for granted. Or, to put it another way, it was because of this new quest for the self that he finally turned to God, whom he did not ask to reveal to him the mysteries of the universe or even the perplexities of Being. He asks to "hear about myself" from God and thus "to know myself." (B:033149)

Arendt then adds these comments a few sentences later: "In a way I already belong to God. Why should I belong to God when I am in quest of myself? What is the relationship, or perhaps, the affinity between self and God?" (B:033149–50). She answers the question much more fully in Copy B than in the original by adding:

> In other words, this God who is *my* God, the right object of my desire and my love, is the quintessence of my inner self and therefore by no means identical with it. Indeed, this relationship is no more identical than beauty, the quintessence of all beautiful bodies, can be said to be identical to any one body. And just as body may be consumed but not beauty, light may be extinguished but not brightness, the sounds come and go but not the very sweetness of music, the dark "abysses" of the human heart are subject to time and consumed by time, but not its quintessential being that adheres to it. To this quintessential being I can belong by virtue of love, since love confers belonging. . . . In finding God [man] finds what he lacks, the very thing he is not: an eternal essence. And this eternal manifests itself "inwardly"—it is the *internum aeternum*, the internal insofar as it is eternal. And it can be eternal only because it is the "location" of the human essence. The "inner man" who is invisible to all mortal eyes is the proper place for the working of an invisible God. . . . Just as my bodily eyes are delighted with light because their proper good is brightness, so the "inner man" loves God because his proper good is the eternal. (B:033150)

Arendt next sharpens the contrast between the eternal essence and human temporal existence by adding new text linking the essence-existence duality to the nature of time:

> However, since this human essence is immutable by definition *(incommutabilis)*, it stands in flagrant contradiction to human existence, which is subject to time and which changes from day to day, from hour to hour, appearing through birth from non-being and disappearing through death into non-being. So long as man exists, he *is* not. He can only anticipate his essence by striving for eternity, and he will *be* only when he finally holds and enjoys *(frui)* it. (B:033151)

Because of the centrality of time in Heidegger's phenomenology, Arendt's emphasis on time in the distinctive Augustinian context of natality and *memoria* indicates her willingness to challenge Heidegger. Augustine understands man as both bound by time and able to transcend it through the "transit." She adds an important interpretation of Augustine to Copy B:

> This anticipation, namely that man can live in the future as though it were the present and can "hold" *(tenere)* and "enjoy" *(frui)* future eternity, is possible on the ground of Augustine's interpretation of temporality. In contrast to our own understanding, time for Augustine does not begin in the past in order to progress through the present into the future, but comes out of the future and runs, as it were, backward through the present and ends in the past. (Incidentally, this was the Roman understanding of time, which found its conceptual framework solely in Augustine.) Moreover, as far as human existence is concerned, past and future are understood as different modes of the present. (B:033152)

A few pages later she adds this succinct comment: "To Augustine, Being and time are opposites. In order to *be*, man has to overcome his human existence, which is temporality" (B:033154).

In the next addition Arendt sharpens the contrast between the imperative to deny human existence and the command to love one's neighbor: "The greatest difficulty which this self-forgetfulness and complete denial of human existence raises for Augustine is that it makes the central command to love one's neighbor as oneself well nigh impossible" (B:033154).

Augustine's paradigm of love as desire founders in this context, as it does when confronted with the notion of *caritas* as expressed by Paul in 1 Corinthians 13. Arendt hints at this other understanding of love in copy A.

In Copy B she heightens the dramatic incompatibility between love as desire and love as Pauline *caritas*. Arendt's additions highlight Augustine's originality in departing from his philosophic roots, as he shifts to a concept of *caritas* grounded both in a journey inward to the Creator and in the givenness of human community.

> For this [love as desire] is not the kind of love of which Augustine, in an altogether different context, writes that it has the power to "make God present." In this context Augustine can write that "if you love God you are in heaven even though you are still on earth." All desire craves its fulfillment, that is, its own end. An everlasting desire could only be either a contradiction in terms or a description of hell. Hence, when Augustine writes that "only *caritas* stays forever" and that "after this life only *caritas* will remain," since instead of believing we shall know and instead of hoping we shall possess, he refers necessarily to a different kind of love. (B:033156)

Part I, Chapter 3 (B:033166–76)

Arendt indulged in major editing of this chapter, incorporating interlinear notes, marginalia, and footnotes from Copy A. She also added entirely new text. Once again, the effect of her revisions is to explicate important points more fully and to provide a dramatic edge to her favorite "contradictions." Since this chapter is a summation, she also returns to her hypothesis that the question about the neighbor's relevance always turns into a simultaneous critique of the prevailing concept of love, that is, the Stoic and Neoplatonic understanding of love as desire. The relevance of the constituted world and the human community was a "matter of course" for Augustine, Arendt notes, as well as the locus of a Christian commandment. How could neighborly love be valued in itself when the world, natural and human, was to be used for the goal of avoiding death in the "absolute future"?

The revisions to Copy A all focus on this "heterogeneous" difficulty by underscoring the following major points: the difficulties associated with "the order of love"; the distinction between use *(uti)* and enjoyment *(frui)*; and Augustine's "terminological inconsistency" resulting from his struggle to shift "terminological contexts" in order to approach his own distinct understanding of neighborly love. For example, the *"ordo"* theme is introduced in Copy A to link the order of love to the object of love.

> This longed-for freedom, which is realized in charity, marks Augustine's view of the world. We relate to the world by using it,

freely and without depending on it. Confined to being "for the
sake of," the world has lost all meaning save the purposiveness
gained in its use . . . the world is set in a specific order. . . . From
the absolute future, to which charity made him surrender, he returns to the world as it now exists, only to find that it has forfeited
its primary significance. Yet in the absolute future he has at the
same time obtained a point of reference that lies, on principle,
outside the world itself . . . a point of reference from which the
world, and its relations to it, can be regulated. (A:033281)

In Copy B, the same main points are sharpened, with more direct references
to the worldly implications of the ordering function of love understood
as craving. Arendt is shifting focus to the sources of moral judgment in
Augustine's thought.

The future freedom, anticipated in *caritas*, serves as guide and
ultimate standard for the right understanding of the world and
the right estimation of everything that occurs in it—things as well
as persons. What should and should not be desired and who should
and who should not be loved are decided with reference to the anticipated future, as is the degree of desire and love to be spent on
whatever occurs in the present. . . . According to Augustine,
some hierarchical order of love always exists. . . . As a Roman,
Augustine calls the right conduct of men in this world their "virtue." He writes in his political work, *The City of God*, that "a brief
and true definition of virtue is the order of love." (B:033166)

The term "community" also makes its appearance in this context, but
only in Copy B. Arendt is attempting to explain the contradiction between
love of neighbor for the sake of God *(uti)*, based on desire as craving, and
love of neighbor for his own sake *(frui)*. Her first attempt was to write:

My neighbor is a neighbor only insofar as he enters into the same
relationship with God as I do. I no longer experience him in concrete worldly encounters . . . as a human being he has his place in
an order that determines love. . . . Use does not mean that the
person comes to be a means; it is only the index for the gradation
established by the order, which accordingly antedates love.
(A:033285)

In revision, however, she is concerned to emphasize the regulatory, ordering effect of the paradigm of love as craving, particularly when the desired

object is transcendent or abstracted from the "concrete." She writes, extrapolating from Augustine:

> Not everything, but only what stands in some relation to myself, is included in the order of love. And this relation is established in the community *(societas)* with those who, like myself, can achieve happiness only in regard to God and the "highest good" and therefore are "closest to me" *(proximi)* my true neighbors. . . . Therefore, there is a difference between the mere use of the world *(uti)* in complete alienation from it and this love that also is directed toward the world, even though it is not permitted to enjoy its objects for their own sake *(frui)*. (B:033169)

As Arendt adds in Copy B, this "is not to say that neighborly love has no place in Augustine's thinking." In fact, the "contrary" is the case. Arendt adds here one of her many "we shall meet it again" promises of things to come, referring to future chapters in Part II in which *caritas* is a "specifically Christian . . . explicit version of the natural, prereligious, and secular law of not doing to others what we would not have them do to us *(quod tibi fieri non vis, alteri ne feceris)*" (B:033169). In discarded footnotes to chapter 3 (added to the text of Copy B), Arendt gives the reader a further glimpse of Part II by suggesting that "aside from the Christian tradition of neighborly love as a divine commandment," Augustine shifts to "an entirely different context . . . to the concept of love obtained precisely from the natural coexistence and interdependence of men" (B:033175).

Arendt adds a substantial and detailed explication of the incompatibility between love defined as craving and Augustine's understanding of *caritas* to make the point that he is aware of the conflict between the tradition of philosophy and the Christian thought:

> Those with whom I live together in this world can be divided between those whom I help and those by whom I am helped. . . . The emphasis in this neighborly love is on mutual help, and this insistence is the clearest sign that love remains harnessed to the "for the sake of" category, which rules out meeting my fellow men (in their concrete worldly reality and relation to me). . . . "It is a great question. . . whether men should enjoy or use each other." (B:033171)

Copy A breaks off in mid sentence. The last page of this chapter and the footnotes were found inserted and worked into Copy B. Arendt must have discarded the rest of the manuscript sheets as she rewrote them. As she completes rewriting the chapter, she reiterates the "objectivity" or "from the outside" aspect of the order of love, which harnesses the present to an absolute future. Each "thing," including other persons and oneself, is assigned "its proper place." This is a fearless love, since desire for the absolute future has stilled desire for present enjoyment: "A consequence of the strange dialectics of the equation of love and desire is that self-oblivion grows eminently real." But such an outcome is not Augustine's intention and is ultimately "pseudo-Christian" (B:033172).

Echoes of *Origins of Totalitarianism*, *The Human Condition*, *Eichmann in Jerusalem*, and *On Revolution*, as well as the preface to *Between Past and Future*, abound in these early 1960s revisions. The problem of abstract categories of judgment imposed on the human community from the "outside" is Augustine's, but also Arendt's. Again she describes him as trapped in the "terminological context" (B:033173) of his Stoic and Neoplatonic predecessors, attempting to analyze experiences they would have found alien. *Caritas*, operating via *memoria*, is the bridge from the absolute future to the present world. But can the bridge be traveled in both directions?

Augustine's "*ordinatio ad unum*," according to Arendt, results in the "degradation of love, which contradicts the central place love occupies in [his] thought." *Caritas* must be derived from a different source if Augustine is to answer the question "'who is my neighbor?'" without offering the "equivocal" response, "'every man,'" because "'they have rational souls which I love even in thieves.'" Worst of all would be for him to say, "I have no right to judge; all men are brothers." *Caritas* must be directed not at men in their "concrete uniqueness" but toward "the most abstract quality of being human" (B:033172–73). Arendt's discomfort in 1929 is heightened dramatically in her revisions, indicating as much or more about her own vantage point as a political theorist than about Augustine's.

Part II, Chapter 1 (B:033181–A:033313)

Arendt adds the term "natality" to Copy B to highlight the original section in which the theme of new beginnings is established. In Copy A the emphasis had been on "man as a creature" and "desire and the fear of death." But the revisions for Copy B take up the whole section (beginning at B:033190) and reposition the argument. These revisions, coincident with her discussion of natality in other works, more effectively link "the decisive fact [of birth] determining man as a conscious remembering being" with her move away from Heidegger's central theme of anxiety in the face of death.

The traditional idea Augustine inherited of man as a craving, appetitive being, entails "fear of death and inadequacy of life" as the "springs of desire."

But his own revisions of the tradition produced "gratitude for life having been given at all [as] . . . the spring of remembrance" (B:033187). In Copy A, the natality theme is established implicitly:

> Looking back at craving from this Creator-creator context, it will be seen why the self-denial arising from it would be called pseudo-Christian . . . because the original assumption of this "referring back" . . . already harbors an intention to comprehend man as "createdness by God" (*a Deo creatum esse*). . . . Whatever the creature is it had first to become. The structure of its being is genesis and change (*fieri* and *mutari*). The Creator is Being as such. (A:033291)

In Copy B, Arendt also notes that the return to the Creator through imitation "is not a matter of will and free decision; it expresses a dependence inherent in the fact of createdness . . . man's dependence . . . relies exclusively on remembrance" (B:033187). Interestingly, the link between dependence and remembrance is not reproduced in her later works in which natality is embedded in an explicitly political context.

In her later works, Arendt transfers the natality theme (*"initium ut esset"*) from its original phenomenological context to its new location as part of her analysis of free will and action in the public space. In *The Human Condition*, she uses the same technique to shift *caritas* from its original definition as love of God and others for the sake of God to the basis of community bonding, albeit "for-the-sake-of." The transition is already at work, however, in the central question of her dissertation: "the relevance of the neighbor" to an "out of the world" phenomenology.

For Arendt, remembrance is a major axis of analysis that links natality to temporality, since memory is the "space" between past and future in which the "questing search" for the Creator takes place. Copy B expands the memory section substantially and clarifies the relationship of memory to the other aspects of individual *Existenz*. In Copy B memory is equated with consciousness, defined as a foundational mode of dependence, and cited as proof of the gap between essence and existence and the fact that God is both "in" and "outside" man. It is clear that in Copy B the quest for a "relation to the source" shifts away from Copy A's emphasis on Heideggerian "Being" and toward Arendt's own emphasis on "natality" and remembrance, achieved via Augustine.

Another "thought train" derived from the central theme of natality is the idea of man as an actor and storyteller. This linkage is absent in Copy A and is present only in brief references in Copy B. Acting and storytelling are developed in conjunction with the natality, *novitas*, and remembrance themes. Discussion of these topics occurs where Arendt is implicitly or explicitly settling accounts with Heidegger. She writes in Copy B:

> It was the sake of *novitas* . . . that man was created. Since man can know, be conscious of, and remember his "beginning" or his origin, he is able to act as a beginner and enact the story of mankind.
> Everything has a beginning . . . a new story begins.
> (B:033190)

Arendt's discussion of *principium* versus *initium* in Copy B is also related to natality. "Beginning" has different names depending on whether it occurs because of human or divine agency. "Augustine distinguishes between the beginning of the world and time, both of which existed before man and the beginning of man" (B:033190). *Principium* suggests the governing role of the Creator, whereas *initium*, symbolized by birth, becomes the capacity of he who is first born—the human individual. Arendt adds an important reference to Heidegger in Copy B, marking her farewell to her mentor.

> It is memory and not expectation (for instance, the expectation of death as in Heidegger's approach), that gives unity and wholeness to human existence. In making and holding present both past and future, that is, memory and the expectation derived from it, it is the present in which they coincide that determines human existence. This human possibility gives man his share in being "immutable." (B:033192)

Evil, which is the opposite of acting *imago Dei*, is a much more developed theme in Copy B. Evil defined as falling away from God "belongs first among the basic structures that rule human conduct," but it is a negative quality rather than a substantive characteristic (B:033190). She writes, "Since no part in this universe, no human life . . . can possess its own autonomous significance, there can be no 'evil' *(malum)*. There are only 'goods' *(bona)* in their proper order, which may *seem* evil from the transient perspective of the individual *(singulum)*. This quality of goodness . . . is bestowed . . . by the universe" (B:033196).

Copy B is also notable for its very long, and substantially revised, discourse on Neoplatonism in general and Greek concepts of the universe in particular. For example, in Copy A harmony is defined as congruence with eternal law. In Copy B, Arendt goes on at length about "eternal law" and introduces a subtle shift:

> And if Augustine . . . says that everything that "is just and lawful in temporal law is derived from eternal law," he does not necessarily think of God as the eternal lawgiver, but rather that the laws determining the motions and actions of the parts are . . . derived from the . . . whole. (B:033196–97)

Beginning in B:033197, entirely new text is added. Arendt's apparent intention is to underscore Augustine's departure from the "tradition" of his time, making his philosophy an example of "natality":

> These speculations about everlasting Being and the universe are Platonic in origin. Augustine's concept of the world partly belongs to a tradition that reached from Plato to Plotinus. And the problem of a beginning of the universe, which becomes so perplexing in Augustine, who knows of a definite beginning through the Creator, had been troubling this tradition from its very start. (B:033197)

Arendt says furthermore:

> It is difficult to overestimate the enormous influence this concept of Being as the all-encompassing universe exerted on Augustine's thought. . . . We shall find that for the creature-Creator relationship the Christian worldview is by far the more important and decisive one. Nevertheless, this is no reason to neglect Augustine's indebtedness to Greek philosophy, which is most apparent in his conception of the universe. Moreover, it was only by deflecting the Christian conceptual context that Augustine could arrive at his notion of the twofold "before." (B:033197, 93)

It is this static concept of a universe created permanently and independently of man that, as Arendt says, is "derived from the Greek tradition, [and] is not really the primary focus of Augustine's later writings." The reason is that "it plainly deflects his concept of the world" (A:033299).

Significantly, in her revisions for Copy B, Arendt did not alter footnote 50 (here footnote 79) describing Heidegger's concept of *mundus*. Did her dissertation committee understand the original note as a veiled criticism of Heidegger's rather passive *ens creatum?* She already had a more active definition of the "world [as] constituted by men" in Copy A, which she retained in

Copy B. The importance of this "thought train" both for the doctoral student and the emerging political theorist is obvious. In the original footnote, Arendt comments that

> Heidegger distinguishes two of Augustine's meanings of *mundus*, . . . *ens creatum* . . . [and] world conceived as lovers of the world. Heidegger interprets only the latter: "World means the *ens in toto*, . . . according to which human existence relates to, and acts toward, the end." While his interpretation is confined to illuminating the world as "living with the world at heart," and the other world concept, though mentioned, remains uninterpreted, the aim of our interpretation is precisely to make this twofold approach understood (B:033208)

Another idea that takes on a heightened significance in Copy B because of the expanded context surrounding it is "foundation." The act of foundation is unchanged from Copy A to Copy B, but in the latter is embedded in a much more developed discussion of Augustine's concept of natality and his "originality" in departing from the tradition of philosophy as he fashions an active understanding of creation. In both versions, Arendt comments:

> When life is viewed in its concrete mortality and createdness, it is understood as life with and in the world. To begin with, life is neither independent of the world (as in "returning" or going back from the world to the source) nor is the world independent of life. Instead, life has a hand in founding the world in which it lives. . . . According to this view it does not matter whether we mean by "world" the lovers of the world or the divine fabric of the world. For even if the man has a hand in founding the world, this foundation always takes place on the ground of the divine fabric . . . as God's creation. This alone makes it possible to establish the world once more in a more explicit sense. Death removes us from both the humanly constructed world and the divine fabric. (A:033310)

Arendt is also concerned to link the founding of the *mundus* to the "encompassing," a term derived from Jaspers that she uses repeatedly in Copy A and Copy B. In her retyped revisions she expands upon the linkage between the created and founded worlds, on the one hand, and between both worlds and the individual's "return" on the other:

> Return to oneself would no longer mean a departure from the world. Instead, the imitation of God would be accomplished

through proper integration into the world by the "well-ordered man," who fits himself into what encompasses him; that is, into the whole that makes him the part he is. . . . It is at the end what it was at the beginning. (A:033311)

All the terms Arendt added or expanded in meaning in Copy B (foundation, *principium, initium, novitas,* natality, and *caritas*) are evocative of her political thought. But in the context of the dissertation these terms do not refer to the "public realm" or the *vita activa.* The discussion of return to the world suggests the reconstitution of community or *societas* rather than the world of "word and deed" Arendt portrayed in *The Human Condition* and *On Revolution.* Nevertheless, this positive idea of society is a vital missing bridge to her free-floating public realm, where politics occurs without roots in personal or social life and "appears" to lack a moral compass. The dissertation grounds her political thought and provides the existential context for her phenomenology of public life—one of the most influential and eloquent arguments for freedom in this century.

3 / Heidegger: Arendt between Past and Future

The rediscovery of Arendt's 1929 dissertation on Augustine, reinforced by her intention to publish it in 1964–65, forces a modification of the standard interpretation not only of Arendt's relationship to the Christian philosophic tradition but also to her first mentor, Martin Heidegger. The dissertation is an extended, but critical, encounter with Heidegger via an inquiry into the "heterogeneous intentions" of St. Augustine, one of the pillars of Western tradition. Because Augustine's own thought was methodologically conflicted, focused on a "turn" to Being from Death, and committed to the "fact" of the world's complexities, he was an ideal subject upon which to test Heidegger's phenomenology.

Arendt was Heidegger's mistress and intellectual companion as well as his student. These facts, however, neither prove direct influence nor are sufficient grounds to posit an esoteric reading of Arendt. The puzzle of authorial intention is not reducible to "history," as Arendt herself would have said. Addressing the problem of whether her intentions were Heideggerian becomes even more problematic in view of her inherently deconstructive premise that "new beginnings," or actions, almost never achieve their purposes. What she meant her audiences to understand by her words may or may not be their underlying truth; that understanding, moreover, may or may not be reflected in the meaning her audiences have constructed. With Augustine as her guide to the puzzle of freedom, Arendt preferred to approach life as a miraculous creative process, the outcome of which was a "story."

Contingency is so central to Arendt's *Existenz* that she insisted on invalidating determinism at every opportunity, especially when pressed to be explicit about the "method" underpinning her own story. Disclosing "who" someone is occurs in speech and action, Arendt argued, and is not related causally to any product of these activities. She adopted the idea of the "facticity" of the individual born into a "given community" from Heidegger and Jaspers. But it was Augustine who allowed her to transform the fact of birth into a miraculous exemplar of "natality" and to begin her own "turn" away from the gridlock of givenness and from Heidegger. Birth regenerates the power of contingency as the newcomer is "inserted" into the existing "web" of "conflicting wills and intentions." In this study of Arendt's encounter with Augustine, "return" is not intended as a reduction. Arendt's first work is not significant because all her later works can be read as footnotes to it, but because it demonstrates that there is more to Arendt's *Existenz* than an ontology of the Holocaust or, as Jean Elshtain termed it, "polis envy" (Elshtain 1988).

Questions haunt the problem of Arendt's indebtedness to Heidegger. In his posthumous "appreciation" of her work, Hans Morganthau wondered "from what philosophic and political point of view did Hannah Arendt approach the disparate topics of her investigations?" The answer eluded him, as it always has eluded both her admirers and her detractors. Morganthau felt certain that although Arendt had studied with Heidegger and Jaspers, "one would have to search very carefully for direct influences traceable to these two giants" (Morganthau 1976, 5–8).

Yet for others the debt to Heidegger is damning. Writing from the vantage point of the Straussian school of political thought in *The Spirit of Modern Republicanism* (1988), Thomas Pangle attacks Arendt as a Heideggerian mole who undermined the American liberal tradition of political thought with the corrosive effects of German nihilism. She was one of the "many thoughtful men and women" of her time who were disturbed by "the growth of 'individualism' [and] the feebleness of civic pride" (Pangle 1988, 48). But she and her mentors reacted with an equally dangerous "nostalgic pining for a heroic, communitarian ancestry," which "encouraged a moral rebellion" against the "bourgeois liberalism" that "defines" the Western republican tradition. Pangle ascribes a mesmerizing effect to Arendt's intellectual presence, which has made her

> the most serious intellectual source of these longings. J. G. A. Pocock and his students make it clear that while some of their key methodologic assumptions may derive from Wittgenstein, Kuhn, or Geertz, the animating moral inspiration for their writings comes from Arendt. (Ibid., 49)

Pangle fears that Pocock, John Diggins, and other intellectual historians on both sides of the Atlantic have missed the *éminence noire* cleverly concealed behind her celebrations of the "lost treasure" of *polis* life. In truth, says Pangle, "Arendt was the popularizer in America of Heidegger's political broodings." Her intention from the beginning of her career was to "effect a rupture with the entire Western tradition," especially the "relation between reason and action." As a Heideggerian fellow traveler, Arendt pursued an "esoteric" methodology of concealed meanings.

> She rarely conveyed her enormous debt to Heidegger, and her humanity compelled her to shrink back, in understandable inconsistency and wavering obfuscation, from the most radical implications of her mentor's new thinking. But she in effect endowed a watered-down version of Heideggerian political thought with an allure that it previously lacked altogether in the Anglo-American world. (Ibid.)

And Heidegger was not the only bad company she kept. Arendt also stands accused of a penchant for Machiavelli, Robespierre, and Lenin, as evidenced by her enthusiasm for "resoluteness" and "decision." While at one level of discourse her study of revolutions seems to validate the American "more restrained and sober" version, "when she enters into a more detailed analysis of the thinking of the leaders," Pangle detects that "her deepest sympathies are with precisely the Roberspierrean activist vision" (ibid., 51).

Pangle's Heideggerian, protofascist vision of Arendt is the most extreme of the published attacks on Arendt's debt to her German phenomenologist mentors. However, since Pangle is himself a highly influential political scientist, his message reaches a wide, receptive audience. Another important critic, Luc Ferry, replicates Pangle's guilt-by-association approach, claiming that Arendt's connection to Heidegger produced a critical theory of totalitarianism that had the ironic effect of undermining the rationalist foundations of Western philosophy. According to Ferry, Arendt, acting under the influence of Heidegger, blames the concept of necessity entailed in modern philosophies of history, particularly Marxism, for the crisis of modernity and its death throes in totalitarian ideologies. Arendt juxtaposes the nineteenth-century "idea that the real was wholly masterable and controllable" to a phenomenology of novelty and mystery, which, Ferry argues, throws causality and moral agency overboard. This was a "new" idea of history based on Heidegger's "deconstruction of metaphysics" (Ferry 1992, 5). Arendt, with her idea of "natality," is the prime agent for a phenomenological perspective that "makes any scientific work in the field of the social and any ethical view of politics and history impossible" (ibid., 4).

Ferry does not name the dissertation as the source of Arendt's first work on natality. Instead he traces the "miracle of being" reference to Heidegger (ibid., 6). Yet he is one of the few Arendt critics to base his case against her on the Augustinian terms her supporters find most compelling: "chain of miracles," the "miraculous," and the "miracle of Being," and "detecting this unexpectedly new." Citing a 1953 article, "Understanding and Politics," in *Partisan Review*, Ferry finds Arendt commenting that "newness is the real of the historian" because he deals with "events which always occur only once." The fault, he admits, is Heidegger's as much as Arendt's. Ferry suggests:

> Let us say for the moment that in Hannah Arendt, a student and disciple of Heidegger (even if this fact is disturbing because of Heidegger's political choices the fact remains inarguable), this new idea of history crystallized around the idea of action. (ibid., 5)

Under this phenomenological rubric, Ferry asks, "what would be the meaning of the 'banality of evil,'" made famous by Arendt, "if human actions are not credited to . . . the human will but only considered 'miracles of being'" (ibid., 7)?

At the other end of the critical spectrum are the works of John Gunnell, which analyze the emergence of the subfield of political theory and the role played by the "crisis" *mentalité* of the German émigrés in the United States, especially Arendt (Gunnell 1986, 99–117; 1993, 177–82, 196–97). Gunnell's approach, while contextualist and historical, is equally negative when it comes to determining the effect Heidegger's students have had on the discipline of political science. However, the effect Gunnell deplores is the complete opposite of that identified by Pangle and Ferry.

Instead of criticizing Arendt and her émigré colleagues for defending "moral relativism" and "nihilism," Gunnell accuses them of attacking American empiricism and pragmatism, and defending instead the morality of political life and the possibility of "normative" political thought.

> Although Arendt does not place as much pointed emphasis on the dilemma of relativism and the need to recover absolute values as Strauss and Voegelin do, relativism is a principal aspect of her analysis of world alienation. . . . Modern philosophy and modern science are, Arendt claims, founded on "Cartesian doubt" and have contributed to "modern nihilism." (Gunnell 1986, 111)

Gunnell argues that rather than eschewing the "tradition" of the Western tradition, Arendt and her cohort deconstruct its modern contradictions in order to restore its classical roots. In the face of ideology and terror, and in response to the stalemate of liberalism, Arendt searches for an alternative method of moral reasoning in phenomenological political thought. Gunnell cites Arendt's lament over the decline of the ability "to think in universal, absolute terms." The result is that the idea of a "transcendent world disappears." Instead of "Being we now find the concept of process." The life of the mind loses its "for its own sake" status and becomes instrumental to other ends on "the assumption that life, and not the world, is the highest good of man" (Gunnell's quotes from Arendt 1958a, 236–38, 246, 262, 266, 270).

Gunnell finds Arendt "caught between 'past and future' "—a mental location he does not trace to the dissertation but to the peculiar validation Arendt, Strauss, and Voegelin accord to their role as theorists. Terms such as "retheorization," "restoration," or Arendt's "thinking what we are doing" refer not only to the "restoration of political philosophy" as an academic pursuit but hint at a role for theory in legitimating political life. Yet, Gunnell argues, positioning of the thinker between past and future does not effectively link him or her to engagement in the public world. That is, Arendt's temporal metaphor, derived from Augustine, suggests both presence in and critical distance from political practice. "Arendt explains, and partly apologizes for, Heidegger's flirtation with the Nazi regime on the grounds that it was an example of thought being enticed into the alien world of practice where it could not authentically reside" (Gunnell 1986, 103). However much Arendt distanced herself geographically and academically, Gunnell concludes, "her deconstruction of the tradition of Western political thought closely parallels Heidegger's analysis of the historical fate of philosophy" (ibid., 113).

The Arendt-Heidegger connection has certainly borne strange academic fruit among American political scientists. Pangle, Ferry, and Gunnell are warriors in the academic, though no less ideological, battle over the link between philosophy and public life. All are critical of the effect of Heidegger's *Existenz* not only on Arendt as his student but, via her broad influence, on American political science from the late 1940s onward. Ironically, both Morganthau, an ardent admirer, and Pangle, Ferry, and Gunnell, ardent critics, agree that if Arendt's debt to Heidegger is considerable it is nonetheless well veiled. They also agree that the Arendt-Heidegger connection was a key factor in a devastating attack on "modernity" launched on both sides of the Atlantic. The reaction to the émigré's critique of the liberal underpinnings of modernity was not only the *gemeinschaft* impulse in political thought, but also a weakened linkage between liberal values and political practice in Atlantic culture.

Divided Paths: Radical Interpretation

Arendt's explicit task in 1929 was to expose the "heterogeneous" layers of Augustine's understanding of love by focusing on love of neighbor as the most "problematic." At the same time, the effect of the dissertation is to find a way out of Heidegger's world by locating points of exit and entry and by suggesting the possibility of "constituting" new worlds based on mutual *caritas*. Validating change as well as repetition, authenticity in both selfhood and community, and a "space" for judgment are her implicit agendas.

When questioned about her vantage point, Arendt confessed to being a "radical," employing a term rich with cultural meaning to the interwar generation in Europe and America. Martin Heidegger also utilized the term, but not as self-definition. It was his ontology of *Dasein* that was designated radical in order to distinguish it from the "tradition" of philosophy running from the Socratic Greeks through Kant. In the last years of the 1920s Arendt, together with a number of future distinguished theorists, attended Heidegger's lectures on "Being and Time," which were premised on his insistence that journeying to the root meaning of Being was a quintessential "radical" task for the "tradition." As a preliminary step, his *Sein und Zeit* lectures would "unevil" the *Existenz*, via *Dasein* (being-in-the-world), of the Being whose essence remains hidden. Elucidating the path to Being was the most important undertaking of "interpretation," since the tradition of philosophy is nothing more than the "universal phenomenological ontology . . . [which] takes its departure from the hermeneutic of *Dasein*." The authentically radical beginning is to "provide ontological grounds for ontology" (Heidegger 1962, 486–87).

In operational terms, the meaning of radicalism Arendt inherited from Husserl, Jaspers, and Heidegger was more of a hermeneutic than an *Existenz*, dedicated to removing textual obstacles to "interpretation" (ibid., 62). In the introductory lectures Heidegger speaks of a need to "grasp the problem of Being in a more radical way" (ibid., 46). To do so it is necessary to "destroy the ontological tradition," which has veiled its "fundamental question" even from itself.

Yet interpretation seemed doomed to chase its tail. Fundamental questions about Being-as-such were trapped in a philosophical discourse of traditional assumptions leading to traditional conclusions, which made it impossible to "come to terms with the things themselves." His phenomenological methodology was intended to bypass standard "technical devices" common to his favorite targets of criticism—realism and idealism—and instead "destroy the traditional content of ancient ontology" (ibid., 50, 57).

His goal was to arrive "at those primordial experiences in which we achieved our first ways of determining the nature of Being—the ways which have guided us ever since" (ibid., 44).

Arendt's lifelong struggle with the hermeneutical impasse was triggered by Heidegger's, and is directly reflected in the dissertation. Arendt had been drawn to him precisely because of his self-proclaimed apostasy, eschewing the constraints of professional philosophical "schools." Heidegger introduces his own phenomenological vantage point, which will "run parallel" to other more traditional ones.

> Adhering to the procedure which we have fixed upon . . . we must
> lay bare a fundamental structure in *Dasein;* Being in the world. . . .
> In the interpretation of *Dasein* this structure is something "a
> priori"; it is not pieced together, but is primordially and
> constantly a whole. . . . Our treatise does not subscribe to a
> "standpoint" or represent any special "direction"; for
> phenomenology is nothing of either sort, nor can it become so as
> long as it understands itself. (Ibid., 50, 65)

Arendt's introduction to her dissertation emphasizes parallel "trains of thought" in Augustine's work, which she will reproduce as three "conceptual contexts in which the problem of love plays a decisive role." Her equivalent of a priori structure is "the question of the meaning and importance of neighborly love," that is, "the question about the neighbor's relevance for the believer who is estranged from the world and its desires." She insists, however, that her vantage point "will never be an absolute critique from some fixed philosophical or theoretical standpoint" (A:033241–42). It derives instead from her choice of research question, and is meant to enhance rather than reduce the "disjointedness" of Augustine's own work. Heidegger's rendering of this tension between the essential question and the complexity of its manifestations was his statement that "the whole of this structure [of interpretation] always comes first; but if we keep this constantly in view, these items, as phenomena, will be made to stand out" (Heidegger 1962, 65).

The methodological unity resulting from a single *quaestio* gave meaning to the multiplicity of *Dasein*'s experience of "thrownness" in the world. Conceptually, however, from Arendt's perspective the problem of *Dasein*'s own self-understanding remained problematic. Heidegger tried to project a path out of *Dasein*'s "submission to the world" in "authentic repetition" of "the possibilities that have come down to one" as conscious choice. This "resoluteness" was to be distinguished from habitual dispersion in the "multiplicity of possibilities, comfortableness, shirking and taking things lightly" that is entailed in the "average public way of interpreting *Dasein* today" (ibid., 437, 435). Arendt turned Heidegger's repetition into Augustine's "imitation," defined it as the foundation of free choice "out of the world," and followed it with a "return" journey back to "community" in a world in which "new beginnings" ("natality") and "foundation" can break out of the hermeneutical trap, both in interpretation and in existence. The condition to be avoided is *habitus*, a term used by both Heidegger and Arendt. Arendt coopted the term from Augustine's analysis of the thoughtlessness of cupidity (see A:033320); later she would employ it to describe the Nazi mentality of Adolph Eichmann ("banality"). *Habitus* appears in the 1929 dissertation and remains unchanged in Arendt's 1960s revisions. Ironically, it was Heidegger who apparently surrendered to the "publicness" of Nazi Germany in the 1930s while his young student fled to France and finally to New York City.

Augustine's pilgrim soul "gathered his self from dispersion and the distraction of the world," much like Heidegger's *Dasein*. However, Arendt warned in 1929 that such withdrawal is not simply alienation but is based upon restructuring the basic *quaestio* (Heidegger's "problematic"). The flight from dispersion provokes further questions.

> For the more he withdrew into himself . . . the more he "became
> a question to himself" *[quaestio mihi factus sum]*. Hence, it is by no
> means a simple withdrawal . . . that Augustine opposes to the loss
> of self in dispersion and distraction, but rather a turning about of
> the question itself. (B:033149)

Heidegger begins his lectures with the same set of Augustinian citations to establish that "in determining itself as an entity," *Dasein* "somehow understands" itself "in the light of a possibility" (Heidegger 1962, 69). In Latin Augustine asks, *"Quid autem propinquius meipso mihi?"* ("But what is closer to me than myself?"). The answer, repeated by Heidegger, is *"ego certe laboro hic et laboro in meipso: factus sum mihi terra difficultatis et sudoris nimii"* ("Assuredly I labor here and I labor within myself; I have become to myself a land of trouble and inordinate sweat"). Though both Arendt and Heidegger mine the *Confessions*, particularly Book X, Heidegger confines his context to the *quaestio* of the earthly *Existenz*.

Arendt's dissertation takes broader aim. At first glance, Arendt's idea of *caritas* is immediately evocative of Heidegger's "care." But a closer look shows that for him, "care" is simply *Dasein*'s Being and does not entail natality. Care's ontological meaning is temporality and is disclosed as the "there of the world." The "ontological constitution of the world," which imposes the unity of significance, is grounded in *Dasein*'s "care-ful" relation to the world as a given. Other terms linked to "care" are "anxiety," "isolation," and "Death." They express *Dasein*'s links to, but alienation from, the "everyday-ness" of the "they" and the "publicness" of the World (ibid., 416–17).

Arendt proposes an alternative definition of care in the dissertation and revisits her premise of "love" repeatedly throughout her career. Central to its meaning is the possibility of "reconstituting" relationships through friendship, forgiveness, and social bonding. *Caritas*, which Arendt used either as "neighborly love," a mental "binding agent," or as the Creature's link to its Creator, is a "miracle" possible despite death, which is the habitu-ated impotence of the will and dispersion in worldliness. Observing Au-gustine's struggle to extract himself from the Greek heritage of ontological rationalism, Arendt applauded his shift to an "entirely different context." Stoic disengagement and Neoplatonic teleologies missed the drama of the human story. The field of memory, (internally) and human community (ex-ternally) facilitated a reversal of the ontology of death. In Augustine, Arendt found her central metaphor of "natality" embedded in the power of love *(caritas)* that, following Augustine, replicates creation in each new birth, each act of moral will, and in each new, contingent "constituting" of the world in action (see B:033157).

Confronted with death, Augustine is beset by fear and seeks perma-nence not in "repetition," in resolute acceptance of tradition, or even in an approach to existential Being. Rather, the soul withdraws inward to the "vast camps of memory" in desirous search for future happiness through a return to God as personal Creator. Arendt writes:

> This self is even more impenetrable than the "hidden works of nature." What Augustine expects of God is an answer to the ques-tion "Who am I?"—the certainty of which all previous philosophy had taken for granted . . . it was because of this new quest for the self that he finally turned to God, whom he did not ask to reveal to him the mysteries of the universe or even the per-plexities of Being. (B:033149)

Caritas is the "Creator's call for obedience in faith" and is therefore "the road which connects man and his ultimate goal." *Cupiditas*, its opposite, craves possession and permanence among the mutable objects of the tem-poral world out of fear of death and the loss of self. Augustine shifts ground from a passion-driven *caritas* that seeks a future union with the Creator to an "entirely different" *caritas* motivated by memory and gratitude for life itself (see B:033147). The *civitas terrena* is the initial setting for the drama of self-definition, but the scene soon changes to the *civitas Dei*. Arendt paraphrases Augustine's related *quaestio*, "Would it not then be better to love the world in *cupiditas* and be at home?" Augustine's negative response reflects "a deep dissatisfaction with what the world can give its lovers" (B:033143).

It is not the world that is evil but the cupidity the individual brings to it. "It is only by its pursuing what is outside that craving turns the neutral 'outside' into a 'world' strictly speaking, that is, into a home for man . . . in which the self gets lost" (B:033148) Evil consists in the habit of worldliness born out of a misdirected desire for permanence. Therefore, Arendt's *Dasein* looks not for Being but for the self in God. "Whoever wishes to say 'I am,' and to summon up his own unity and identity and pit it against the variety and multiplicity of the world, must withdraw into himself" (B:033149).

Withdrawal leads eventually to return, first to the remembered past of the creature-Creator relationship and finally to the "community" in the world, which can be reborn in freely willed acts of "natality." Heidegger attempted to extricate *Dasein* from the world, enough to produce at least a resoluteness toward appropriating its givenness. Arendt asks how Augustine can relate *caritas* as love of God to *caritas* as love of community: "How is it possible for their [our neighbors'] equality, based on the Christian sense of sin . . . to become obligatory for one gripped by faith? The creature knows itself dependent on the source, the epitome of being out of the world, that is, on the Creator. How can duties be derived from a past that is to be totally eradicated?" (A:033356).

The answer is as distinctly Arendt's as it is Augustine's. Fellowship in the *civitas Dei* on earth is not only the result of historical contiguity or genealogy but also of "indirect" love "for the sake of divine grace." "Mutual love . . . *(diligere invicem)* replaces mutual dependence." The human community "is no longer a mater of course." The "new society" becomes "explicit" and grounded in "imitation" of individual relationships to God (A:033361).

> Love extends to all people in the *civitas Dei*, just as interdependence extended equally to all in the *civitas terrena*. This love makes human relations definite and explicit. . . . Thus, love [in the *civitas Dei*] does not turn to humankind but to the individual, albeit every individual. In the community of the new society the human race dissolves into its many individuals. (A:033364)

Heidegger's multiplicity is transcended in Arendt's plural community. A precursor of her later concept of "plurality," Arendt's indirect community preserves the individual's singularity. "Any human community envisions the being of the human race, but not that of the individual" (A:033365). But the "very possibility of isolation" before God allows the freedom of detachment "from human history and from its irrevocable enchainment by generation" (A:033367). Free will calls the individual from the world and "severs his essential social ties," but the equality of common descent from Adam and of individual ties to God's creation is equally given. The equality of interdependence is transformed into the equality of "love of neighbor." The "coexistence" of human beings is no longer "everyday" but is "freely chosen" and entails obligations to the neighbor (A:033353).

Evidence of Arendt's linkage between 1929 and her American odyssey is clear (see chapter 2 above). Moving far from her mentor's preoccupations, Arendt entered the public world of academic political theory, taking Augustine with her. In 1951 *(Origins of Totalitarianism)* Arendt applied the *Existenz* of *caritas*-inspired new beginnings to political life. She raised the "radical" possibility of a totalitarian world by juxtaposing it to the counterworld of public life based in "natality." In closing her famous chapter "Ideology and Terror," which she added to the text in 1958, Arendt invokes Augustine directly. After lamenting the appearance of "an entirely new form of government" in totalitarianism brought on by "the crisis of our time," she balances her pessimistic prognosis with a more positive rendering of "new beginnings."

> But there remains also the truth that every end in history necessarily contains a new beginning: this beginning is the promise, the only "message" which the end can ever produce. Beginning, before it becomes a historical event, is the supreme capacity of man; politically it is identical with man's freedom. *Initium ut esset homo creatus est*—"that a beginning be made man was created," said Augustine. This beginning is guaranteed by each new birth; it is indeed everyman. (Arendt 1958b, 479)

In *The Human Condition*, also from 1958, Arendt presented a full exposition of the paradigmatic *polis* as a matter of collective power "between men" and then insisted on juridical "fences" between it and the "society" of economic production and class conflict. At the same time she began to revise the translation of her dissertation for publication.

In America, the *Existenz* veiled by the "tradition" of political thought was not Being but the *vita activa*. According to Arendt, the natality of political word and deed, not Parmenides' vision of Being, was "the greatest early experience" of the Greeks (Arendt 1953a, draft 2, p. 46). In her 1953 Christian Gaus lectures at Princeton, which were never published but later incorporated in *The Human Condition*, Arendt was again radically reconfiguring a Heideggerian theme. She asserted that what is concealed behind the tradition's discourse is not Being as the essence of *Dasein* but contingent political action as existential evidence of human collective power and natality.

> Political thought itself is older than our tradition of philosophy, which begins with Plato and Aristotle, just as philosophy is older and contains more than the Western tradition eventually accepted and developed. At the beginning, therefore, not of our political or philosophical history, but of our tradition of political philosophy stands Plato's contempt for Politics. (Ibid.)

Heidegger claimed that the "tradition" had forgotten its pre-Socratic vision of pure Being. His "problematic" is the concealed nature of Being in historicity and in human "everydayness." In the context of America, after war and Holocaust, Arendt used Heidegger's "destructive" method to define the modern dilemma as the concealed nature of freedom's essence in the politics of mass society. By privileging a vantage point "in but not of" the world, Arendt achieved an Archimedean point denied to Heidegger's *Dasein* because of its immersion in the "publicness" of the "they."

The emphasis the dissertation places on return, natality, and foundation signal Arendt's early interest in the moral dilemma of the observer with respect to the public world, even though there are no direct political references. The idea of founding new moral communities in the Germany of 1929, using Augustine's *civitas Dei* as a guide, led eventually to Arendt's expressly political natality of new "committees," "public spaces," and "soviets" in America. In Arendt's hands, the tradition's failure to understand Being became its failure to understand the phenomenology of creativity, spontaneity, and freedom.

Divided Paths: Memory as the Seat of Consciousness:

Augustine taught Arendt that "it is memory and not expectation (for instance, the expectation of death as in Heidegger's approach) that gives unity and wholeness to human existence" (B:033192). In memory the future flows through the present to the past (see B:033182–86). "Time for Augustine does not begin in the past in order to progress through the present into the future, but comes out of the future and runs, as it were, backward through the present and ends in the past" (B:033152). Augustine uses *memoria* to designate that "space" (*nunc stans* or *stans aeternitatis*) between past and future to which the creature retreats from the world, and defines space as "the seat

of consciousness." Heidegger's "clearing" or "path" is now Augustine's vantage point between past and future. Arendt's Augustine says that "when I
look for God or the happy life, I actually 'walk in the space of my memory
and I do not find [them] outside it.'" Memory "transforms the past into the
future possibility" and likewise "throws back" the creature from a future expectation of death to the past memory of happiness and of the Creator as its
source. (B:033183). "Only in referring back from mortal existence to the
immortal source of this existence does created man find the determinant of
his being" (B:033185). Remembrance, therefore, "is primarily recollection"
or "'collecting myself from dispersion,'" and means the same thing as "confession" (B:033184).

The contrast between Arendt's Augustinian continuum of the future
thrown back to the "aboriginal past" and Heidegger's parallel but distinct
understanding of time is significant.

> Only an entity which, in its Being, is essentially futural so that it is
> free for its death and can let itself be thrown back upon its factical
> "there" by shattering itself against death . . . can, by handing
> down to itself the possibility it has inherited, take over its own
> throwness and be in the moment of vision for "its time." (Heideg-
> ger 1962, 437)

In undated notes in the Library of Congress (Box 68) prepared for a series of
Yale lectures, it is interesting to observe Arendt selectively copying citations
from *Sein und Zeit*. She picks out Heidegger's statement that "the past in a
certain way arises from the future" (ibid., 326). But she also notes his comment that "we intentionally avoid the term, 'act'" (ibid., 347).

The full citation from Heidegger is even more illustrative of the contrast between their understandings of action in temporal context. To "take
action" must be interpreted broadly, Heidegger observed, and must include
"the passivity of resistance." Otherwise *Dasein* will be misunderstood "as
if resoluteness were a special way of behavior belonging to the practical
faculty as contrasted with one that is theoretical" (ibid.). Arendt took a
more radical position than her mentor. In Germany in 1929, just as later in
America, an *Existenz* built upon a division between consciousness and action
did not please her. For Arendt, to act in the world and to dwell in the space
of memory were both examples of contingent "natality" and denoted more
than simply "being in the Situation."

Arendt expressed her vantage point once again in 1946 when she wrote
"What Is Existenz Philosophy" for the "little" New York journal *Partisan
Review*. Distinguishing the *Existenz* from French existentialism, which

she quickly dismissed as a "French literary movement of the last decade," Arendt traced its German lineage, running from Schelling through Kierkegaard, Nietzsche, and Bergson to the postwar generation of Scheler, Husserl, Heidegger, and Jaspers. Classic philosophy had assimilated being to thought. Since Kant, however, a rupture had appeared and the attempts at repair had failed until the emergence of the *Existenz*.

In 1930 Arendt had described Augustine's philosophy of freedom as proceeding by means of a "detour through pietism" (Young-Bruehl, 1982, 81). In 1946 she would apply the metaphor to Husserl, who "sought to reestablish the ancient relation between Being and Thought which had guaranteed man a home in the world" by means of "detour through the intentional structure of consciousness." For Husserl "a reconstruction of the world from consciousness" would "equal a second creation." For in observing the contents of thought as the contents of reality, the world was no longer a "given" but rather "created by [man]" (Arendt 1946b, 36–37).

Although Augustinianism is not the occasion of her analysis, the methodological revisionism already evident in the 1929 dissertation becomes explicit in 1946. Modernity has produced a "feeling of homelessness in the world," Arendt claims. "Classicists," such as Husserl and Hofmannsthal, responded by trying to find "a home out of the world which has become alien," a substitute for the "being at home in the world" of the Greek *polis* (ibid., 36). However, Arendt argues, Husserl and his successor Heidegger were significant not only methodologically but also because they waged a battle against "historicism," which she understood as the entrapment of philosophy by its particular historical contexts. The *Existenz* became the philosophy of "the things in themselves"—phenomena experienced by human beings rather than products of "progress," historical flux, or the laws of history.

It would seem, therefore, that in tracing Arendt's turn, Pangle's discontent seems singularly misdirected. Not only did she consistently critique "historical or natural or biological or psychological flux" as the defining context for human existence, but she also rejected Heidegger's "nihilism." Indeed, the dissertation, with its themes of *caritas*, natality, foundations, and plurality within community, provides significant evidence of Arendt's early decision to travel by a different "thought train" toward the phenomenological horizon.

In her *Partisan Review* article, Arendt brought to the surface some of her earlier (implicit) disquiet with Heidegger's path. References to *Sein und Zeit* are amplified by references to *What Is Metaphysics?* Heidegger must be taken seriously, she warns, because his methodology proposes to negate a negation—the "destruction begun with Kant of the ancient concept of Being." Even if the result is not a new positive ontology, Heidegger's *quaestio* compels attention. Indeed, it may be that "no ontology in the traditional sense can be re-established" at all in the modern world. The void opens up beneath Heidegger's *Existenz* because

> to the question concerning the meaning of Being he has given the provisional answer . . . that the meaning of Being is temporality. With this he implied, and with his analysis of human reality . . . which is conditioned by death, he established, that the meaning of Being is nothingness. (Ibid., 46)

The thought that Being is nothing enables man to "imagine himself," to "relate himself to Being that is given, no less than the Creator before the creation of the world," which was created *ex nihilo*. The givenness of the world is resolutely defied by embracing its source as a void. Man becomes a Creator trapped in his creation. "This is the real reason why in Heidegger the Nothing suddenly becomes active and begins 'to nothing.' " In man, as previously in God, essence and existence coincide—but in a worldly entrapment (ibid., 47).

The vantage point for *Dasein*'s self-consciousness collapses. The power of action and creativity is replaced by anxiety and care. "Heidegger's philosophy is the first absolutely and uncompromisingly this-worldly philosophy," asserts Arendt. Because it is based on "homelessness and fearfulness," it cannot reconstruct a positive ontology (ibid., 49). The result is "modern nihilism" that, contrary to Pangle, Arendt judges to be an ironic "revenge" of the very tradition that phenomenological radicals sought to overturn (ibid., 47).

As might be anticipated, Arendt's *Partisan Review* critique of Heidegger's nihilism and will-oriented *Existenz* was not her last word on the subject. In 1971, four years before her death, Arendt composed a surprisingly celebratory retrospective on Heidegger's life and works, "Martin Heidegger at Eighty." In a dramatic "return" to her own origins as well as his, though with no direct reference to the dissertation, Arendt began with one of her favorite Platonic utterances: "The beginning is also a god; so long as he dwells among men, he saves all things." Her point was that the beginning of Heidegger's "woodpath" or "trail marks" was not a private event, for his public life as a teacher of "extraordinary influence" was already well established by 1927 when *Sein und Zeit* was published. Arendt's notes "something strange" about it, "stranger perhaps than the fame of Kafka or Braque and Picasso," who were also "unknown to what is commonly understood as the public," but who nonetheless had an "extraordinary influence" in the intellectual community (Arendt 1978a, 293).

Arendt definitely did not consider herself one of the "common" public, but she nevertheless understood her choice of Heidegger as a teacher to be a public statement of discontent with the academic status quo. She says that the students who flocked to Marburg did not do so in order to join a secret "circle," but to bear witness to a "widespread discontent with the academic enterprise of teaching and learning." Heidegger promised them they could do so by moving "away from theories, away from books," to philosophy "as a rigorous science (ibid., 294). Other students would follow different paths to sciences, among them Horkheimer and Adorno in Frankfurt. But for Arendt and her cohort, only Heidegger could preside over the funeral of "the tradition" and the coming of "dark times" (ibid., 295). He did so from within the traditional itself "as a credit to philosophy, a tribute" from one who had a "share" in its collapse but who "thought [it] through to its end" (ibid., 297), and did so in the name of thought itself.

Jaspers is entirely absent from this retrospective ode to the German masters of the 1920s. In 1971 Arendt did not hesitate to compare Heidegger to Plato and Aristotle because of his commitment to "passionate thinking" and "pathos." For Heidegger, "thinking and aliveness become one" because of the "simple fact" of "being born-in-the-world." Each of his works "reads as though he were starting from the beginning" (ibid., 297, 298). Because constant revision is implied, he avoids the trap of system building in which thinking is "measured . . . by its results." Terms like "restlessness," "beginning ever anew," "retrogression," and "imminent criticism" are cited, as if Arendt were attempting to rescue her mentor from the unfortunate consequences of his teachings and actions.

Arendt identifies Heidegger's abode as the realm of thought and describes the phenomenology of his *nunc stans* in terms derived from the dissertation and suggestive of the Gifford Lectures soon to come.

> This addition seems to be decisive for reflecting on who Martin Heidegger is. For many . . . are acquainted with thinking and the solitude bound up with it; but clearly, they do not have their residence there. When wonder at the simple overtakes them and, yielding to the wonder, they engage in thinking, they know they have been torn out of their habitual place in the continuum of occupations in which human affairs take place, and will return to it in a little while. The abode of which Heidegger speaks lies there-

fore, in a metaphorical sense, outside the habitations of men.
(Ibid., 299)

Problems arose, however, when Heidegger attempted "to change his residence," to leave behind the world of passionate thought and "get involved in
the world of human affairs," where "he was served somewhat worse than
Plato because the tyrant and his victims were not located beyond the sea, but
in his own country" (ibid., 302). Arendt's awkward phrasing does not iden-
tify a precise agent of moral responsibility either in Heidegger's temporary
change of address, or in Heidegger himself. Instead, she says that the shock
of the "collision" between his philosopher's sensibilities developed "out of
the world" and the "reality of the Gestapo cellars and the torture-hells"
after "ten short hectic months thirty-seven years ago drove him back to his
residence," where he proceeded to "settle in his thinking what he had experienced" (ibid., 303).

   In an extensive footnote, replete with poetry, Arendt elaborates her ex-
oneration of her mentor and lover as a philosopher temporarily lost in the
world. She gently faults Heidegger for a "misunderstanding" of National
Socialism, which he shared with "so many other German intellectuals" who
never read *Mein Kampf* but instead preferred the Italian futurists, "who
indeed had some connection with fascism as distinct from National Socialism." As Arendt portrays him, Heidegger lacked a relevant reading list and
therefore was unprepared to appreciate the existential reality surrounding
him. The impulse to inappropriately intellectualize the Holocaust, Arendt
insists, continues today as the moral equivalent of Heidegger's "error" of
an earlier time: too many "so-called scholars" find Plato, Luther, Hegel,
Nietzsche, Junger, Stefan George, and Heidegger more to their taste than
the historical evidence of Nazism. Nevertheless, Arendt's Heidegger "took
more risks" and "corrected his own 'error' more quickly and more radically
than many of those who later sat in judgment over him" (ibid., 302). His was
a regrettable, but forgivable, "déformation professionelle" that leads those
whose abode is thought to admire tyrants. Apparently, "wondering at the
simple" and "taking up this wondering as one's permanent abode" (ibid.,
301) leads to strikingly simpleminded conclusions about the connections
between thought and action.

   The subtext of Arendt's ode to Heidegger is in fact the problem of
Augustine's *nunc stans*, or the "place of stillness" where thinking abides. In
1971 Arendt spun her own Penelope's web—a modern cave analogy de-
signed to recuse Heidegger, though not excuse him from the implications of

his philosophy both for the "tradition" and for the political world. Since Being has itself "withdrawn" from the cave, leaving shadows on the wall, the thinker must withdraw inward to an "abode" where the world is distant but Being is imminent. For Heidegger, as for Arendt and Augustine, the next step of return would prove most problematic.

Heidegger made thinking "come to life again" by unearthing "the cultural treasures of the past," which have been "made to speak." "Nearness-remoteness . . . presence-absence . . . concealing-revealing" pervade Heidegger's work, according to Arendt (ibid., 300). In fact, since these qualities of being "in but not of" the political world are characteristic of her own work as well, Augustine was a particularly apt starting point for Arendt's struggle with her Heideggerian heritage. A return to the world as a reconstituted community, and even as a community of fallen humans, was morally entailed in the relationship between Augustine's creature and Creator. Did Heidegger manage to achieve a credible "return" to the world, not as a "political" thinker or even as rector but as the founder of a philosophic *civitas Dei?* Arendt's metaphorical view of Heidegger's vantage point is suggestive.

> The *hidden king* reigned therefore in the realm of thinking, which,
> although it is completely of this world, is so concealed in it that
> one can never be quite sure whether it exists at all; and still its
> inhabitants must be more numerous than is commonly believed.
> For how, otherwise, could the unprecedented, often under-
> ground, influence of Heidegger's thinking . . . be explained,
> extending as it does beyond the circle of students and disciples
> and beyond what is commonly understood by philosophy.
> (Ibid., 295–96)

Heidegger's philosophy itself did *not* entail founding new communities, taking public action in the old *civitas terrena*, or in any way moving beyond the *nunc stans* of thought. His "authenticity" required simply that *Dasein* hear the "call" of "understanding," and acknowledge inevitable "anxiety" and separation from the world of "they." By contrast, in her dissertation Arendt fastened on Augustine's requirement that the divided will, liberated from impotence by *caritas*, reconstitute the world as a community of "neighbors" bound by personal grace and collective values. Equally significant is the fact that the protagonist in her odyssey is not *Dasein* as an exemplar of Being, but a particular philosopher-bishop who exemplifies the human condition in "dark times." Arendt confronts good and evil through the tragic vision of a public figure, a Christianized Roman living at the geographical periphery and historical end of the Roman *res publica*.

Arendt's critics, such as Pangle and Gunnell, note her preference for individual "heroes" who together constitute the *gemeinschaft* (Pangle 1988, 50; Gunnell 1986, 108). Arendt's "founders" occupy a privileged position accorded to idealized action and actors. But while Pangle worries that Arendt is too drawn to the Jacobin mentality as a result, Gunnell reads her heroes as philosophers who are deluded that they might be kings.

> She still maintains the assumption of the privileged place of thought and mind, really of the academic intellectual in the modern world where ideas have become ideology. The crisis (of freedom in modernity) has freed thought . . . for a "critical interpretation of the past" that may save the present. (Gunnell 1986, 106)

The problem of the source and status of thought, both for thinkers and the "masses," remained with Arendt throughout her professional life, fueling charges of elitism, amorality, and a historical belief in the central role of philosophical discourse in cultural change. Arendt was particularly appalled that Eichmann understood himself to be a Kantian "little man," since he was neither a philosopher nor politically inconsequential. Capitulating to the world of *das Man* or the "they," and using philosophy as an instrumental justification, was clearly a subversion of moral reasoning and, significantly, a corruption of Kant's philosophy. As she argued in her dissertation and more concretely in the Eichmann study, surrender to habituated behavior, and the resulting avoidance of responsibility, define the death of free will and moral judgment—Augustine's sin of *cupiditas*. It was not love of the world as such which was wrong, but the resulting failure to "think what we are doing" or failing to do, as a result.

In America, reacting to the dismay of the Jewish community over her reportage on Eichmann, Arendt insisted on her own *nunc stans* and, by implication, reiterated the idea of *caritas* she had developed in 1929. Her understanding of the role of love in binding individuals to their communities was not the *gemeinschaft*-laden version of the later Heidegger or the death-driven one of the earlier Heidegger; it was also not the classically Christian version later espoused by her friend Wystan Auden. What she did *not* intend by "love" was made very clear in correspondence with Gershom Scholem.

> I am not moved by any "love" [of the Jewish people] . . . for two reasons: I have never in my life "loved" any people or collective,

neither the German people, nor the French, nor the American, nor the working class. . . . Secondly this "love of the Jews" would appear to me, since I am Jewish . . . rather suspect. I cannot love myself or anything which I know is part and parcel of my own person. (Arendt 1974a)

In the *Partisan Review* article, in her 1971 tribute to Heidegger, in the Christian Gaus lectures, and throughout her career, Arendt returned to the antitraditional genealogy of the *Existenz*. In 1953, in an unpublished letter to Dolf Steinberger preserved among her correspondence in the Library of Congress, Arendt repeated comments she had made in other, more public venues. The occasion was a discussion of Heidegger's *Introduction to Metaphysics*. "You accuse Heidegger and his often desperate willfulness of those exaggerations which we find in their clearest and most evil form in Nietzsche," she argued. His efforts were desperate because he was not altogether successfully "using the conceptual means of tradition to write against tradition." Like a frightened child, asking questions of the icy silence, Heidegger "beg[an] to talk too loudly" and took up "whistling in the dark." Inevitably, "wrong notes slip in." Arendt insisted that Heidegger's "attempt" took "tremendous courage" and "deserves our respect," though she herself remained silent about the substance or consequences of the Heideggerian project (Arendt 1953c).

Yet in the dissertation and in her subsequent politicized discourse of alienation and engagement, Arendt would break new ground in a phenomenology of "constituted" worlds, displaying her own courageous resolve. In Arendt's works the "prepolitical" and the "pretheological" are the existential context for both action and judgment in the public world. *Caritas* bridges not only the "monstrosity" of a will divided against itself, but also the realms of human experience. *Caritas*, like power in Arendt's explicitly political terminology, negates the negations of nihilism and sovereignty. The negative social phenomenology of modernity—materialism, mass society, and violence—that besets the city of man can be reconstituted in a temporal city of *caritas*.

Divided Paths: The Return

In her 1973 Gifford Lectures, which would be published posthumously as *The Life of The Mind*, Arendt returns to her own beginnings. Rephrasing Augustine's *quaestio* from the dissertation in terms appropriate to another age of public moral quandary, Arendt returns to the *Existenz*, at least in the introduction. The Eichmann trial presented the problem of "thoughtless-ness" as an operational definition of evil and, for Arendt, suggested a parallel to the dichotomy of habituated *cupiditas* versus freely willed *caritas*. The *vita activa* forces upon the thoughtful observer, as well as upon the actor, the pressing need to repair the ontological rupture Husserl and Heidegger had identified. Citing the twelfth-century Augustinian Hugh of St. Victor, Arendt states the problem: "the active way of life is 'laborious,' the contem-plative one in the 'desert'; the active one is devoted to 'the necessity of one's neighbor,' the contemplative one to the vision of God" (Arendt 1978b, 1:6). In the dissertation *caritas* is a bridging, enabling power that links the self to God, to temporality through memory, and to community in plurality. In the Gifford Lectures, Hugh of St. Victor's "necessity of one's neighbor" in the "desert" of the world are really Augustine's terms pulled from the dissertation. However, unlike the dissertation and the *The Human Condition*, Augustinianism is used in the lectures to validate traditional polarities be-tween mind and the world, and between the impulses of willing and not willing. *Caritas* heals the divisions of the mind and facilitates moral choice but is not defined as "love of neighbor"

Arendt's 1974 study of the "life" of the mind explored its encapsulation rather than its active role in the foundation of community. A parallel 1974 publication, written for a book of tributes to Auden, spoke again of old themes: love, praise, and memory. She had met Auden in 1958, at a time when she had completed *The Human Condition* and the new chapter on "Ide-ology and Terror" for *Origins of Totalitarianism*. Arendt celebrated the "mys-teries of language" unveiled by poets like Auden, and Heidegger, whose works "disappear[ed] in a cloud of banality" when they were "wrenched from their original [textual] abode" (Arendt 1974c, 181). Goodness for Auden was "an irresistible inclination" resulting from a late conversion to Christianity. Auden came to politics out of love for *"les malheureux,"* not out of "any need for action, for public happiness, or the desire to change the world" (ibid., 184). Like Robespierre, therefore, he was a revolutionary of a dangerous sort. Yet his Christianity took him "out of the world" and never facilitated total reentry. Rather than change the world, Auden praised it. Still, his praise was a form of defiance, since it pitched "itself against all that is most unsat-isfactory in man's condition on this earth" in order to suck "strength out of the wound." As Arendt paraphrased Auden, the gods give men unhappiness "so that they may be able to tell the tales and sing the songs" (ibid., 186).

Arendt's ode to Auden interwove themes of the "monstrosity" of the will divided against itself, of the healing power of *caritas*, and of the *nunc stans* of memory and the *poesis* of praise. All come directly from the dissertation through the refractive prisms of her late 1950s and early 1960s work on the *vita activa* and *vita contempliva*. Similarly, in the Thinking section of the Gifford Lectures, Arendt observes that Augustine provides the best description of the inner vision of the mind, "the vision which was without when the sense was formed by a sensible body" and which "is succeeded by a similar vision within" (Arendt 1978b, 1:77). What is "decisive," she argues citing Augustine, is "what remains in the memory" as an image of what is external, which gives rise to "something else when we remember." This, literally, is imagination and "is in no way different from men's need to tell the story of some happening . . . or to write poems about it." Thinking based on "withdrawal from the world of appearances" is presented in Augustinian terms and frames of reference. It is implicitly comparable to the journey of the creature to the Creator and the return to the reconstituted world. The journey takes place in the *nunc stans* of *memoria*, which in the dissertation Arendt had termed the "seat of consciousness." The *nunc stans*, she says here, is always "implied" in all thinking (ibid., 1:78).

In the following paragraphs, Heidegger himself returns. As Sheldon Wolin remarked in his review of *The Life of the Mind* in the *New York Review of Books*, Heidegger's "presence haunts the pages of these volumes." But this time, the ghost is kept at arm's length. Arendt does not repeat the very positive view expressed in "Martin Heidegger at Eighty" (1971), probably, in part, because the occasion is not that of a Festschrift. Wolin considers *The Life of The Mind* an "important work," but he struggles to "find the proper terms for understanding it without glossing over its faults." He notes Arendt's return to Augustine, reminding his readers that this is "less surprising than [it] seem[s] at first glance: Augustine, for example, had been the subject of her dissertation." Duns Scotus, too, Wolin notes, was the subject of her mentor's first publication. Arendt's final work is so full of wonderful "excesses—an outrageous scope, magisterial tone, peremptory judgment and occasional mockery of 'professional thinkers,'" says Wolin, that she herself "has no place to hide" (Wolin 1978, 16).

Indeed, Arendt had always preferred to hide in plain sight, meaning precisely what she said and no more. In *The Life of The Mind*, Heidegger is summoned up only to reinforce the "out of order" nature of thought that is inherently "contrary to the human condition" of "sheer thereness." Her last public word on Heidegger is a careful comment noting the "fallacies and absurdities" of "two-world theories" and of the "very curious notion" of ancient lineage that there is an "affinity between death and philosophy." The Heidegger of *Sein und Zeit*, she reminds her readers, "treated anticipation of death" as the necessary and sufficient condition for achieving authenticity of selfhood and liberation from the "They." In 1929, Arendt countered with the paradigm of *caritas* as grace-empowered free will. The resulting "natality" in mind and action became the only truly liberating outcome of death-driven anxiety. In the 1974 Gifford Lectures, Arendt obliquely referenced both her own 1929 critique of Heidegger and the irony of his later role as Nazi rector of Freiberg, noting that he seemed "quite unaware of the extent to which this doctrine sprang . . . from the opinion of the Many" (Arendt 1978b, 1:80).

The dissertation became a bridge between her future and her past, between Heidegger's suspicion of *das Man* and the world of the "they" and her own growing sense of being "in" but not completely "of" the public world of late modernity. The intersection of Heidegger, her study of Augustine, and her thoughts on publicness was already on her mind in 1930, long before emigration and the Holocaust. That year Arendt published a review essay on Karl Mannheim's *Ideology and Utopia*, one of the most controversial books of 1929. In it she explores the emerging field of "sociology" and praises Mannheim for his attempt to apply "critical theory" to the problem of ideas in historical context. Mannheim, unlike Lukács, searches for "reality," not "socio-economic interest," as the "foundation of theory." But though he argues that "every intellectual position" is expressive of socio-economic positioning, he himself "adopts none of these positions." Inadvertently, therefore, Mannheim's sociology "has something to say to philosophy," which is also searching for a reality beyond or inherent in the everydayness of existence. "The spiritual" retains its significance, Arendt suggests, by virtue of the positioning of the social scientific observer. This is Heidegger's and Jaspers's terrain, but Mannheim uses a different map.

> In philosophic terms, the problem which lies at the heart of Mannheim's sociology is the uncertain nature of the relationship of the ontic to the ontological. Where philosophy inquires after the "being of the essent" (*Sein des Seinden*, Heidegger) or the self-understanding of 'existence' (*Existenz*, Jaspers), in its detachment from everyday life, sociology, by contrast, inquires after the "essent" which is the basis for this "existential interpretation." It is interested precisely in what philosophy judges to be irrelevant. (Arendt 1930, 197)

Arendt faults Mannheim mainly for posing an absolute duality between "utopian consciousness" which achieves "freedom from 'public existence'" through transcendence, and "ideology," which is "existentially bound" to the particulars of historical circumstance and action but proposes to alter them radically. Mannheim, as Arendt reads him, loses his neutrality and clearly prefers the contextual rootedness of the ideology because "it is always inextricably bound to community" (ibid., 205). For Arendt, however, this option entails an inevitable "distrust of the spirit" and preference for a "collective subject" to which "the individual is not only relegated but toward which he "exists in a state of separation" because he is "no longer in tune with social existence." The "actual historical world," stimulates "detachment" as a reaction (ibid., 204).

Returning to the dissertation, completed a year earlier, Arendt suggests that there is a "third possibility" derived from Christianity.

[It] was a crucial element in the formation of Christian love in ancient Christianity: this is the possibility of living in the world while believing that Christian love cannot be realized on earth. . . . Such a detachment from the world does not lead to a desire to change it; yet it is also no flight from the historical world. (Ibid., 205)

Her example, in this instance, is Saint Francis of Assisi. Max Weber is also summoned to establish the point that a public ideology, like capitalism, "arises from a particular form of solitude." That is, "a state of bondedness, originally religious in nature (Protestantism), creates a world of everyday life which leaves little room for the unique individual." By implication, there are other varieties of Christian religious experience that can legitimate the individual and public worlds simultaneously. Arendt concludes that when the "religious bond," the "third possibility," has lost its legitimacy, the "public sphere becomes so powerful" that what she terms solitude (the *nunc stans* of the dissertation) is possible only in alienation and "flight." "Nowadays we are perhaps so much at the mercy of this public state of existence that even the possibility of our detachment from it can only be defined indirectly as 'being free from it'" (ibid., 206).

In analyzing Mannheim, Arendt equates the public realm with the "economic power structure," not with either the social or public realms of *The Human Condition* or with the *civitas* of her dissertation. Mannheim's world, in other words, looks like Heidegger's. Its dominance forces "the spirit" to "become 'ideological superstructure.'" In such a world the individual's meaning is "based on economic status rather than tradition" and so, concludes Arendt, "he becomes homeless." Out of this sensation, which in the dissertation she called "being lost in a desert," comes the possibility of thought and of a question. The stance of the questioner is that of the theorist who asks about "the justness and meaning of social position." However, the question of meaning itself, Arendt reminds Mannheim, "is far older than capitalism. It arises from an earlier experience in history of human uncertainty in the world—from Christianity" (ibid., 207).

4 / Jaspers: Arendt and *Existenz* Philosophy

Hannah Arendt had the good fortune to study with two of the most prominent philosophers of the twentieth century—Martin Heidegger and Karl Jaspers. She also took courses with Edmund Husserl. Once at the University of Heidelberg, she wrote her dissertation on Augustine under Jaspers's direction. A latecomer to academic philosophy, Jaspers was just beginning to write his three-volume masterpiece *Philosophy* (1931) when Arendt began her studies with him. He greatly influenced her intellectual questions and concerns. Moreover, the community of scholars and friends that she found in Heidelberg provided a marked change from the year of relative isolation she spent at Marburg during her studies with Heidegger.

Heidegger is a giant among the major philosophers of the twentieth century. Arendt's development of *Existenz* philosophy, with its theme of *caritas* and the journey "out of the world" impelled by anxiety over death, is in many ways a direct reflection of Heidegger's project (Boyle 1987; see also chapter 3 above). However, she was also, if less visibly, a student of Karl Jaspers, whose life-affirming orientation won out over Heidegger's "death-driven" vision of *Dasein*. Arendt's understanding of temporality and "encompassing" are clear echoes of her collaboration with Jaspers.

What began as a fruitful association of professor and student evolved into a life-long friendship that lasted until Jaspers's death in 1969. From the beginning of their association—first in Germany, then while Arendt was in Paris and finally in the United States—Arendt and Jaspers conducted a frequent, lively, and multifaceted correspondence whose course was broken only during World War II (Arendt and Jaspers 1992). Shared philosophical and political concerns, mutual respect and affection, and what Jaspers called "loving struggle" bound them together in abiding friendship.

After the publication of *Eichmann in Jerusalem*, Jaspers's friendship provided Arendt welcome support in the midst of the storm of controversy. Jaspers painstakingly reviewed the introduction Arendt wrote for the German edition of *Eichmann* and promised her that he would write his own book about the Eichmann affair after her German edition had been published. By 1967 it became clear that Jaspers did not have the strength to complete the task, and Arendt released him from his promise. That same year Jaspers had published what was to be his farewell to politics, *The Future of Germany*, for which Arendt wrote the foreword.

Arendt's dissertation set the stage for their friendship and professional association. Even though Arendt did not directly acknowledge it, the influence of her mentor and dissertation director can be seen throughout the work, both in her approach and in her thematic concerns.

Arendt's approach to Augustine's thinking shows more than a passing reference to Jaspers's new *Existenz* philosophy. While setting out to explore one of the central concepts of Augustine's philosophy—love—Arendt would in the process reveal and elucidate the tensions and oppositions in Augustine's thinking. Both Parts I and II of the dissertation come to a close with the tensions laid bare but not meditated or resolved in any fundamental way. Arendt describes this approach in the introduction as an effort to "interpret even seemingly heterogeneous statements and trains of thought in the direction of a substantially common base. In this attempt, the substantial base itself may come to manifest heterogeneous intentions" (A:033243). Arendt's effort to seek a common base owes much to Jaspers, as does her refusal to force an alien resolution onto the tensions in Augustine's thought. In acknowledging these oppositions in Augustine, Arendt writes at the end of her introduction that "we must let the contradictions stand as what they are, make them understood as contradictions, and grasp what lies beneath them" (A:033248).

Other parallels with Jaspers are apparent. Arendt begins Part I of her work by describing love as appetite, proceeds to examine the twofold expression of love as *caritas* and *cupiditas*, and then elucidates the order of love. From the perspective of the order of love, Augustine's emphasis on the Christian commandment to "love one's neighbor as oneself" founders and cannot bear the full weight of meaning with which Augustine endows it in other contexts. In Parts II and III of the dissertation, Arendt then takes up the issue of love, in particular love of neighbor in other Augustinian contexts, and proceeds to elucidate and examine them. Arendt's approach of starting with a description of experience, moving along the path of exploration and analysis to see where it leads, and then beginning the process anew has much in common with Jaspers's philosophical project. For him, the task of philosophy is not to set out a complete system of knowledge and reality, but to engage in the process of illumination and disclosure that often

reveals oppositions, contradictions, limits, and boundaries, and to share
these philosophical reflections through communication.[1]

Jaspers's influence on his student can be seen not only in Arendt's approach to philosophy, but in the concepts she chose to examine in Augustine. Her focus on the human states of freedom, responsibility, love, fear,
guilt, sinfulness, redemption, and death clearly reflects Jaspers's concern to
give a philosophical account of the radical finitude and precariousness (and
at the same time the fundamental *givenness*) of human life. Jaspers calls these
states "limit situations" and describes them as follows:

> Situations such as: that I am always in situations, that I cannot live
> either without struggle and without suffering, that I ineluctably
> take guilt upon myself, that I must die—these I call limit situa-
> tions. They do not change except in their appearance; as applied
> to our existence they possess finality. We cannot give an over-view
> of them; confined within our existence we see nothing else behind
> them. They are like a wall against which we butt, against which
> we founder. They cannot be changed by us but merely clarified.
> (Jaspers 1970, 78)

Augustine's thinking lends itself particularly well to the *Existenz* approach Arendt learned from her mentors, especially Jaspers. Using love as
the focal point, she explores man's situation in the world, including both his
extramundane source and destiny. She also explores man's four basic relationships: to God, to the world, to himself, and to his neighbor. One's relationship to one's neighbor, in the context of Christian ambivalence toward
the *civitas terrena*, is the fundamental *quaestio* which drives Arendt's exploration of Augustinian *caritas*.

The Encompassing

One of Jaspers's central concepts is what he terms "the Encompassing" *(das
Umgreifende)*, which he first fully articulated in *Reason and Existenz* (1935).
There he writes:

---

1. Elisabeth Young-Bruehl calls this exploration "spatial tracing" (Young-Bruehl 1982,
490). See also Kurt Hoffman, who writes: "Since knowledge for him [Jaspers] is always a quest
that arrives only at intermediary stations, never at the end, fully determinate concepts are often
dispensed with in his philosophy and hence, quite purposely, the sharp clarity of a system
that uses determinate concepts and a strictly univocal terminology is not aimed at" (Hoffman
1957, 96).

> We always live and think within a horizon. But the very fact that it
> is a horizon indicates something further which again surrounds
> the given horizon. From this situation arises the question of the
> Encompassing. The Encompassing is not a horizon within which
> every determinate mode of Being and truth emerges for us, but
> rather that within which every particular horizon is enclosed as in
> something absolutely comprehensive which is no longer visible as
> a horizon at all. (Jaspers 1955, 52)

According to Jaspers there are two modes of the Encompassing: "either as
Being itself, in and through which we are—or else as the Encompassing,
which we ourselves are, and in which every mode of being appears to us."
Jaspers calls these modes "two opposing perspectives." In doing so he attempts to overcome Kantian epistemological and ontological dualism by
positing the oppositional as well as the interlocking and interpenetrating
nature of these two modes. The philosophical temptation is to make the
Encompassing into a definite object of our experience instead of considering "the whole as the most extreme, self-supporting ground of Being,
whether it is Being in itself, or Being as it is for us." (ibid.).

The dissertation provides evidence of both linguistic and conceptual
similarities between Jaspers's notion of the Encompassing and Arendt's own
use of the term. In the German text of the dissertation Arendt employs three
different words—*das Umschliessende, das Umfassende,* and *das Umgreifende*—
all of which are translated as "the Encompassing." Arendt is here drawing
on Jaspers's mode of the Encompassing as "Being as such" or "the ground of
Being." Clear connections exist between Jaspers's concept and Arendt's use
of phrases like "the 'well-ordered man' who fits himself into the encompassing." (A:033311). Arendt notes that "in this view Being is equated with the
universe and is the encompassing whole where time is not" (B:033196).
Again, the " 'end' is simultaneously the source, the encompassing being, and
eternity as such" (A:033311). Hints of Jaspers's other mode of the Encompassing can be detected in the way Arendt presents Augustine's understanding of the human being's relationship to God (especially in the theological
sense) as creature to Creator. Here the case can be made for a conceptual similarity between the way in which Arendt via Augustine understands
man's true being as ultimately grounded in God (creature in Creator) and
Jaspers's mode of the Encompassing understood as consciousness in which I
understand myself as transcending ordinary, empirical existence.

Jaspers's mode of the Encompassing appears in the dissertation as Augustine's notion of man grounded in God's immutable and eternal Being

(A:033312–13). Full understanding of the individual's being results only from an arduous process fraught with risks. Arendt's Augustine requires the Christian believer to question himself out of this world ("I have become a question to myself"), and in so doing to find his true source and destiny. Analogously, the *Existenz* philosopher engages in genuine thinking about the Encompassing "without losing himself in the void of the mere universal of the understanding, in the meaningless facticity of empirical existence, or in some empty beyond" (Jaspers 1955, 76). In Arendt's view, Augustine's effort is simultaneously both otherworldly and of this world, so that even the Christian who has effected the "transit out of this world" can discover a basis for human community in humanity's "common descent from Adam." For Jaspers, the philosopher's task is less riddled with ambiguity: "Man can seek the path of his truth in unfanatical absoluteness, in a decisiveness which remains open" (ibid.).

Arendt's use of terms that hark back to Jaspers's notion of the Encompassing can be seen in all layers of the text and throughout the history of its revisions: first in the original German version, then in the unedited English translation (Copy A), and then in the material Arendt edited in the late 1950s/early 1960s (Copy B). A few examples from each layer will suffice to illustrate the case.

First, in Part II, chapter 1 of the German original, Arendt uses Jaspers's term *das Umgreifende* to refer to the universe as the "encompassing whole": "The whole is by definition the totally encompassing and as such is indifferent to its parts. . . . In this view Being is equated with the universe and is the encompassing whole *[das Umfassende und Umgreifende]* where time is not" (B:033195–96). Second, references to the encompassing are simply translated as such and appear in the sections of the English translation that Arendt did not revise; for example, references to "encompassing being, . . . eternity as such," and "beginning and end are no longer absolutely separated but have become identical in the concept of the encompassing" (A:033313). Arendt also writes about God as the encompassing: "The Creator, as encompassing eternal Being, no longer determines only the beginning and the end of the creature's life" (A:033324). Third, in the sections of the dissertation Arendt revised, several changes occur: Arendt deletes one parenthetical reference to "the encompassing pure and simple" (A:033394) while adding four new references to the encompassing that did not appear in the German original. These four additional references occur on two consecutive pages of the revised version (Copy B) where Arendt is discussing Augustine's indebtedness to the Greek notion of Being and his efforts to understand evil within that ontological framework: "That person is wicked who tries in vain to escape the predetermined harmony of the whole. It is the structure of this all-encompassing harmony/that as the 'eternal law is impressed upon us.'" Further, in discussing the relationship between temporal and eternal law, Arendt adds that Augustine "does not necessarily think of God as the eternal lawgiver, but rather that the laws determining the motions and actions of the parts are necessarily derived from the law of the encompassing whole" (B:033196–97). Then Arendt adds further reflections on Augustine's deep reliance on Greek ontology, which also did not appear in the German original:

> It is difficult to overestimate the enormous influence this con-
> cept of Being as the all-encompassing universe exerted on
> Augustine's thought. This is most manifest in passages in which
> the perfection of man or other created things is derived from the
> Creator and not from Being as such. Even in such an obviously
> Christian context, the other strictly "Greek" thought echoes
> through. (B:033197)

Here Arendt uses the term, "encompassing," to elucidate the Greek ontological influences on Augustine's thinking even when he is developing an argument within a Christian framework. The twentieth-century concept is being fitted to ancient Greek ontology in order to clarify the thinking of the Christian Church father of late antiquity. That Arendt was influenced by Jaspers's *Existenz* philosophy in the late 1920s when she was writing the dissertation is clear; what was not so clear, until the layers of the dissertation text were sorted out, was that, instead of repudiating this early influence, Arendt continued to use *Existenz* language during the entire course of her revisions.

Jaspers on Arendt and Arendt on Jaspers: The Lifelong Conversation

Communication was one of the central themes of Jaspers's *Existenz* philosophy and of his long and distinguished life. There were few friends with whom Jaspers conducted as rich, wide-ranging, and enduring a conversation as he did with Hannah Arendt (the only exception was his wife Gertrud). Jaspers and Arendt engaged in a continuous and incisive commentary on one another's works that was mutually supportive, reflective, and challenging (see Arendt and Jaspers 1992). In their later years both happily acknowledged the influence each had on the other's works without either having to sacrifice independence of thought and a critical stance. For

Jaspers, communication entails what he terms "loving struggle." In his explanation of this phrase, we perhaps may catch a glimpse of the essence of
the Jaspers-Arendt friendship.

> We are dealing with utter openness, with exclusion of all force
> and superiority, with the self-being of the other as well as my own.
> It is a struggle in which both sides dare, without reserve, to lay
> themselves open and to let themselves be called into question. . . .
> There exists an incomparable solidarity in the struggle of commu-
> nication. It is this solidarity that makes possible the most extreme
> questioning because it sustains the venture, turns it into a joint
> one and is coresponsible for the result. It limits the struggle to
> existential communication, which always is the secret of two; thus,
> those who are the closest of friends, as far as the public is con-
> cerned, are the ones who wrestle with each other in a struggle in
> which both share gain and loss. (Jaspers 1970, 60–61)

Jaspers's Comments on the Dissertation

Jaspers takes a balanced approach in assessing Arendt's dissertation, praising
its obvious merits (what he calls "the occasional shining pearls"), and pointing to areas that need further attention (Arendt and Jaspers 1992, 689–90
n.2). He commends her method of staying within "intellectual structures,"
in marked contrast to that of other contemporary authors he mentions.
Jaspers writes that his student avoids a "reductive and softening approach"
while her own work "draws distinct lines, and the positions Augustine takes
within them are let stand in all their sharpness" (ibid., 689). Jaspers then
takes a more detailed look at each section of the dissertation, calling Part I
"absolutely clear and in every point complete and flawless." Parts II and III
are also assessed:

> The second part, more difficult and interesting in its subject mat-
> ter, tends to wander in some passages; in others, ideas remain
> undeveloped. In the quotations some errors appear, some of
> which have been corrected, other of which require more work.
> The third section is not finished yet but clearly shows the path the
> study will follow. (Ibid.)

Clearly, Jaspers approves Arendt's overall approach to the topic. He comments that "neither historical nor philosophical interests are primary here

. . . [and] the author wants to justify her freedom from Christian possibilities which also attract her." Jaspers agrees with Arendt's claim that a system cannot be forced on Augustine's views and praises her effort to reveal the discrepancies "and so gain insight into the existential origins of these ideas" (ibid., 689–90).

Jaspers notes that "some of these errors have been corrected as a result of our discussions," but that in the final analysis "this otherwise impressive work, outstanding in its positive content, can unfortunately not be given the highest grade" (ibid., 690). Even though Arendt does not seem to have responded to her mentor's assessment of her dissertation, there are a few references in their correspondence of 1929 indicating that Arendt was preparing the dissertation for publication in the light of some of the changes Jaspers had suggested (ibid., 8–9).

Arendt on Jaspers's *Existenz* Philosophy

In her 1946 article "What Is Existenz Philosophy?" Arendt considers Jaspers's contribution to the new philosophical movement that was well underway in Europe between the two wars and that was just being introduced to American readers. Specifically, she extols the *Existenz* philosophy of Jaspers over Heidegger by acknowledging Jaspers's *Psychologie der Weltenshauungen* (1919) as "undoubtedly the first book of the new school" (Arendt 1946b, 51; see also chapter 3 above). In heightening the contrast between her two former professors, Arendt asserts that even though Jaspers's three-volume *Philosophy* was published five years after *Sein und Zeit*, "Jaspers' philosophy is not really closed and is at the same time more modern." She goes on to explain that "either Heidegger has said his last word on the condition of contemporary philosophy or he will have to break with his own philosophy. . . . Jaspers belongs without any such break to contemporary philosophy, and will develop and decisively intervene in its discussion" (Arendt 1946b, 55).

Arendt remarks on Jaspers's efforts to confront man's problematic relationship to the world, especially since Kant and the loss of traditional ontological bearings:

Instead of [traditional ontology] the "discordance of Being" . . .
can be admitted; and the modern feeling of alienation in the
world can be taken into account, as well as the modern will to
create a human world which can be a home within a world which
is no longer a home. (Ibid.)

Arendt's interpretation of Jaspers's struggle with "tradition" parallels her account of Augustine exploring man's paradoxical relation to the created and man-made world, albeit in a premodern, Christian context. Moreover, Jaspers's notion of "failure," in which man "experiences the fact that he can neither know nor create Being and that thus he is not God" (ibid., 54), can be compared to Arendt's interpretation of Augustine in which man discovers his radical dependence as a creature upon the Creator and comes to understand his source, his destiny, and his true nature in this new light.

In her essay on *Existenz* philosophy, Arendt notes Jaspers's view of "extreme situations" *(Grenzsituationem)* in which "the limits of this island of human freedom are traced out . . . and in which man experiences the limitations which immediately become the conditions of his freedom and the ground of his activity" (ibid., 55). In her dissertation, Arendt had located Augustine on a similar philosophical path: man questions himself "out of the world," comes to know his "limits" (as his source and destiny), and then reappropriates his relationship to the world and the community in this new light. Similarly, Arendt emphasizes Jaspers's insistence on the relationship between the individual and the community. She writes that "*Existenz* itself is never essentially isolated; it exists only in communication and in knowledge of the *Existenz* of others. . . . It can only develop in the togetherness of men in the common given world" (ibid., 56). Similarly, the dissertation had emphasized Augustine's understanding of the individual in the context of the Christian commandment of neighborly love.

Arendt's Augustinian approach to grounding the human community and to understanding its constitution as a result of a particular kind of "love of the world" shares with Jaspers neither content nor context but rather a methodological congruity. In Arendt's view, Jaspers takes up the contemporary challenge to come to terms with human alienation in the face of the loss of our ontological bearings. She in turn thinks she has discovered the seeds of the analogous philosophical project already at work in Augustine's thinking.

Arendt and Jaspers: The Augustine Connection

Could it have been sheer historical coincidence that Arendt and Jaspers were both working on Augustine at roughly the same time (mid to late 1950s and early 1960s)? Augustine's philosophy plays a prominent role in the first volume of Jaspers's *Die grossen Philosophen*, which was published in Germany in 1957. By the late 1950s, Arendt was beginning the work of reviewing and revising her dissertation for publication in the United States. At the same time she was editing sections of Jaspers's *Die grossen Philosophen* for an English translation that would be published in 1962. One volume would be called *Plato and Augustine.*

In the section called "Modes of Augustine's Thinking," Jaspers emphasizes Augustine's method of introspection and cites the Augustinian text that served as the leitmotif of Arendt's early work: "I have become a question to myself" (Jaspers 1962, 70–71). Further, as Arendt herself had done in her dissertation, Jaspers acknowledges the tensions and oppositions in Augustine's thinking and proceeds to list some of these "grave contradictions" (ibid., 109–112). As his student did many years earlier, he finds in these contradictions a philosophical richness that he then compares to the modern philosophical guides who had exerted such a profound influence on his earlier philosophical formation—Kierkegaard and Nietzsche. Of Augustine, Jaspers writes:

> Nothing is easier than to find contradictions in Augustine. We take them as features of his greatness. No philosophy is free from contradictions—and no thinker can aim at contradiction. But Augustine is one of the thinkers who ventures into contradictions, who draw their life from the tensions of enormous contradictions. He is not one of those who strive from the outset for freedom from contradictions; on the contrary, he lets his thought run aground on the shoals of contradiction when he tries to think God. Augustine faces the contradictions. And more than that: he presses them to their utmost limits. He makes us aware of the provocative question: Is there a point, a limit, where we are bound to encounter contradiction? And of the answer: Yes, wherever moved by the source of being and the unconditional will within us, we seek to communicate ourselves in thought, that is to say, in words. In this realm, freedom from contradiction would be existential death and the end of thinking itself. It is because Augustine took up these essential contradictions that he still exerts so provocative a power. (Ibid., 111)

During 1957 and 1958 Arendt wrote two essays about Karl Jaspers. The first, entitled "Karl Jaspers: Citizen of the World?" was written for a volume on Jaspers's philosophy for the Library of Living Philosophers series (1957), then reprinted in Arendt's *Men in Dark Times* (1968). The second was an address that Arendt delivered on the occasion of Jaspers's receipt of the German Book Trade's Peace Prize (1958), called simply "Karl Jaspers: A Laudatio" (Arendt 1968, 71–80). The first essay contains one explicit reference to Augustine (to the *quaestio mihi factus sum*). Arendt places Augustine in the great "axial period," which she describes as "the time when mankind first discovered the human condition on earth, so that from then on the mere chronological sequence of events could become a story and the stories be worked into a history, a significant object of reflection and understanding" (ibid., 89).[2] Further, in these two essays Arendt touches on themes that appear both in her dissertation and in Jaspers's work on Augustine. In the last paragraphs of "A Laudatio," Arendt praises Jaspers's ability to converse with the great philosophers (including Augustine) across the great divides of time and culture. Jaspers, says Arendt, has succeeded in establishing with these other philosophers the "realm of the spirit" to which "everyone can come out of his own origins." Similarities can be seen here with Arendt's discovery of Augustine's "transit" out of this world to the *nunc stans* where past and future meet. And just as in Augustine, there is a "return" to the world. Arendt sees Jaspers's realm of the spirit as "worldly" and yet "invisible," one "in which Jaspers is at home and to which he has opened the way for us; [it] does not lie in the beyond and is not utopian; it is not of yesterday nor of tomorrow; it is of the present and of this world" (Ibid., 80). Arendt also praises Jaspers's notion of communication, its relation to establishing the human community and the conditions necessary for political action (ibid., 90–91).

In an introductory essay called "Philosophical Autobiography," written especially for the Library of Living Philosophers collection, Jaspers speaks in glowing terms of Hannah Arendt. Reflecting on the immediate aftermath of World War II, he writes that

> my wife and I found Hannah Arendt-Blucher, whose longtime affection had not waned through the decades, very helpful. Her philosophical solidarity remains among the most beautiful experiences of those years. She came from the younger generation to us older ones and brought us what she experienced. (Jaspers 1957, 66).

Bringing their friendship into the present, Jaspers writes movingly of their association and of the "loving struggle" that their friendship entailed:

> Since 1948 she visited us repeatedly for intensive discussions and in order to make sure of a unanimity which could not be rationally defined. With her I was able to discuss once again in a fashion

2. Arendt added this sentence to the 1968 version of the essay.

which I had desired all my life, but had from my youth on—with
the exception of those closest to me, who shared my fate—really
experienced with only a few men: In (an atmosphere of) complete
unreservedness which allows no mental reservations—in abandon
because one knows that one can overshoot the mark, that such
overshooting would be corrected and that it demonstrates in itself
something worthwhile, viz., the tension of perhaps deep-seated
differences which yet are encompassed by such trust that to differ
does not mean a lessening of affection,—(in such an atmosphere
to realize) the radical and mutual letting-free of the other, where
abstract demands cease because they are extinguished in factual
fidelity. (Ibid., 67)

In a lengthy essay called "Reply to My Critics" at the close of the 1957
volume *The Philosophy of Karl Jaspers*, Jaspers first singles out Arendt's essay
for comment. He writes:

Hannah Arendt seems to me to have written such an excellent
report on the present world situation and on the idea of a world-
citizen which emerges from this situation, that I fear that, in the
form of reporting my thoughts, she has often presented me with
her own. (Ibid., 751)

Jaspers asserts that because their ideas are so close, it is Arendt's own
thoughts that really shine through her commentary on him. (Other commentators have used less flattering terms to describe Arendt's less than
literal interpretations of texts and traditions.) In remarking on their affinity,
Jaspers is able to illustrate both the similarities and the important differences in their views, in this case about the present world political situation.
He accepts Arendt's views on philosophy as the *ancilla vitae* (in a reworking
of one of Kant's remarks) and then proceeds to interpret the relationship
between life and philosophy in the following light: "He who, in the process
of philosophizing carries the torch ahead of those others and seeks justice,
knows—in disappointment and in hope—that he is dependent upon what is
beyond his knowledge" (ibid., 755). In Jaspers's terms, we are confronting a
limit situation from which there is no turning back and beyond which there
is no certain knowledge, but at that point the illumination of *Existenz* can
take place.

During the Eichmann controversy Jaspers was one of Arendt's strong-
est European supporters. When Arendt sent Jaspers the draft of the introduction for the German edition of *Eichmann in Jerusalem*, he reviewed it in

detail and made ample suggestions for changes (Young-Bruehl 1982, 354).
Jaspers had also promised to write a book inspired by the Eichmann controversy, for which he sketched some sections under the heading "On the Independence of Thought" (Jaspers 1986, 513). Instead, in failing health and
having been released from his promise by Arendt, Jaspers wrote his last
major work, *The Future of Germany* (1967), for which Arendt wrote the foreword. In a 14 February 1965 interview, Jaspers had commented exten-
sively on the Eichmann debate and praised Arendt for her "independence of
thought." Asked for his overall assessment of the Eichmann book, Jaspers
replied: "For me the book as a whole represents a marvelous testimony to
the independence of thought. Hannah Arendt cannot be categorized as to
her area of competence. One cannot say she is a writer. One cannot say she is
a scholar" (ibid., 520).

He then proceeded to comment on Arendt's dissertation and on her
early work on Rahel Varnhagen:

> When she finished her doctorate, with a brilliant dissertation—a
> thorough piece of work philosophically as well as speculatively—
> about the concept of love in St. Augustine . . . she was still very
> young, I believe twenty-two; she was offered the opportunity to
> lecture at the university. She refused. Her instincts resisted the
> university, she wanted to be free. What did she do then? First of
> all, before 1933, she wrote a book about Rahel Varnhagen that
> was as good as finished but was not published until the fifties.
> This book, too, cannot be classified; in any case it was based on
> the most exact knowledge of the sources (in this process she man-
> aged to preserve material that was later lost). This book already
> bears the same characteristic as the later ones: dispassionate, but
> passionate in the cause of truth. (Ibid., 520–21)

Jaspers also replies to the critics who had castigated Arendt for the
"tone, the irony, this cold soul, this laughter" that they detected in *Eichmann
in Jerusalem*. Jaspers looks at her approach in quite another light when he
comments:

> I like this tone of Hannah Arendt's. Since I have known her
> for many decades, I see in it again her independence. When
> Eichmann reveals himself as this nullity, then she laughs, because
> this denouement is like a joke. She amuses us that when she read
> the transcripts of the Eichmann interrogation, she laughed—not
> once but often—loudly to herself. What does this mean? One can

discuss back and forth how, in life itself, laughter and irony can be
founded in an extraordinary seriousness. Plato says: Only a great
writer of comedies can be a great writer of tragedies. (Ibid., 521)

Just as Jaspers remarked that Arendt's words about his philosophy also revealed her own thought, Jaspers's praise of Arendt revealed his own philosophical characteristics: independence of thought and dispassion, but passion in the cause of truth. Propelled by their own intellectual bent and by
the "cunning of history" beyond narrow national concerns, both Jaspers and
Arendt, in their own lives and in their thinking, challenged their contem-
poraries to new assessments of politics and the world order. Each called the
other "citizen of the world." And both—together in conversing and alone in
thinking—strove to attain the "realm of the spirit" that Arendt described as
"of the present and of this world. Reason has created it and freedom reigns
in it" (Arendt 1968, 80).

References

Arendt, Hannah. 1930. "Philosophy and Sociology." In *Knowledge and Politics: The Sociology of Knowledge Dispute*, ed. Volker Meja and Nico Stehr, 196–207. London and New York: Routledge, 1990.

———. 1946a. "No Longer and Not Yet." *The Nation*, September 14, 300–302.

———. 1946b. "What Is Existenz Philosophy?" *Partisan Review* 13:34–56.

———. 1950. "Religion and the Intellectuals: A Symposium." *Partisan Review* 17:113–116.

———. 1953a. "Christian Gaus Lectures: Karl Marx and the Tradition of Western Thought." Manuscript Division, Library of Congress. Drafts 1–2.

———. 1953b. "Understanding and Politics." *Partisan Review* 20:377–90.

———. 1953c. Dolf Steinberger Correspondence. 28 November. Trans. Sue Fischer. Library of Congress. Ms. 010118–19, Box 14.

———. 1958a. *The Human Condition*. Chicago: University of Chicago Press.

———. 1958b. *Origins of Totalitarianism*. Rev. ed. New York: Meridian Books.

———. 1964. George McKenna Correspondence. 13 January. Arendt Papers, Library of Congress. Ms. 020690, Box 12.

———. 1965. *Eichmann in Jerusalem: A Report on the Banality of Evil*. New York: Penguin Books.

———. 1967. Foreword to *The Future of Germany* by Karl Jaspers. Trans. E. B. Ashton. Chicago: University of Chicago Press.

———. 1968. *Men in Dark Times*. New York: Harcourt, Brace, & World.

———. 1973. *On Revolution*. New York: Penguin Books.

———. 1974a. Gershom Scholem Correspondence. Xerox copies of January 1974 exchange in *Encounter* and Arendt's notes. Arendt Papers, Library of Congress. Box 64.

———. 1974b. "The Gifford Lectures." Manuscript Division, Library of Congress.

———. 1974c. "Remembering Wystan H. Auden." In *W. H. Auden: A Tribute*, ed. Stephen Spender, 181–87. London: Weidenfeld and Nicolson Ltd.

———. 1977. *Between Past and Future: Eight Exercises in Political Thought*. New York: Penguin Books.

———. 1978a. "Martin Heidegger at Eighty." In *Heidegger and Modern Philosophy: Critical Essays*, ed. Michael Murray, ed. 293–303. New Haven, Conn.: Yale University Press.

———. 1978b. *The Life of the Mind: Thinking and Willing*. 2 vols. New York: Harcourt Brace Jovanovich.

———. 1982. *Hannah Arendt: Lectures on Kant's Political Philosophy.* Ed. Ronald Beiner. Chicago: University of Chicago Press.

———. 1994. *Essays in Understanding: 1930–1954.* Trans. and ed. Jerome Kohn. New York: Harcourt, Brace & Co.

———. Undated. Notes *Sein und Zeit.* Trans. Sue Fischer. Manuscript Division, Library of Congress. Box 68.

Arendt, Hannah, and Karl Jaspers. 1992. *Hannah Arendt/Karl Jaspers Correspondence, 1926–69.* Ed. Lotte Kohler and Hans Saner. Trans. Robert and Rita Kimber. New York: Harcourt Brace Jovanovich.

Arendt, Hannah, and Mary McCarthy. 1995. *Between Friends: The Correspondence of Hannah Arendt and Mary McCarthy, 1929–75.* Ed. Carol Brightman. New York: Harcourt, Brace & Co.

Barnouw, Dagmar. 1988. *Weimar Intellectuals and the Threat of Modernity.* Bloomington: Indiana University Press.

———. 1990. *Visible Spaces: Hannah Arendt and the German-Jewish Experience.* Baltimore: Johns Hopkins University Press.

Berlin, I., and Ramin Jahanbegloo. 1991. *Recollections of a Historian of Ideas.* New York: Charles Scribner's Sons.

Boyle, Patrick. 1987. "Elusive Neighborliness: Hannah Arendt's Interpretation of Saint Augustine." In *Amor Mundi: Explorations in the Faith and Thought of Hannah Arendt,* ed. James Bernauer, 81–114. The Netherlands: Martinus Nijhoff.

Canovan, Margaret. 1992. *Hannah Arendt: A Reinterpretation of Her Political Thought.* Cambridge: Cambridge University Press.

Caputo, John D. 1993. "Heidegger and Theology." In *The Cambridge Companion to Heidegger,* ed. Charles Guignon, 270–88. Cambridge: Cambridge University Press.

Eger, H. 1930. Review of *Der Liebesbegriff bei Augustin* by Hannah Arendt. *Zeitschrift für Kirchengeschichte* 49:257–59.

Elshtain, Jean. 1988. Remarks presented as discussant for panel on Hannah Arendt at American Political Science Association convention, 3 September, Washington, D.C.

Ferry, Luc. 1992. *The System of Philosophies of History.* Trans. Franklin Philip. Chicago: University of Chicago Press.

Gunnell, John G. 1986. *Between Philosophy and Politics: The Alienation of Political Theory.* Amherst: University of Massachusetts Press.

———. 1993. *The Descent of Political Theory: The Genealogy of an American Vocation.* Chicago: University of Chicago Press.

Heidegger, Martin. 1962. *Being and Time.* Trans. John Macquarrie and Edward Robinson. New York: Harper & Row.

Hessen, J. 1931. Review of *Der Liebesbegriff bei Augustin* by Hannah Arendt. *Kantstudien* 36:175.

Hoffman, Kurt. 1957. "The Basic Concepts of Jaspers' Philosophy." In *The Philosophy of Karl Jaspers,* ed. Paul Arthur Schilpp, 95–113. New York: Tudor Publishing Co.

Honig, Bonnie. 1992. "Toward an Agnostic Feminism: Hannah Arendt and the Politics of Identity." In *Feminists Theorize the Political*, ed. Judith Butler and Joan Scott, 215–56. New York: Routledge.

Issac, Jeffrey C. 1992. *Arendt, Camus, and Modern Rebellion*. New Haven, Conn.: Yale University Press.

Jaspers, Karl. 1955. *Reason and Existenz*. Trans. W. Earle. New York: Noonday Press.

———. 1957. *The Philosophy of Karl Jaspers*. Ed. Paul Arthur Schilpp. New York: Tudor Publishing Co.

———. 1962. *Plato and Augustine*. Ed. Hannah Arendt. Trans. Ralph Mannheim. New York: Harcourt, Brace, & World.

———. 1970. *Philosophy*. Vol. 2. Trans. E. B. Ashton. Chicago: University of Chicago Press.

———. 1986. *Basic Philosophical Writings*. Ed. Edith Erlich, Leonard H. Erlich, and George B. Pepper. Athens: Ohio University Press.

Jay, Martin. 1985. *Permanent Exiles: Essays on the Intellectual Migration from Germany to America*. New York: Columbia University Press.

Jonas, Hans. 1990. Telephone interview. 2 May.

Kateb, George. 1983. *Hannah Arendt: Politics, Conscience, Evil*. Totowa, N.J.: Rowman & Allenheld.

Krell, David Farrell. 1986. *Intimations of Mortality: Time, Truth and Finitude in Heidegger's Thinking of Being*. University Park: Pennsylvania State University Press.

Morganthau, Hans. 1976. "Hannah Arendt: An Appreciation." *Political Theory* 4, no. 1 (February): 5–8.

Pangle, Thomas. 1988. *The Spirit of Modern Republicanism: The Moral Vision of the American Founders and the Philosophy of John Locke*. Chicago: University of Chicago Press.

Wolin, Sheldon. 1978. "Stopping to Think." *New York Review of Books*, 26 October, 16–21.

Young-Bruehl, Elisabeth. 1982. *Hannah Arendt: For Love of the World*. New Haven, Conn.: Yale University Press.

Zepf, Max. 1932. Review of *Der Liebesbegriff bei Augustin* by Hannah Arendt. *Gnomon* 8:101–5.

Index

Abel, Cain and, 103n.21

acting, 168–69

action: labor and work and, 151, 152; as miraculous, 176; natality as spring of, 146, 167, 185; reason and, 175. *See also vita activa*

Adam, 95, 100, 102–4, 109, 112

agape, 38

American Revolution, 153, 175

amor: amor amoris dei, 48–49; meaning for Augustine, 38, 39

amor sui. See self-love

appetitus. See craving

Arendt, Hannah: as abstracting those parts of Augustine useful to her, 122–23; accused of Jacobinism, 175, 191; accused of narrowly selective use of historical texts, xvi; Augustine as an old friend, 115; Augustine as paradigm for assault on tradition by, 155; on axial age, 143, 208; Barnouw on, 127–28; at Berlin, 116–17; Isaiah Berlin on, 126; *Between Past and Future,* x, 115; Canovan on, 131–34; challenge to Heidegger on time, 163, 185; Christian Gaus lectures, 145, 183–84, 192; continued use of *Existenz* language, 203; *Crises of the Republic,* xiv; as drawing a line between her early concerns and later interests, 128; an early versus a mature Arendt, 126–27; editing of Benjamin's *Illuminations,* xiv; encounter with Augustine not accorded attention it merits, xi; favorite pas-

sage from Augustine, 138, 147, 168, 183; feminist readings of, 131; Ferry on, 127, 175–76, 177; Gunnell on, 176–77, 191; as Heideggerian mole, 116, 174; Heidegger's death-driven phenomenology abandoned by, 124–25, 198; Heidegger's influence on, 117–18, 173–97, 198; on Heidegger's Nazism, 177, 189; at Heidelberg and Marburg, 198; the Holocaust and, 126, 127, 131, 174; interest in Christian theology, 116; interpretative paradigm of, 123; and Jaspers working on Augustine at same time, 206–11; on Jaspers's *Existenz* philosophy, 205–6; Jaspers's influence on, 117, 118, 198–211; Jay on, 127; "Karl Jaspers: A Laudatio," 207–8; "Karl Jaspers: Citizen of the World?" 143, 207–8; key terms of, 116; on love of the Jewish people, 191–92; "Martin Heidegger at Eighty," 117, 187–90, 194; *Men in Dark Times,* 115, 207; as more than a transmitter of German phenomenology, 160; "No Longer and Not Yet," 118; Pangle on, 127, 174–75, 177, 186, 187, 191; on philosophy, ix, 188; physical presence and intellectual aura of, vii; political writings accorded canonical status, 125; the politics-only Arendt, 130; preference for individual heroes, 191; as a radical, 178; relativism and, 176–77; status relative to the tradition, ix; "Understanding and Politics," 176;

Made in the USA
Las Vegas, NV
01 June 2021